MW00324915

Language and Literacy Teaching for Indigenous Education

BILINGUAL EDUCATION AND BILINGUALISM
Series Editors: Professor Nancy H. Hornberger, *University of Pennsylvania, Philadelphia, USA* and Professor Colin Baker, *University of Wales, Bangor, UK*

Other Books in the Series
At War With Diversity: US Language Policy in an Age of Anxiety
James Crawford
Cross-linguistic Influence in Third Language Acquisition
J. Cenoz, B. Hufeisen and U. Jessner (eds)
Dual Language Education
Kathryn J. Lindholm-Leary
English in Europe: The Acquisition of a Third Language
Jasone Cenoz and Ulrike Jessner (eds)
Foundations of Bilingual Education and Bilingualism
Colin Baker
Identity and the English Language Learner
Elaine Day
An Introductory Reader to the Writings of Jim Cummins
Colin Baker and Nancy Hornberger (eds)
Language Minority Students in the Mainstream Classroom (2nd Edition)
Angela L. Carrasquillo and Vivian Rodriguez
Languages in America: A Pluralist View
Susan J. Dicker
Language, Power and Pedagogy: Bilingual Children in the Crossfire
Jim Cummins
Language Revitalization Processes and Prospects
Kendall A. King
Language Use in Interlingual Families: A Japanese-English Sociolinguistic Study
Masayo Yamamoto
Learning English at School: Identity, Social Relations and Classroom Practice
Kelleen Toohey
Learners' Experiences of Immersion Education: Case Studies of French and Chinese
Michèle de Courcy
Power, Prestige and Bilingualism: International Perspectives on Elite Bilingual Education
Anne-Marie de Mejía
Reflections on Multiliterate Lives
Diane Belcher and Ulla Connor (eds)
The Sociopolitics of English Language Teaching
Joan Kelly Hall and William G. Eggington (eds)
Studies in Japanese Bilingualism
Mary Goebel Noguchi and Sandra Fotos (eds)
Working with Bilingual Children
M.K. Verma, K.P. Corrigan and S. Firth (eds)
World English: A Study of its Development
Janina Brutt-Griffler

Please contact us for the latest book information:
Multilingual Matters, Frankfurt Lodge, Clevedon Hall,
Victoria Road, Clevedon, BS21 7HH, England
http://www.multilingual-matters.com

BILINGUAL EDUCATION AND BILINGUALISM 37
Series Editors: Nancy H. Hornberger and Colin Baker

Language and Literacy Teaching for Indigenous Education

A Bilingual Approach

Norbert Francis and Jon Reyhner

MULTILINGUAL MATTERS LTD
Clevedon • Buffalo • Toronto • Sydney

Library of Congress Cataloging in Publication Data
A catalog record for this book is available from the Library of Congress.

British Library Cataloguing in Publication Data
A catalogue entry for this book is available from the British Library.

ISBN 1-85359-601-9 (hbk)
ISBN 1-85359-600-0 (pbk)

Multilingual Matters Ltd
UK: Frankfurt Lodge, Clevedon Hall, Victoria Road, Clevedon BS21 7HH.
USA: UTP, 2250 Military Road, Tonawanda, NY 14150, USA.
Canada: UTP, 5201 Dufferin Street, North York, Ontario M3H 5T8, Canada.
Australia: Footprint Books, PO Box 418, Church Point, NSW 2103, Australia.

Copyright © 2002 Norbert Francis and Jon Reyhner.

All rights reserved. No part of this work may be reproduced in any form or by any means without permission in writing from the publisher.

Typeset by Wordworks Ltd.
Printed and bound in Great Britain by the Cromwell Press Ltd.

Contents

Preface

A bilingual approach to language and literacy teaching for Indian education flows from a premise that any language a child understands can be an effective medium of instruction, including languages that have in the past been excluded for one reason or another from school. At the same time, languages that children want to learn, but still do not understand, can also be an integral part of the teaching program, in many ways. In the case of indigenous languages, we can broaden this premise: incorporating a community's language into the school program can provide for a number of important benefits from the point of view of academic achievement. And in addition, we can propose a corollary: excluding one of the languages of a bilingual community from school, aside from restricting access to the benefits of bilingualism, limits language learners' options in the area of academic language development and literacy. The idea that language learning and literacy can be enriched with the inclusion of indigenous languages is what this book is about.

Certainly, a book like this could not have been written without the help and inspiration of innumerable others, first and foremost the children with whom we have worked over the many years in communities throughout the United States and Mexico. It is to them and their families that our first acknowledgement is gratefully extended: for their generous disposition and unselfish patience that accompanied us in our work as educators and researchers. As guests and visitors to their communities, we want to express our gratitude for the hospitality that was always extended to us, and in particular during periods of fieldwork and study, the tolerance toward and understanding of our research objectives. We thank the teachers and principals of the following schools for access to their classrooms and for the many hours they shared relating to us their experiences about one or another aspect of language learning and language teaching: the Escuela Xicohténcatl (Tlaxcala), the elementary schools of Pozuelos and Santa Teresa (Municipality of Cardonal in Hidalgo state), and San Isidro (Michoacán state) in Mexico, and Rocky Boy and Heart Butte Elementary Schools in Montana, and Havasupai, Cibecue, and Rock Point Community Schools in Arizona.

Special thanks go to Archie Phinney for the recording and translation of

Coyote and the Shadow People, and to Jarold Ramsey (1983) for permission to reprint the text in its entirety from his study *Reading the Fire: Essays in the Traditional Indian Literatures of the Far West;* to Pedro Atzatzi for the transcription of *Los Vaqueros Vasarios,* to Reyes Arce for his narration of *Tlacual uan Coyotl (The Opossum and the Coyote),* and to Pablo Rogelio Navarrete Gómez for many of the translations and transcriptions of Náhuatl language texts, and for commentaries and observations about indigenous language bilingualism in his community that have contributed to the refining of a number of concepts discussed in this book. The staff of the Dirección General de Education Bilingüe (DGEI), Mexico's national department of indigenous education, has over the years been a consistent point of support: answering questions, providing materials, letters of introduction, and invaluable advice about doing field work in bilingual communities; thanks to Rafael Nieto Andrade in particular for his collaboration in the development of the *Entrevista Bilingüe* [Bilingual Interview], and to the DGEI we offer a formal acknowledgement for permission to reproduce a selection of the graphic materials from this assessment instrument; thanks also to Harrison Henry, Bert Corcoran, Jimmie C. Begay, Sally Old Coyote, Harry Lee, Jeanne Eder, Dick Heiser and Gina Cantoni for their collegial guidance and the numerous consultations of all kinds over the years. To the editors of Multilingual Matters, and an anonymous reviewer, we are especially grateful for the many helpful observations, suggestions and corrections, and in particular to the latter, for a careful and thoughtful reading of an earlier draft, and for posing a good number of hard questions and challenging critiques.

We acknowledge the financial support of a number of agencies and foundations that have supported our work: the Ford Foundation, the US/ Mexico Fund for Culture, the Office and Grants and Contract of Northern Arizona University, and the Consejo Nacional de Ciencia y Tecnología of Mexico through its funding of two research projects directed by Rainer Enrique Hamel of the Universidad Autónoma Metropolitana.

And to our families: our wives, Marie and María Natalia, our children, Deborah, Tsosie, and Zoraida, and niece Yvonne, we will always be grateful for their support and encouragement to this project.

Abbreviations

BIA   Bureau of Indian Affairs

BICS   Basic Interpersonal Communicative Skills

CALP   Cognitive Academic Language Proficiency

DGEI   Dirección General de Educación Indígena (Mexico)

ESL   English as a Second Language

HLI   Hawaiian Language Immersion

IL   Indigenous Language

INEGI   Instituto Nacional de Estadística Geografía e Informática (Mexico)

L1   First Language

L2   Second Language

LAD   Language Acquisition Device

LEA   Language Experience Approach

LLSD   Language Learner Sensitive Discourse

NCC   Navajo Community College (now Diné College)

NL   National Language

NSL   Navajo as a Second Language

PEEB   Proyecto Experimental de Educación Bilingüe (Peru)

UG   Universal Grammar

UNESCO   United Nations Educational Scientific and Cultural Organization

WROLT   Window Rock Oral Language Test: Navajo/English Bilingual Proficiency

Part 1

A Survey of Indigenous Languages in Education in the Americas

Chapter 1

Prospects for Learning and Teaching Indigenous Languages

European explorers and conquerors of the 16th century encountered hundreds of indigenous languages spoken on the American continent. Today, it is estimated that over 500 languages, belonging to 20 different linguistic families, have survived (Saguier, 1983; Silver & Miller, 1997). In the United States alone, 154 indigenous languages are still spoken (Grimes, 1999); however the estimates regarding their short-term prospects for survival paint a stark picture of the crisis that all Amerindian languages face today. Of these 154 languages, at current rates of language shift,* 45 are on the verge of extinction, and another 90 are projected to disappear by the year 2050 (Crawford, 1995; Krauss, 1996). A similar situation prevails for many languages in Canada and Latin America.

While the last 500 years have witnessed the permanent loss of many, and the continued erosion of virtually all the remaining indigenous languages, responses to this loss have taken many forms. In recent years the resistance to language erosion has began to shift toward more active strategies involving the first attempts at language planning and the implementation of language revitalization programs, more and more involving the active participation of members of the indigenous speech communities themselves.

Concentrated, for the most part, in the same regions they occupied prior to the European conquest, some of the major language groups are well known. In the Andean region (Peru, Bolivia, Ecuador, Northern Argentina and Southern Colombia) Quechua, the *lingua franca** of the former Inca empire, is spoken by as many as 12,000,000 people, Aymara by one million. In Paraguay 3,000,000 speak Guaraní, in Mexico and Guatemala, Maya is spoken by one million, and Náhuatl, mainly in Mexico, by over one million by conservative estimates[1] (Varese, 1990; DGEI, 1990). Maya and Náhuatl played a role in Mesoamerica similar to that of Quechua in South America. Their function as languages of wider communication, among other factors, led to the early development of writing systems (more advanced in the case of Maya). In the United States, Navajo is still spoken in the home by as many as 150,000 adults and children (Crawford, 1995, citing a 1993 US Census report).

3

In Canada, Cree, Ojibwa, and Inuktitut have maintained a certain degree of linguistic vitality with more than 10,000 speakers each. However, as in the United States, language loss seems to have accelerated in recent years. According to census figures, in 1951, 87.4% of aboriginal people indicated their tribal language as their first language; in 1981, it was the mother tongue for only 29.3%. By 1991, the prospects for Canada's sixty Native languages seems precarious at best, with 71% of First Nations' children reporting never having spoken an indigenous language (Burnaby, 1996).

Far from an issue that primarily concerns anthropologists and linguists, indigenous communities themselves have in recent years come forward and proposed language policies with the aim of reversing the erosion of their ancestral languages. In 1984 the Northern Ute Tribe Tribal Business Committee passed a resolution declaring:

> The Ute language is a living and vital language that has the ability to match any other in the world for expressiveness and beauty. Our language is capable of lexical expansion into modern conceptual fields such as the field of politics, economics, mathematics and science. Be it known that the Ute language shall be recognized as our first language, and the English language will be recognized as our second language. We assert that our students are fully capable of developing fluency in our mother tongue and the foreign English language and we further assert that higher level of Ute mastery results in higher levels of English skills. (Northern Ute Tribe, 1985: 16)

The same year, the Navajo Tribal Education Policies were approved by the Tribal Council, reiterated recently as part of a broader "Diné Cultural Content Standards for Students":

> The Navajo language is an essential element of the life, culture and identity of the Navajo people. The Navajo Nation recognizes the importance of preserving and perpetuating that language for the survival of the Nation. Instruction in the Navajo language shall be made available for all grade levels in all schools serving the Navajo Nation. Navajo language instruction shall include to the greatest extent practicable: thinking, speaking, comprehension, reading and writing skills and study of the formal grammar of the language. (Education Committee of the Navajo Nation Council, 2000)

In a declaration to the United Nations Working Group on Indigenous Populations in 1987, the Alliance of Indigenous Bilingual Professionals (Mexico) pointed to the positive efforts made by the Department of Indian

Education in the area of investigation, materials development, and bilingual teacher preparation; but called attention to the fact that:

> In practice these actions have remained at the experimental level, they have not had real consequences, nor have produced real changes. In practice, the education that the indigenous people receive continues to be ineffective and ethnocidal. The education that is available to the 56 indigenous peoples of Mexico does not correspond to their necessities because the programs, textbooks, and curriculum materials continue to be foreign to the indigenous reality and destroy their languages ... Until the federal and state governments take into account the participation of the indigenous people on educational policy, we will not be able to achieve the conservation of our indigenous languages and our culture. (Alianza de Profesionales Indígenas Bilingües AC, 1992: 207).

But perhaps a more immediate concern for the thousands of indigenous communities of the Americas is the linguistic and academic development of pre-school and school-age children who continue to speak their ancestral language. Independent of their opinions regarding the possibility of preserving the ancestral language, parents view improvements in the local schools that their children attend as a major priority, at times taking precedence over most other social, economic, and cultural issues. Reforming past language policies and practices is often an important ingredient in the upgrading of the educational programs in *Native** American communities. As part of this effort, since the late 1960s, a growing number teachers working with indigenous children have been experimenting with different models of bilingual education that explicitly incorporate the Indian language into the school day.

In some school districts, the indigenous language is an integral component of an established bilingual program; in others, teachers have taken the initiative on their own, experimenting with new ways to teach literacy, integrating cultural content with language teaching, or simply introducing isolated capsules of language when they can. It is to these educators and the communities that they serve that we offer this review of the research and curriculum guide for indigenous languages. Our purpose is to contribute to the important discussion among community leaders, teachers, parents, and school administrators on the critical issues of school language policy and community language planning, and to outline a series of practical strategies in the area of language teaching. It is to the classroom-based educator, and the preservice teacher that this book is primarily directed, in large part because there is no substitute for the professionally trained language teacher, and the systematic and well designed language learning program that he or she implements in the formal setting of the classroom. However, this does not imply that the classroom teacher and the school program are sufficient for attaining the language learning objectives that parents and communities set or aspire to attain. Especially in the case of communities that have decided to include the revitalization and preservation of their indigenous language as one of the language learning objectives for children, teachers and academic programs will need to seek out many points of support outside the classroom. It may even be true, as some researchers have suggested, that the school might turn out to be only a secondary or complementary component (see the discussion in Reyhner *et al.*, 1999, 2000; Crawford, 1996). As such, the principles of language teaching discussed in the following chapters should be of wider interest. From this perspective, communities will be in a better position to collectively reflect upon the complex processes of language and cultural change, and ultimately begin to intervene directly in policy and planning decisions that will affect their future; see Ruiz (1995) and McCarty and Watahomigie (1999) on the tasks that a communiy might undertake in "language planning."

Part 1 briefly describes the current state of indigenous languages in a representative sample of regions, followed by a review of various initiatives in the area of bilingual indigenous education, and a discussion of the role that schools can play in language preservation. A series of maps indicates the approximate location of language communities mentioned in Chapters 1, 2, and 3. This will help place the discussion in an overall geographic context; the reader should be cognizant, however, that the selection of languages represents but a small sample of the hundreds of Amerindian languages. For complete maps with precise locations of all languages, readers can consult *Ethnologue: Languages of the World*; see Chapter 9 for the website.

Part 2 is devoted to an overview of classroom language activities, curriculum, materials and methods that, if applied, can begin to realize the great untapped potential of a more inclusive language teaching program in our schools. The bilingualism that both students and teachers bring to school represents a vast knowledge store that, to date, has been only partially exploited, even in the best programs. Ultimately, this new additive bilingualism could enrich the entire curriculum and open up new linguistic, cultural, and academic horizons for our students.

The theory and practice of bilingual education has developed largely through research that has not taken into account the specific contexts of indigenous languages and the communities in which these languages continue to be spoken. However, this does not invalidate or render inapplicable the general conclusions about how children learn second languages most effectively when the situation involves the sharp inequalities of indigenous language/national language bilingualism. This assumption, or hypothesis (if the reader prefers) represents one of the central themes of this book. Therefore, the chapters on Language teaching (Chapters 4 and 5), Literacy (Chapter 6), and Assessment (Chapter 7) will tend to emphasize how second language teaching principles can be applied to the special, or different, circumstances of indigenous language bilingualism. For each chapter in Part 2, we recommend four additional readings that teachers can consult. In regard to the authors' suggestions on methods and materials, and how they might be applied to indigenous language programs, we have little to add and even less, if anything, to take away. Our discussion in these areas will attempt to avoid as much recapitulation as possible. For some of the finer points of the theory of language learning and language teaching we refer the reader to the Notes section where more citations can be found for further more in depth study. Glossary terms are marked in the chapters with an asterisk (*like this**). Specifically for this reader in mind, we include a brief study guide at the beginning of the Notes that groups the notes by theme.

The reader will also take note of a series of enclosed inserts, set aside for reflections on language and language learning, verbal art, thought, and ways of knowing. We took the liberty to cite a number of representative voices from different indigenous communities, some from the past, others from the present; some are historical or public figures (identified by name), others, anonymous "Voices from the Communities" ("Voices" for short).

In our discussion of the educational and language learning issues that parents and educators might consider as they begin to chart a course toward language revitalization, we have chosen to include all the Americas (Canada, United States and Latin America) given the broad common ground that we share. In fact, the present political boundaries that separate Mexico from the US Southwest, and separate Canada from the northern states, represent arbitrary divisions both historically and culturally from the perspective of the indigenous peoples of each region. For too long, an unnecessary distinction has been maintained between what is narrowly conceived of as "American Indian education" and the experience of educators and researchers in Latin America and Canada. This dichotomy has limited our ability to learn from each other's work.

The vast region of the US Southwest and Mexican Northwest is a case in point. The area has been a crossroads of languages and cultures ever since the first immigrants arrived thousands of years before the modern era. The first European newcomers introduced Spanish (early sporadic contacts with military expeditions in 1528 and 1539 occurring soon after the conquest of the Aztecs). English speakers did not arrive in significant

---

Voices 1 (Cree)

Selected glossary for speaking and thinking terms

âyimômiso	discuss oneself, speak unguardedly about oneself
itwêstamaw	say thus for someone, speak for someone; interpret for someone
kitot	address someone, speak to someone, lecture someone
naskwêwasim	speak to someone in response
pîkiskwât	speak about something with concern; speak a prayer over something
tâpowê	speak correctly, recite one's prayer correctly
wîci-pîkiskwêm	speak together with someone
ispîhtêyimiso	think thus highly of oneself
kihcêyim	think highly of someone, hold someone sacred
kiskisopayi	think of something, suddenly remember
kotêyiht	try something in one's mind, think strenuously about something, test or challenge something
mâmitonêyihtamih	cause someone to think about it/him
mâmitonêyim	have someone on one's mind
misawâc	whatever might be thought

Freda Ahenakew (in Ahenakew & Wolfart, 1998: 374–75)

---

numbers until the 19th century. Today, the region is perhaps one of the most culturally and linguistically diverse in the world, continuing to occupy one of the center stages in the massive migratory movements of the modern day international labor market. But if one can imagine the current political boundary between the United States and Mexico on Map 1, it is noteworthy that (1) the first cultures that settled the area today continue to inhabit their historical homelands, and (2) the indigenous communities themselves are often transnational, the most extensive of the Indian lands to be divided in such a way being that of the Tohono O'odham. Other historical ties (e.g. the Hopi, Pima, Tarahumara, and Náhuatl, among others, belong to the same linguistic family), and common social circumstances vis-à-vis the respective national languages of each country underline the necessity to share experiences and perspectives across our borders.

While our review of bilingual educational programs will, by necessity, be far from comprehensive (mainly considering the United States, Mexico,

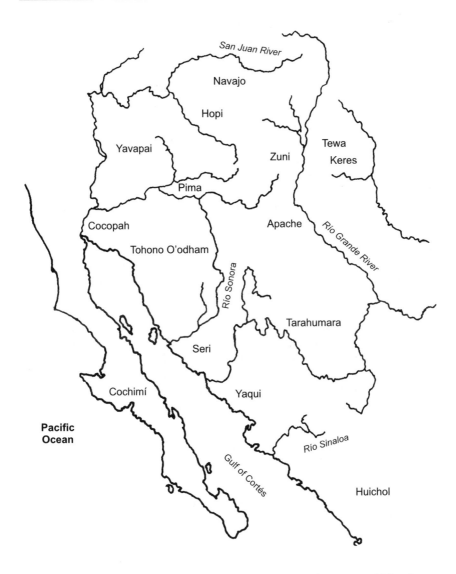

Map 1 Indigenous peoples of the Southwest United States and Northwest Mexico in the 16th century

Source: *Ethnologue* (http://www.ethnologue.com/web.asp); León-Portilla (1976)

and the Andean countries) we recognize the important contribution to the field made by our colleagues in Canada and other regions of Central and South America.

Bilingualism as a Resource for Schools and Children

Conceivably, three broad groups of children, or categories of language learners, would benefit from the systematic and academic use of indigenous languages in the classroom. For some, instruction will involve developing an indigenous language that they already speak natively; for others, it will involve learning the community's ancestral tongue as a second language.

Within the indigenous speech community itself, two categories of language learners come to mind:

(1) children who acquired the Indian language at home, who are either monolingual or dominant in the language and who will be learning the national language (NL) in school as a second language.
(2) children who are dominant or monolingual in the national language, or who are bilingual. Their families and the community, together with the school, may choose to implement a language revitalization program for enrichment purposes. Today, in most indigenous communities, it is this second category that would represent the greater fraction of indigenous language speakers among children, monolingualism in the indigenous language (IL), in this age group, having decreased significantly in virtually all regions.

Outside the community:
(3) non-Indian children or indigenous children from other IL communities in close geographical proximity whose families perceive the need for more effective interethnic communication.

Within these categories a number of finer distinctions could be made. Among IL-speaking children in category 1 it is important to distinguish between bilinguals with adequate comprehension ability in the NL (for example for the purpose of understanding NL-medium instruction) from children who are at the very initial stages of learning the NL as a second language. In many regions the latter still represents an important sector of the community, for whom the use or non-use of the IL in school is posed as a fundamental question of Linguistic Human Rights (Maffi, 2001; Skutnabb-Kangas, 2000; Nahmad Sittón, 1999; Hamel, 1993), or what we could propose as the first order or most fundamental right (Francis & Nieto Andrade, 2000): that elementary school-age children have access to at least some instruction (ideally a significant component of the curriculum plan) in a language that they understand. For the bilingual IL-speaking child, who understands the NL but is more proficient in his or her first language (the IL), this fundamental right would apply to the use of the language he or she understands *best*.

For indigenous children in our second category (the NL is the primary language and the IL is, or could be, the L2), their right to have access to an additive bilingual development that involves the recuperation or revitalization of the IL would depend on the community's decision, willingness, and capability to work toward this language learning objective. As an aspect of the struggle against discrimination and inequality, and for full access to the opportunity structure of society, the right to develop one's ancestral/community language would be one that any democratically minded educator would actively support. In any case, the common ground among all these groups of language learners is a general educational right: access to the optimal conditions for academic and cognitive development, the foremost component here being the highest level of literacy development comparable with that of the school population as a whole.

In the past, it has been the first group (language learner category 1) that has been viewed by the broader society and the indigenous community alike as most in need of one form or another of bilingual education. Most often, in actual practice, the variant of bilingual education received has fallen far short of the minimum requirements for effective dual language teaching. Under the best circumstances, the use of the indigenous language in school has usually been restricted to short-term, transitional, models that neither attributed any intrinsic value to the indigenous language nor ever envisioned their preservation within a developmental program that would promote a well-rounded additive bilingual proficiency. Of course, as a rule, the language-learning model that the great majority of educational programs still adhere to is the monolingual, exclusionary model, English-only (or French-only) in the US and Canada, or Spanish-only, or Portuguese-only, in Latin America.

Based on our research and first-hand experience working in Indian community schools, we are convinced that the same benefits can potentially be realized for bilingual Indian students that have been demonstrated for bilingual children in more favorable social situations. In one sense (a very narrow one) the "need" for bilingual education for Indian students has diminished thanks to the broader economic and cultural changes that have brought public schools, radio, television, wage employment, and so forth, into the great majority of indigenous communities. If the use of the indigenous language is viewed simply as a means to teach the national language, then bilingual instruction becomes less and less necessary for the growing number of communities where young children, in greater and greater numbers, are acquiring the national language before they enter school. But if the expansion of the national languages has almost eliminated, for many, the function of the transitional use of indigenous languages, it has, at the same time, highlighted new opportunities; primary among them would be to question the limited, early-exit, transitional models that contribute little, if anything, to indigenous language development. Indeed, indigenous young people acquiring high levels of proficiency in English, French, or Spanish can be viewed only in the most positive terms: a perspective, as a rule, that is broadly shared by their families.[2] Precisely, the opportunities, for bilingual children, lie in the areas of cognitive, academic, and language development (Bialystok & Cummins, 1991; Bialystok & Hakuta, 1994; Cummins, 1996; Yelland *et al.*, 1993; Lambert, 1990).

The bilingual teaching curriculum model proposed in Chapter 4, and the sample language learning activities described in Chapters 5 and 6, apply to both of the broad categories of language learners: the IL-speaker who is learning the NL as a second language (category 1), and indigenous children who are competent speakers of the NL, with varying levels of proficiency in the IL (category 2). But clearly, any language learning or literacy lesson in the IL, for example, would be implemented in a different way depending on the level of IL proficiency that each child may possess, aspects of proficiency in the NL from which he or she will be able to draw, contextual factors that constrain in different ways the use of the IL in the academic domain, etc. On some activities the advanced IL speaker and the NL monolingual IL beginner will be able to work together, on other activities this may not be appropriate. Regarding these matters of lesson planning and teacher judgment we will offer some general guidelines; however, it is difficult to specify in advance the different ways teachers should on some occasions integrate, and on others differentiate. Nevertheless, a fundamental rule should apply: children of widely different language proficiency backgrounds should not indiscriminately and at all times be provided with the same instruction. In a similar way, there is no single universal bilingual approach that can be implemented uniformly in contexts that range from the situation of the IL community whose language is in the final stages of extinction, to the still-vital speech community with virtually no written record, to indigenous languages encompassing millions of speakers and a long tradition of formal discourses, literature, and other written forms. General principles of language learning would be applied creatively and with a keen eye to the vast diversity of IL/NL contact situations. However, our point of view is that, in the last analysis, the general principles still apply; i.e. there is no indigenous language community to which they do not apply, on one level or another, or in one way or another. This, in fact, is part of the story that we want to tell, especially in Part II – what these principles are and how they may be applied.

In addition, promoting additive bilingualism opens up new opportunities in the area of cultural and ethnic self-affirmation. We mentioned the 500 years of resistance by Native peoples to the displacement of their languages by English, Spanish, French and Portuguese; but also, by consciously taking on the task of learning and perfecting one's indigenous language, young people resist the *externally imposed conditions* for *integration** into the broader society. Students and their families would begin to see themselves less as objects of more powerful outside forces beyond their control, and more as subjects of language planning and development. Integration itself, in the broad sense, will not be focal point of resistance, but rather it will move forward, as it inevitably must, but on different terms. Learning and developing one's ancestral language, as well as achieving high levels of proficiency in the national language, is one way of leveling the presently very uneven playing field.

A growing body of research evidence is pointing to the academic benefits that bilingual children are in a position to take advantage of if both languages are allowed to develop (Bialystok, 1991; Bialystok & Hakuta, 1994). We believe that these same favorable circumstances apply to indigenous language bilingualism despite the important differences that characterize the situation of language contact with their respective national language: discrimination and social stigma, sharp imbalances in the access to cultural resources, the oral–literate division of functions that has effectively reserved writing for the national language, and differences (real and perceived) in social *prestige** and functional value.

The Indigenous Language Speaking Community: Domains of Language Shift and Language Revitalization

Language activists and researchers have pointed to the necessity of conscious and persistent community-wide planning efforts to begin to reverse the tendency toward monolingualism in the national language. Only an active language policy, focused on the development and expansion of the indigenous language, can have any measurable impact. Here, the school represents one of the central institutions at the community level that can play such an active role since, potentially, educational and language policy can be subject to some degree of control by the community itself.

Historically, religious institutions (despite the many contradictory aspects of their mission and actual practices in the New World) have often participated in the promotion and even limited expansion of indigenous languages. Religious institutions, like schools, bring people together, provide an opportunity to use language in a different way, and allow for different social functions of language to develop. And, as with the educational institutions, the degree of influence that communities can exercise over these social functions will determine how useful this domain turns out to be for language preservation.

Civic and traditional governing institutions vary widely in their use of the national and indigenous languages. However, in general, official and ceremonial uses of the IL have been progressively displaced, with the NL increasingly penetrating into the most traditional domains of community life. Often this shift has been the source of tension and conflict at local government meetings, judicial/reconciliation proceedings, agrarian reform convocations, town assemblies, civic celebrations, and political rallies. The unequal balance will continue to tip in favor of the national language if conscious language planning measures are not introduced. A balance of rights and responsibilities between indigenous language and national language speakers is possible (for example, the promotion of inclusionary practices such as translation for monolingual English or Spanish speakers).

However, it is the immediate and extended family unit, together with its wide network of ritual kinship ties that remains the primary vehicle of intergenerational transmission of the indigenous language. On the question of early language acquisition, evidence from studies of children's linguistic development and second language learning lends support to sociolinguistic perspectives on reversing language shift that emphasize the role of the primary care givers.[3] Early childhood, particularly the preschool years from 18 months through entry into primary school, represents the most favorable opportunity for bilingual development that will eventually lay the foundation for future growth and consolidation of the indigenous language. The observation by many community language activists that school-based programs are too little too late is consistent with what we know about the unique opportunity that early childhood language acquisition represents. Although there may be a considerable range in terms of the optimal proficiency level that children entering first grade should possess in the IL, it would be safe to say that the totally monolingual English or Spanish speaking six-year-old faces the greatest challenges in learning and maintaining the indigenous language. Given the sharp imbalances in utility, availability of learning resources, and the relative social status associated with each language, for most youngsters these challenges would turn out, sooner or later, to be insurmountable. However, as we will argue in the following chapters, minimizing or discounting the role that language learning in school plays, posing an opposition between school-based and community-based language revitalization, is unnecessary and counterproductive (for further discussion, see Cantoni, 1997).

While for the most part we will examine the research from school-based programs, the perspective that we propose (one which, in fact, appears to be the only viable alternative) will require a convergence of language planning efforts, coordinating and combining the various strands of a community-wide revitalization movement among active participants in each language use domain (see Figure 1). In Part 2 our proposals for curriculum and methods are primarily addressed to educators, however, they form part of what should be an integrated language development program bringing together the school, community, and family in one concerted effort. Beginning in Chapter 4 in particular, we continuously refer to *teachers* and *classrooms* (in part, perhaps, because we still identify ourselves professionally with the former, and owe our first experiences as educators to the latter). The references to teachers and classrooms also betray our theoretical and practical inclination on the issues of reversing language shift. However in this book, the reader should take *teacher* as any person who engages in the act of helping to guide the learning of another. It may seem that some of the suggested language-learning activities are appropriate or workable only in a school, led by a professional educator. In most cases this is not true. In some form or another, and on some level, the proposed teaching strategies would be in good hands with any speaker of an indigenous language with a sincere vocation to take on an apprentice. "Classrooms" can be found, or set up, anywhere, under the aegis of any one of the different community-based institutions, as well as in informal situations of all kinds. The story told to a granddaughter requires only a very small room; listening to an indigenous language radio program requires none at all.

In Figure 1, a number of the interacting domains of language use and aspects of language development are portrayed schematically:

(1) early childhood (preschool) and late childhood (school years);
(2) acquiring or learning the IL and or NL as a first language or a second language (also see Figure 2);
(3) the important distinction between: (a) acquiring or learning the language itself (grammatical knowledge and vocabulary specific to the language), and (b) learning the key aspects of "*discourse** competence," in this case referring to the knowledge structures that underlie higher-order language abilities associated with academic discourse (see

Language use domains and language learning

Figure 1 attempts to represent, in a very summary form, two dimensions of language learning and language proficiency. These are: (1) on the one hand, *early* (preschool) and *late* childhood – the upper and lower bubbles, respectively, and (2) acquisition and learning of the *language itself* (related to the ability to master its basic grammatical structure and use the language for everyday conversation, for example – the left-side balloons); this is in contrast to the learning of academic-related *discourse** competencies that underlie *higher-order language abilities* associated with schooling and literacy, and the various formal and elevated forms of language use in IL communities (narration, ceremony, etc. – the right-side balloons). The reader will notice that we do not divide discourse competence (the right side) into indigenous language and national language components. Rather, the strategies, abilities and skills that make up this aspect of language proficiency are largely not specific to either linguistic system, i.e. they do not "belong," strictly speaking, to either IL or NL. Once learned, these discourse competencies are always available (unless for some reason they are forgotten or otherwise lost). This model of the relationship between the two dimensions of language is meant to be compatible with the theories of Cummins (1989, 1996), which we will have the opportunity to revisit in Chapter 4. The right-side arrows emphasize that there are, potentially, two primary sources of this kind of discourse competence. With the erosion of the traditional discourses in many indigenous communities, this source will vary significantly from one community to the other, and within communities, from one family to another. In this case, other institutions, primarily the school, must compensate for this shift (usually the result of the penetration of the electronic media – which we wish to point out is far from devoid of value from the point of view of language learning).

On the left side of Figure 1, we find a number of features of the language contact situation that are peculiar to bilingual indigenous communities: (1) none of the domains is typically monopolized by the IL, while the same cannot be said of the NL; (2) the media play a pre-eminent role in both early acquisition and late language learning; with the exception perhaps of Quechua and Aymara in South America, the NL enjoys a virtual monopoly in this domain. With the advance of technological innovations in the area of access to the electronic media, this imbalance may shift slightly to include some participation of the IL in years to come. (3) In regard to the institution of public schooling, our inclusion of "NL and IL" clearly reflects *potential* rather than actual practice; and with the expansion of "preschool" educational programs, both NL and IL will be able to take advantage of the special conditions of early childhood language acquisition.

Among the various combinations of interacting factors involved, we can point to some of the more common ones: (1) early childhood acquisition of IL or NL, or both, plus extensive contact with higher-order discourses (narratives, ceremony, poetry); (2) early childhood acquisition of IL or NL, or both, with limited early contact with higher-order discourses; (3) early acquisition of IL and partial acquisition of NL, the NL consolidated in later childhood upon entry to school, or vice versa; (4) a situation of language loss/replacement where NL takes the place of IL in later childhood. Note that the converse would rarely, if ever, occur.

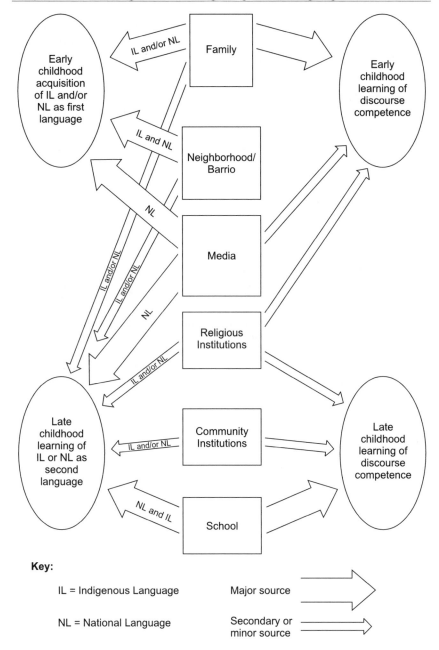

Figure 1 Domains of language use and sources of input for language learning

the glossary entry for "discourse").The rectangular elements (Family, Neighborhood, Media, School, etc.) represent the sources of the above competencies and abilities. Some are "major" or primary sources, others are usually (although not always) "minor" or secondary sources.

In the final analysis, only the indigenous community itself can put into motion the critical resources necessary to reverse the shift toward national language monolingualism. Outside agencies, researchers, and non-indigenous educators can make important contributions to the language policy

---

Child bilingual development

Figure 2 illustrates the different combinations that are possible in children's bilingual development.

(1) The national language (NL) is the first language (L1) or primary language, and the indigenous language (IL) can be learned as a second language (L2).

(2) The IL is the L1, or primary language, and the NL can be learned as a L2.

(3) Sufficient, sustained, and early exposure to both IL and NL result in a balance of linguistic competence; in effect the child possesses two primary languages. In this case the diagonal arrows do not apply, unless IL or NL suffers a significant loss in competence, for example, during the elementary school years.

Note: All three situations, (1), (2), and (3), refer to the fluent command of the language(s) as evidenced in basic conversational abilities, and face-to-face verbal interaction, not academic language proficiency

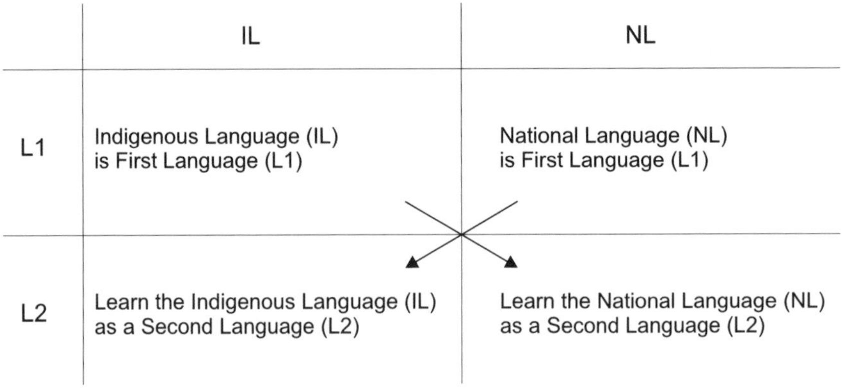

	IL	NL
L1	Indigenous Language (IL) is First Language (L1)	National Language (NL) is First Language (L1)
L2	Learn the Indigenous Language (IL) as a Second Language (L2)	Learn the National Language (NL) as a Second Language (L2)

Figure 2 Child bilingual development

discussions and debates, and even actively collaborate on projects of language planning, curriculum development and teacher training; however, they can never substitute for the autonomous, independently directed, and consciously organized cultural mobilization of the speakers themselves.

The legal and constitutional measures taken in various countries to grant official recognition of indigenous language rights have resulted in establishing important precedents and new democratic principles. Indeed, local initiatives in bilingual education today can point to national or ministerial decrees, legal decisions, and legislated public laws that justify and sanction their efforts in the face of persistent and deep-rooted resistance from powerful forces that oppose language pluralism. But again dependence on outside government institutions and the formal recognition of the nation's Indian language heritage can serve only as an adjunct to an active community-based language revitalization project.

In a very literal sense, the speech community itself has the "final word" on the question of language preservation, up to and including the option to not prioritize the task of linguistic continuity. Depending on the circumstances, even the active managing of language shift can become a valid alternative. Needless to say, such a decision should correspond exclusively to the community of speakers in their struggle, for instance, against the broader society's unwillingness to participate in a collaborative way in the community's economic, social, and cultural integration. Different kinds of heritage language development and revitalization projects may be appropriate (K. King, 2001); and different kinds of objectives would be evaluated depending on the circumstances that indigenous language communities themselves are in the best position to judge.

Chapter 2
State of the Languages

This chapter provides a brief survey of the state of indigenous languages, beginning with the countries that, together, are home to the vast majority of indigenous peoples of the Americas. Bilingual Paraguay aside, the largest concentrations of Amerindian languages today coincide geographically and historically with the great pre-Columbian civilizations of the Náhuatl-speaking peoples, most notably the Aztecs, the Maya in Mesoamerica, and the Inca empire (Andean region of South America). Within these regions, the countries from which the most information is available on bilingual programs are Mexico, Ecuador, Peru, and Bolivia.

In Mexico, Central, and South America the initial contact with the European languages occurred early and developed rapidly. Tenochtitlan fell in 1521, and within fifteen years full-fledged bilingual schools (Náhuatl and Latin, with Spanish as a third language) were operating in the former Aztec capital, now Mexico City. A similar course of events characterized the relations between Spanish and Quechua with the conquest of Peru in 1532. The first contacts between the English colonists and the North American tribes occurred a century later, and developed under distinctly separate circumstances. Nevertheless, our survey of the state of the Native American languages north of the Río Grande reveals important parallels with the present day situation to the south.

We examine these parallels, briefly focusing on each of the following countries: Mexico, Ecuador, Peru, Bolivia, and the United States. Each group of indigenous language speakers faced different challenges; although the social and historical circumstances of language contact varied from one region to the next, our interest in this chapter is to identify some of the common threads and broad tendencies. Following a brief and condensed survey, the discussion will focus on applying the concept of a continuum of *ethnolinguistic vitality** following the model developed by Joshua Fishman (1991, 2001) in his sociolinguistic study of language maintenance: *Reversing Language Shift*.

Mexico

Officially corresponding to 7.5% of the country's population, the 56 different *autochthonous** languages of Mexico represent the largest concentration in any single country, in absolute numbers, of non-European languages in the Western Hemisphere.[4] Differing estimates of the actual population aside, the figures appear to confirm recent observations of a certain demographic stabilization of the language groups as a whole. In part due to increased access to national health care programs, the total population has grown by 2,000,000 persons in the last 20 years. In 1930 16% of the national population was estimated to be indigenous; in 1950 – 11%, 1970 – 7.8%, 1990 – 7.5% (INEGI, 1990).[5] Demographers of the indigenous languages will be especially attentive to the next federal census report. Since average birthrates in the general population have declined more rapidly than those in Indian communities, the apparent leveling tendency of the last 20 years at 7.5% may continue well into the coming decades. While some of the smaller languages continue to face the prospect of extinction in the relatively short term, growth rates for several of the major groups recorded percentages above the national average of 2.6% (e.g. Huichol, Tarahumara, Tzeltal, Tzotzil). Interestingly, aside from Tzeltal, the five languages with the greatest number of speakers (Náhuatl, Maya, Zapoteco, Mixteco and Hñähñú) all registered growth rates below the national average.

During the same period, monolingualism in the indigenous language has seen a significant decline: from 27.6% down to 15.8% of all speakers, ranging widely from 36% for Tzeltal in Chiapas to virtually 0% for some groups further to the north. Reported illiteracy remains high at 41% (more than three times the national average), concentrated among the same sectors where Indian language monolingualism is highest: women who work in the home and elders. Among school-age children, while the expansion of educational programs in the rural areas has dramatically increased the number of Spanish speakers, the largest indigenous language monolingual age group remains the 5 to 9 year old, primary school, population (26%), falling, however, to 8% by age 11 and 12. In general, it is important to take note that even in the most remote regions (in the states of Chiapas and Guerrero), on the average, two-thirds of all indigenous language speakers are bilingual (Manrique Casteñeda, 1988; Valdéz & Menéndez, 1987; INEGI, 1990b).

Contradictory tendencies

In addition to the relationship among the different sectors of monolinguals and bilinguals (from the educational planning point of view) the issue of dialectical variation within each language poses interesting problems, an issue that we will return to when we discuss language and literacy learning. As with all languages, indigenous language dialects reflect the naturally occurring diversity in forms of social organization, regional cultural differences, and geographical dispersion (Díaz-Couder, 1990) that are an important aspect of community identity. Intercomprehensibility among dialects varies; for example, differences may be analogous to those between Spanish, Portuguese, and Italian as in the case of Zapoteco – considered to be one language. On the other hand, variation often involves superficial differences of pronunciation, and vocabulary; the distinction between the categories language and *dialect** being one of historical circumstance and cultural difference (Tzeltal and Tzotzil, and Tohono O'odham and Pima are considered different languages despite their respective linguistic affinities). In the United States, for example, a similar relationship exists between Navajo and Apache.

However, the social relations that the contact with the European languages imposed also tend to exacerbate dialectical fragmentation (Citarella, 1990). The historical example of Náhuatl perhaps represents a special case, but some of the same factors operate in other situations as well. During the period immediately prior to the Spanish Conquest in 1521 and for a brief period after, Náhuatl played the role of a region-wide *lingua franca*, losing this function by the 17th century. Henceforth, and continuing to this day, the geographical and cultural isolation of the different Náhuatl-speaking communities appears to have widened the distance between one dialectical variant and another. Having lost (for the communities of *native** speakers) the literary domains in which it briefly flourished, the language also lost one of the stabilizing forces that tends to counteract fragmentation. On the other hand, recent economic and technological developments have introduced potentially *unifying factors*. Greater mobility has increased contacts between formerly isolated towns and regions, indigenous language radio programs project local dialects beyond their "traditional" radius, in the same way, although on a still very limited scale, that expanded telephone service does for the conversational domain. For some of the more ethnolinguistically vital groups (e.g. Zapoteco of the Isthmus region) the availability of desktop publishing has provided an impetus for local writers to begin to standardize orthographic conventions (de la Cruz, 1992; Bernard, 1992).

In this century, sweeping economic changes have introduced new and previously unforeseen developments in the relationship between indigenous communities and the broader society. The expanding national and international labor market has created a new (and in many cases numerically predominant) social class within the indigenous communities: wage workers whose migration ranges from daily commuting to nearby urban centers, to long-term cyclical movements to the United States. With the

Voices 2 (Náhuatl)

Quinenequi xochitli zan noyollo,
zan nomac on mania.
Zan nicuicanentlamati,
zan nicuicayeyecohua in tlalticpac,
ni Cuacuauhztin,
niononconequi xochitl,
zan nomac on mani,
In ninentlamati.

(Flowers my heart desires
that they be in my hands.
With verses I am afflicted,
I only rehearse verses on this earth.
I, Cuacuauhtzin,
with anxiety I desire the flowers,
that they be in my hands,
for I am dispossessed.)

Cuacuauhtzin de Tepechpan, mid-15th century
(in Leander, 1972: 144)

greater Los Angeles area being the primary destination, it has been estimated that as many as 250,000 indigenous migrant workers reside, at one
time or another, in the Southwestern states of the US. (Varese, 1990).

Immigrant workers' experiences with wage labor, different forms of
economic and social organization, and cultural diversity have transformed
individual perspectives and worldviews. Returning from the United
States, or from similar sojourns in Mexico City, new perceptions and attitudes come into contact, and conflict, with traditional ways. Generally, this
phenomenon has been viewed as a factor that undermines language maintenance; however, the growing economic interdependence and resulting
broader consciousness of interethnic and class relations also allows for the
contemplation of new alternatives, in particular new cultural and linguistic
prerogatives. The progressive "proletarianization" of the indigenous
communities has gone hand in hand, for example, with the emergence of a
class of young bilingual educators, itself, in part, a product of changing
expectations and social and ethnic consciousness on the part of the indigenous communities themselves. During the decade of the 1980's, the
number of indigenous elementary school teachers grew from under 14,000

to over 30,000, with representation in all executive bodies of the Indian education bureaucracy at the state and national levels (Varese, 1990).

Today, in many communities, the prestige of the indigenous language has benefited from the new requirements for the highly regarded position of bilingual teacher (keeping in mind that increments in prestige are always relative, as are the competitiveness of classroom teacher salaries). Not surprisingly, opportunities in other areas have availed themselves: increased access to elementary and secondary education for girls (and opportunities for young women to work outside the home), more frequent and expanded contact with other indigenous communities as well as Hispanic society beyond the limited domain of the weekly regional market. While generally these socioeconomic and cultural shifts have been associated with *language shift* (in this case, from the indigenous language to Spanish) within these broad tendencies (historically inevitable in all cases) new domains and fields of action emerge that provide contexts for indigenous *language development*.

Map 2 Indigenous languages of Mexico

Source: *Ethnologue* (http://www.ethnologue.com/web.asp)

Ecuador

Some 25% of Ecuador's 10 million citizens speak an indigenous language. The central mountainous region is home to the great majority of Quechua, upwards of 2,000,000, and another 60,000 share the lowland Amazonia region with the culturally and politically active Shuar. Numbering only 42,000, the Shuar have maintained a cohesive territorial organization that they have been able to take full advantage of in their struggle for greater control over local resources and equality. Smaller ethnic groups remain along the coastal regions (Chachi, Awa, Tsáchila, Siona-Secoya, A'i and Huaorani) for the most part in one or another advanced stage of dissolution and assimilation into the multicultural communities and large urban centers of Western Ecuador (Chiodi, 1990).

Despite the impact of a certain degree of dialectical differentiation, Quechua has maintained its strong presence in the highlands. This situation is in many ways comparable to that of Náhuatl in Mexico; both enjoyed the status of regional *lingua franca*, respectively, of the Inca and Aztec empires, and later, that of post-colonial vehicles of Christian missionary work.

Parallel to the generalized democratization process in Ecuador during the 1970s, the indigenous peoples of the Amazonia and the highlands have made significant advances in both ethnic-wide and interethnic organization, mobilizing their communities around a program of cultural, linguistic and even limited political self-determination. Their self-identification as *nationalidades* has promoted, for example-conscious and concerted efforts toward unification of the Quechua alphabet, a limited publication of Quechuan language materials, and formal control over bilingual education programs by the CONAIE, Confederación de Nacionalidades Indígenas del Ecuador (Moya, 1990).

The history of the Shuar merits special attention, in particular their efforts to maintain a measure of ethnolinguistic and cultural cohesion in reaction to the ever-expanding industrial and commercial penetration of their traditional territory. The Federación Shuar was founded in 1964 with the help of a group of Salesian advisors, and soon achieved national recognition as the official interlocutor of the confederation of the Centros Shuar based on local villages and extended family units. It is noteworthy that the Salesian missionaries, who have promoted the integration of the Shuar into Ecuadorian society, came into contact with the communities relatively recently. The Federation evolved into a truly ethnic-wide and language-wide (i.e. cross-dialectical) force that promoted the self-identity and unity of the Shuar as a people, by 1972 organizing one of the most extensive and effective radio/distance education networks in Latin America. From an

Map 3 Indigenous languages of the Andean countries

Source: *Ethnologue* (http://www.ethnologue.com/web.asp)

initial enrollment of 506, the program today serves over 90% of the school-age population (5700 students in more than 200 centers, staffed by 10 bilingual *telemaestros*, 56 *teleauxialares* and 14 supervisors). The Sistema de Educación Radiofónica Bicultural Shuar (SERBISH), under the direction of the Federación, represents a major linguistic unifying agent that is far more significant in its actual impact on the language than the limited and sporadic coverage that, for example, indigenous radio programming in Mexico has been able to attain. Kendall King (2001) provides a recent report from the field on the SERBISH program, and the impact it has had on thinking about bilingual education among the majority Quechua-speaking communities.

Peru

Quechua and Aymara are the predominant languages of the Peruvian Andes, with monolinguals (Quechua 7.64%, Aymara 0.84%) and bilinguals (14.21% and 1.62% respectively) comprising 25% of the total population, the southern department of Puno has the highest concentration – 90% speaking one or the other of the two major indigenous languages. The eastern region, the Amazonia, is home to more than 50 ethnolinguistic groups belonging to eleven different language families (Arahuaca, Cahuapana, Harakmbet, Huitoto, Jibaro, Pano, Peb-yagna, Tacana, Tucano, Guaraní and Zaparo) many of whom find themselves today, as in Ecuador, in the final stages of extinction (Citarella, 1990).

The Quechua and Aymara, far from being isolated, have maintained continuous contact with the coastal Hispanic society for the last 400 years. The Puno region (the most indigenous of the Andes, and the department of greatest Aymara concentration) is representative of the current, ever shifting, balance between Spanish and the languages of the former Inca Empire. Already in 1940, 62% of the Aymara were bilingual. Today 84.5% are bilingual, with the Spanish monolingual sector at almost 10% compared with a negligible 1.5% 50 years ago (López, 1989). Nationally, language shift has been even more dramatic: in 1940, indigenous language speaking monolinguals plus bilinguals amounted to 35 + 16.5%; in 1961 the figures were 20 + 20%. In 1981, 73% of all Peruvians spoke only Spanish (Citarella, 1990).

The case of Peru stands out in regard to one particular aspect of its language policy. During the populist military regime of Velasco Alvarado (1968–75) the indigenous languages were accorded formal national recognition in the Federal Education Code. With the stated goal of incorporating the country's marginalized sectors, the Education Ministry's 1970 Annual Report called attention to:

The necessity of overcoming the present violent Castellanization and degradation of the aboriginal languages by [establishing] a system of bilingual literacy teaching, as a more effective, secure, and permanent Castellanization, and comprehension and revalorization of the cultural patterns of each ethnic group. (quoted in Citarella, 1990: 47)

Teacher preparation included required courses in a "Peruvian *vernacular** language," and in 1975, by government decree, Quechua was declared an "official language." While this precedent in language policy represented an important formal acknowledgment of indigenous peoples' linguistic rights in general, actual implementation remained at a virtual standstill for many years.[6] By 1981 still only 3.7% of the total bilingual school population was receiving one form or another of dual language instruction (Zúñiga, 1990).

In Chapter 3, we will review the important findings of one of the best-documented pilot programs in bilingual education in Latin America, the Proyecto Experimental de Educación Bilingüe de Puno (PEEB-P).

Bolivia

From a cursory examination of the census figures, Bolivia seems to depart from the pattern of rapid language shift that is evident in Mexico, Ecuador, and Peru. As in all of Latin America, the national language has registered significant gains, extending its reach into all predominantly indigenous language speaking regions. While 50 years ago Spanish could be considered the language of a minority elite, today more than 65% of the population is Spanish speaking. However, the increase in societal bilingualism, to date, has not been at the expense (at least numerically) of the indigenous languages, with the percentage of Quechua and Aymara speakers maintaining their majority status: 1946 – 54%, 1960 – 63%, 1976 – 63%. What investigators have characterized as a kind of coincidence, or confluence, of high levels of bilingualism with persistent language loyalty is evidenced in a detailed national population survey that actually examined some key sociolinguistic patterns (Montoya, 1983). The national survey analyzed, separately, which language is used "habitually" in the home, and which language(s) respondents reported as knowing or speaking. For example in La Paz, while 20.8% indicated monolingualism in Aymara, for 46.6% it is the habitual language of family conversation – evidence that the indigenous language fulfills important functions related to ethnic identity (Amadio & Zúñiga, 1990; López, 1995). The authors, citing a study by Albó, point to the broad base that Quechua and Aymara maintain among both recent immigrants to the capital, and long-term residents, especially in domains tied to cultural expression, religion, and the family and its extended ritual kinship network. Bolivia's unique nation-wide indigenous language radio programming – the most extensive in all of Latin America, at 50% of total national radio kilowatt output – is testimony to the social weight of the majority languages of the country. Especially in rural areas, language learning, for example, apparently involves large numbers of Spanish-speaking monolinguals becoming bilingual, as well as a significant number of Aymara learning Quechua (in many departments, the more prestigious of the two).

Among the "minority languages" of Bolivia (30 in all, numbering approximately 100,000 speakers) special note should be taken of the Guaraní. On the one hand these 58,000 indigenous residents of Santa Cruz department represent a small percentage of the indigenous majority. However, their proximity (geographically and linguistically) to the Guaraní of Paraguay (the country's majority language, that is reserved the status of "national," alongside the "official" Spanish) is not unrelated to the high levels of cultural and linguistic consciousness in the community on issues of bilingual education (Albó & D'Emilio, 1990). For a review of recent changes regarding national language policy in education, see López (1995).

Amadio and Zúñiga introduce a note of caution regarding the apparently stable bilingual balance in Bolivia. Despite high levels of ethnolinguistic loyalty among all the major groups, in school, the exclusive use of Spanish remains the norm in all departments, with advances in bilingual education still at the most incipient level. Comparing the percentage of school-age Spanish monolinguals (between 45 and 50%) with the national average (37%) an all-too-predictable tendency can be projected if major reforms in the area of language teaching are not put into practice. The authors predict that:

> If the discriminatory treatment of indigenous languages and cultures favoring the dominant language continues the result will be the progressive advance of Spanish, but with a deficient proficiency on the part of bilinguals, accompanied by the gradual loss of the ancestral languages and cultures of Bolivia that, to date, have demonstrated their forceful presence, and whose vitality distinguishes Bolivia from the other countries of the Andean region. (Amadio & Zúñiga, 1990: 245)

The United States

Less than 1% of the current population of the United States identifies itself as having American Indian, Alaska Native, or Native Hawaiian ancestry, this represents a total of over 2 million, of which an estimated 361,978 still speak their heritage language (Grimes, 1999). After four centuries of precipitous population decline, owing mainly to epidemics caused by diseases brought from Europe for which indigenous Americans had no immunities, recent US Census reports show the American Indian population growing rapidly. The estimated ten million indigenous inhabitants of what is now the United States declined to less than 250,000 in 1900

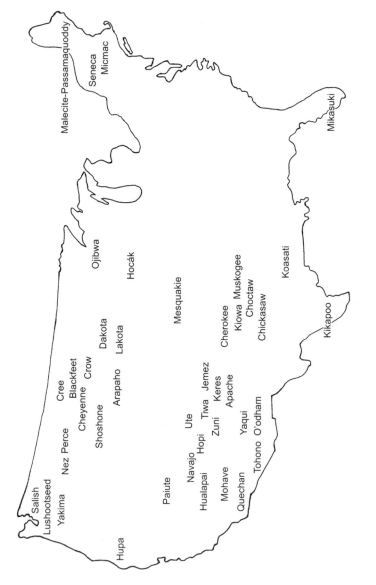

Map 4 Indigenous languages of the United States ("lower continental 48")

Source: *Ethnologue* (http://www.ethnologue.com/web.asp)

(Thornton, 1987). Over the course of the 20th century, the indigienous poulation began to grow again: and the last 30 years has seen a doubling of the population that claims American Indian ancestry.

Of the 154 indigenous languages that are still spoken in the United States (about half the estimated pre-Columbian count), only about 20 of these are still being transmitted to children by their families. The Navajo, with 148,530 speakers, represent the largest group; at the other extreme, seven languages have only one speaker left. In California these most severely threatened languages are Coast Miwok, Plains Miwok, Pomo, and Serrano, in Oregon, they are Coos and Kalapuya, and in Alaska, Eyak. Within the continental United States and Alaska, most American Indian languages fall into one of several broad language families, including Algonquian, Athabaskan, Eskimo-Aleut, Uto-Aztecan, Muskogean, Siouan, Iroquoian, Penutian, Salishan. A few languages, such as Zuni, appear to be unrelated to any of the larger families.

As in Mexico and South America, early European missionaries and traders learned an Indian language for the purpose of evangelization or commerce. For example, the Reverend John Eliot, with the help of Nesuton and other Massachusetts informants, was able to print 1,500 copies of an Indian Bible in the Algonquian language at Harvard University in 1663. This missionary activity continues into the present day, with the Summer Institute of Linguistics working to translate the Christian Bible into the indigenous languages still being spoken in the United States. Although not as significant as the Latin American experiments in bilingual education of the 16th century, the use of Indian languages in some schools during the late 1800s and early 1900s stands as an important historical precedent (Lockard, 1995). Most notably in Hawaii, in many schools, all subjects were taught in the Hawaiian language before the Hawaiian monarchy was over-thrown in 1893.

Missionary writings in the indigenous languages, such as those by Eliot, are sometimes the only remaining record of the language. From these archives, present-day descendents of the communities that the mission-aries served have attempted to "recreate" languages that have no living speakers; a study by Amery (2000) reviews a similar project in Australia. Other archival sources on indigenous languages can be found in the work of anthropological linguists dating to the second half of the 19th century.

Unlike some of the language preservation work of missionaries, the efforts of the US Government generally worked toward the suppression and eradication of Indian languages. One of the most active was led by US Commissioner of Indian Affairs J.D.C. Atkins, who in the 1880s banned the use of Indian languages in both church-sponsored schools and public schools. This suppression was fairly consistent up until the Great Depression of the 1930s when President Roosevelt's Commissioner of Indian Affairs John Collier promoted initiatives in self-government through the Indian Reorganization Act of 1934, and a few experiments in bilingual education were attempted again.

After World War II, a conservative reaction set in that led to an unsuccessful attempt to terminate the system of Indian Reservations. The Civil Rights movement of the 1960s, however, contributed to another policy shift. In 1968 the US Congress passed the Bilingual Education Act that, while mainly providing for speakers of Spanish and other European and Asian languages, was also extended to include bilingual programs that supported the teaching of American Indian and Alaska Native languages. In 1975 Congress passed an Indian Self Determination and Educational Assistance Act that promoted more Indian self government, and provided for the establishment of locally controlled schools, which sometimes taught Indian languages (Reyhner & Eder, 1989). However, most of the efforts to teach Indian languages in schools were limited to less than an hour a day, and usually did not go beyond the level of teaching basic vocabulary, how to count, greetings, and so forth.

Another step towards the revitalization of indigenous languages was marked by the beginnings of the Tribal College movement, with the founding of Navajo Community College in 1968. By 2001, the American Indian Higher Education Consortium included 32 members in the United States and one in Canada. Most of these colleges today teach at least one indigenous language. In the 1980s several tribal governments approved official language policy statements that required or recommended the teaching of the indigenous language in schools, but in part because schools are funded either by the federal or state government, these resolutions had little impact on actual classroom practice. In 1990, at the urging of indigenous language activists, the US Congress passed the Native American Languages Act (PL. 101–477) which made it US Government policy to preserve, promote, and protect American Indian languages. While the Act provided no funding to teach indigenous languages, it has been helpful in turning back efforts in the 1990s to end bilingual education and enforce "English Only" legislation for schools at the state level (Reyhner, 1993; Reyhner & Tennant, 1995).

In the 1980s and 1990s US indigenous language activists began learning about immersion teaching methodologies; visits to New Zealand's Maori "Language Nests" have been especially compelling. Native Hawaiians, who share a Polynesian ancestry with the Maori of New Zealand, were the first to establish their own immersion preschool language programs starting in 1984. Immersion teaching was then extended first into the elementary, and then into the secondary education levels. Also, as in New Zealand, university level courses were offered to teach both the Hawaiian language and immersion methodologies to teachers who were needed to staff the new immersion schools. Through indigenous language conferences like the one held in 1994 in Hilo, Hawaii, mainland language activists learned about the second language immersion approach to teaching indigenous languages, and have applied it to a number of experimental programs in their communities. One noteworthy example is the Piegan Institute's Cut-Bank Language Immersion School on the Blackfeet Indian Reservation in Montana (Kipp, 2000).

While in some ways the indigenous language speaking population of the United States is the most dispersed (118 out of the 154 languages have fewer than 1,000 speakers, with only eight above the 10,000 mark; Grimes, 1999), the number of active demonstration projects and ongoing bilingual programs in the United States singles it out among all the other countries reviewed so far. In any case, the same principle of Linguistic Human Rights (see Chapter 1) applies to all speech communities, regardless of their size or short-term prospects of survival.

Stages of Language Preservation and Revitalization

As we have been able to see from our selective overview of the state of indigenous languages (IL) in the Americas, not a single exception exists to the overall tendency toward language displacement by either Spanish or English. While the historical continuity of Quechua, Aymara, Náhuatl, and Maya seems secure for the foreseeable future, even languages with millions of speakers face the immediate problem of erosion and loss in many of their traditional regional strongholds, where the shift to the national language is occurring at an accelerated pace. Many enclaves or pockets of the IL, in close proximity to major metropolitan areas, face the prospects of total loss in the short term despite the demographic weight and vitality of the language on a national or region-wide level.

The loss of speakers "in the periphery" aside, all indigenous languages face the challenge of both preserving their existing expressive capacities, and adapting to the new requirements of a post-agrarian, increasingly market-driven social organization. Various researchers have called attention to the necessity of actively intervening in the process of language planning at the level of the actual structure of the languages that for 400 years have progressively ceded, together with domains of use, one grammatical, lexical, and discourse feature after another to the national languages

Table 1 Stages of language revitalization

Stage 1

- Speakers of IL restricted to a few grandparents and elders only.
- Speakers are socially isolated.
- Grandchildren are not IL speakers, a few young adults and children may be limited passive bilinguals.
- Language is moribund or on the verge of extinction.
- No intergenerational transmission.
- Archival language rescue efforts may be appropriate to maintain an historical record of the IL.
- A small nucleus of ethnolinguistically conscious language activists may participate in language study groups.

Stage 2

- Most IL speakers are not socially isolated, but are beyond childbearing age.
- Grandparents and elders use the IL among themselves.
- Young adults are mostly monolingual in the national language; many are passive bilinguals.
- Some intergenerational transmission, mainly grandparents to grandchildren.
- "Language nest" type programs are able to put grandchildren (IL learners) in contact with elders.
- Limited IL use at home, especially in presence of grandparents.
- Communities are characterized by pockets of IL use (the most "traditional" or "conservative" barrios).
- Elders are often addressed in small businesses in the IL.
- IL is not used in the school (sometimes actively excluded).
- Written functions virtually nonexistent, except for occasional private possession of some written material or book (e.g. Bible), but written material in IL does not circulate.

Stage 3

- Language is "alive," active intergenerational transmission.
- IL in school:
  - at higher levels IL is used for instruction in academic subjects;
  - schools enjoy a degree of community control, but not complete, most often only incipient;
  - IL used as medium of communication among students, and occasionally between teachers and students outside of instructional contexts;
  - use in school is still short of widespread communicative functions, IL and NL alternate or compete in regard to preference, actual use, conditioned by large number of indigenous children who are dominant in the NL.
- IL used in written functions (still limited) outside of school (e.g. church).
- Limited use of IL in writing for interpersonal communication (letters, notes, etc.) (see McLaughlin, 1992)
- Limited reading in IL (e.g. religious literature), national language literacy still predominates in all domains, "special diglossia" predominates.
- Some use of IL (including, possibly, writing) by community organizations.

Stage 4
- Intergenerational transmission during early childhood between parents and children in the home.
- IL use in government services (lower and higher).
- Introduction of IL into the mass media:
  - print;
  - electronic.
- IL use in school for academic subjects (as language of instruction) is institutionalized.
- Use of IL in higher education:
  - language as object of study (as in departments of Modern Languages);
  - language as medium of content instruction.
- "Special diglossia" begins to break down:
  - some records are kept in IL, IL enjoys a certain legal status (as in court proceedings, titles, documents);
  - oral/written division of language functions is undermined.
- IL use in the workplace:
  - at higher levels by supervisors;
  - at lower levels by employees only;
  - IL use is normal in small businesses.
- IL use is normal in government offices and community organizations:
  - among IL-speaking workers;
  - serving IL-speaking clients.

(Chiodi, 1993; López, 1989). Thus, on one level or another, the linguistic and cultural project of *revitalization* becomes a necessary language-planning objective for any indigenous language community that has taken on the task of language preservation.

Reyhner and Tennant (1995) and Slate (1993) have adapted and applied the eight stages of language loss, proposed by Fishman (1991), to the situation of Native American languages in the United States. For the purposes of this review, we have combined the eight categories into four (see Table 1), and inverted the continuum to indicate, beginning with the lowest stage, *levels of ethnolinguistic vitality*. Stage 4 represents the highest level of *language preservation*. Given the wide variation of sociolinguistic contexts in which Amerindian languages find themselves in contact with their respective national languages, we propose viewing the stages more as an analytical tool (in the sense of *levels* or *contexts*) than as a series of successive *stages* that a language would pass through. Except for languages on the verge of extinction, approaching a kind of *level zero* where perhaps the most pressing task is the compilation of "archival material" (Fishman, 1996), most indigenous languages that have not completely lost the capacity of transmission actually combine features from more than one stage. In the case of some of the well-established indigenous languages (e.g. Náhuatl in

Mexico, Navajo in the United States) we would be able to identify individual communities and regions that correspond to some aspects of the lowest stage where dislocation of the IL is immanent, others that share features of the intermediate stages, passing directly to isolated situations that pertain to the highest levels of language maintenance - use of the language in literature and higher education.

Table 1 represents an attempt at conceptualizing the various phases and contexts of loss, continuity, and development. To each would correspond policy and planning tasks that not only overlap, but also should be applied to each situation of language contact in a way that exploits the actual resources available to the community. In the following section we will refer to two specific contrasting situations of IL revitalization that illustrate the need to view any kind of stages model as one tool among others for understanding the complexities of language contact, as opposed to an instruction manual for applying "appropriate" remedies in some situations and avoiding "inappropriate" ones in others.

In Chapters 4, 5, and 6 we will discuss specific instructional strategies for reversing language shift. While school seems to be the most logical community institution for implementing language-teaching programs, it is not the only one. Language learning occurs naturally and spontaneously in some situations, and requires special teaching contexts in others. If the indigenous language is a frequent and integral part of the daily communicative interchange that surrounds the preschool child, some level of conversational fluency will be assured in most cases by the age of 6 or 7. No "instructional strategy" is necessary for this language acquisition objective. For this child the school offers other opportunities: learning the national language if the child's access to this domain has been limited, and developing the indigenous language along two different, but related, lines:

(1)   extending the use of the IL to new contexts of use and to include new language functions that will make it available as a tool for higher-order thinking, including reflecting on cultural change and the role that the community's indigenous culture and language will play in this change;

(2)   for those children who come to school with only partial knowledge of the IL language system, teach the indigenous language as a second language. Given the social pressures to abandon the language (outlined in our five-country survey at the beginning of this chapter), maintenance of IL grammatical competence would remain an important task for children, including those who enter first grade with complete native-speaker knowledge of the IL.

School is not the only community domain to which these tasks correspond, but it is among the principal ones. In our modest contribution to this complex discussion, the argument that we will present goes somewhat further: school is among the indispensable domains of indigenous language revitalization, on some level, in all circumstances.

Table 1 implies that different formal language learning strategies and activities become more prominent or salient in one or another stage (e.g. where all community institutions in stage 4 are bilingual as a matter of policy and practice, as opposed to stage 2). However, it would be a mistake, once an IL community (or a significant sector of it) committed itself to language preservation and development, to exclude any one agent or domain from the overall "language shift reversal strategy." Again, as we pointed out earlier, actual IL speaking communities, more often than not, do not fall neatly into any single category, the Navajo language being a prominent example. Within the geographical boundaries of its vast reservation, there exist communities that approach the situation of stage 2. On the other hand, there are isolated features that we can point to from stage 4: Diné College, a limited presence in newspaper and electronic media, official recognition and use by the tribal government, extensive intergenerational transmission in some communities. Perhaps most bilingual contexts on the reservation can be characterized by stage 3, (again in general terms), combining features from stage 2, and to a lesser degree from stage 4.

In a similar way, the recent progress that has been made in reviving the Hawaiian language stands as a case in point for viewing the stages of language revitalization in a non-prescriptive way. That is, the stages are useful in analyzing current trends toward language shift or language preservation, not as a fixed set of guidelines that prescribe certain intervention strategies for each stage. As we will see in the following case study, this would be a mistake.

The Hawaiian language, the indigenous language of the 132 island Pacific Ocean archipelago would be considered by all accounts as an endangered language in an advanced state of erosion. Today, as little as 20% of the population identifies itself ethnically as Hawaiian; among these, only a small minority (less than 5%) speaks of the language – 8,872 mostly elderly persons, according to the 1990 census (Kamaná & Wilson, 1996).

As a historical note, the indigenous language of Hawaii, during the 19th century monarchy, was the medium of instruction of an extensive public education system. By 1830, it is estimated that as many as half of all adults were literate in Hawaiian. The existence of a sizable archive of indigenous language literature stands as a modern day testimony to this "Golden Age" of written production and widespread literacy. The reader will take note here of the analogy with Mexico and the flourishing of writing in Náhuatl, and other Mesoamerican ILs, after the introduction of the *alphabetic** system. In Hawaii the social experiment in IL literacy was also short-lived, for similar reasons. Only recently, in 1978, was the legal status of the language reinstated (Slaughter, 1997), and not until 1986 was the restriction against Hawaiian as an instructional language in public schools rescinded (Ka'awa & Hawkins, 1997).

Before the founding of the first immersion preschools on 1984, the state of the language most closely corresponded to stage 1, combined with some elements of stage 2. Nevertheless, revitalization efforts targeted those domains where language teaching could be consciously and deliberately planned: school programs and literacy. Having won the right to control curriculum decisions, language activists were able to circumvent the obstacle of a virtual break in intergenerational transmission. Because language use can be planned within the *boundaries** of the school, Hawaiian immersion was able to launch the program with a teaching staff that was primarily composed of non-native speakers.

From 40 students in two schools the program has expanded to more than 1,700 in full-day K-12 and preschool immersion, 3,500 children in non-immersion K-12 programs, and over 3,000 in community college and university classes, many of which are IL-medium content courses (Jacobson, 1998; Ka'awa & Hawkins, 1997). Research on learning outcomes indicates similar positive findings to those registered in Canadian immersion. The more difficult assessment, however, will involve measuring the impact of this school-based program on actual trends in the reversal of language shift. But evidently, any revitalization movement that would not have placed such a preeminent emphasis on the educational institutions would have had much less to show (Wilson & Kamaná, 2000). For more discussion on the critical issues in Hawaiian language immersion teaching, see Warner (2001).

A final note on literacy and writing: the existence of an archival record (the preservation, in books, of traditional IL literature, much of which otherwise would have been irrevocably lost) has played no small role in the Hawaiian language revival. The re-editing of the material has provided the present-day generation of bilingual students with both an invaluable L2 learning resource and an inherent motivation to maintain high levels of biliteracy. This particular auxiliary project will provide critical lessons for other indigenous languages that have at their disposal extensive archives, to date, inaccessible to the actual speech communities.

The Hawaiian immersion experiment was in large part inspired by the successful experience of the Moari *Te Kohanga Reo* (Language nest), a New Zealand government-funded program for young preschool children. As with Hawaiian, the Maori language revitalization effort could not employ a complete cadre of native speakers from the parents' generation. In this case, grandparents have comprised the greater part of the teaching staffs (Shafer, 1988), institutionalizing, in a sense, the stage 2 intergenerational pattern characteristic of endangered languages. Apparently, the critical factor in reversing the decline of Maori was not the primary school language programs, but the *preschool* Language Nests. Beginning second language instruction in an IL in first grade may be insufficient, as evidenced in the meager results of bilingual education in New Zealand previous to the establishment of the *kohunga reos*. On the other hand, today, between two and three thousand children enter school each year with significant levels of fluency in Maori, which in turn has had a kind of multiplier effect on the primary school programs (Spolsky, 1989; Bratt Paulston *et al.*, 1993).

At the other extreme, at least in demographic terms, we can point to the circumstances of languages such as Quechua (over 10 million according to Silver & Miller, 1997). Some key features of stage 4 are virtually guaranteed by Quechua's broad population base alone, above all intergenerational transmission during early childhood. In hundreds of communities in the highland regions of Ecuador, Peru, and Bolivia, language socialization in the IL is *direct*, between parents and children, as opposed to the stage 2 transmission that depends on extensive child–grandparent contact. Quechua, which enjoys "official" status in many areas, can be heard in some lower-level government agencies, workplaces, and extensively on the air waves in regions of highest density (e.g. Bolivia). The reader will notice here that even when the central requirements of language maintenance are assured (i.e. intergenerational transmission), the IL's diminished presence in the other domains of stage 4 represents a kind of "opening" for this space to be occupied by the NL. In the past, these domains were in fact left "empty," so to speak. Today, fewer and fewer communities, even among the most remote and isolated, remain cut off from the public educational system, communication with the NL-speaking society, radio and television, basic governmental services, and wage employment. With this new distribution of language functions in mind, Quechua must begin to negotiate and consolidate a shared space with Spanish in the new arenas of language use, because they are *at the same time*: (1) opportunities for language learning, and (2) points of language erosion. As Figure 1 in the previous chapter suggests, it becomes progressively more difficult, and eventually impossible, to parcel out the languages, to rigorously compartmentalize them at the community level among Family, Neighborhood, Media, Church and School.

Thus, bilingual education in Peru, for example, is faced with challenges that would have been unthinkable only two or three generations ago when there was little or no "competition" for language use domains between IL and NL. Today educators are discussing questions that include the development of elementary school textbooks and curriculum in Quechua, the standardization of an alphabetic writing system, developing the language itself to allow it to express new concepts, and training teachers in methods of teaching an indigenous language in school (Jung, 1992; Chatry-Komarek, 1987; Chiodi, 1993; Llanque Chana, 1992).

In conclusion, we would propose that there is no one-to-one correspondence between stages of language revitalization and pedagogical approaches. It is still not well understood what relationship night obtain between the sociolinguistic factors related to the different defining characteristics of each stage and the range of effective learning strategies for children at one or another level of IL proficiency. Rather, teachers should be guided by what kinds of learning task are appropriate for each child: what grammatical pattern, vocabulary/concept unit, discourse strategy, etc. each child seems ready to master next. This or that socio-contextual aspect of language displacement or language shift reversal may constrain curriculum planning, but it should not be the starting point for disqualifying or postponing what may turn out to be effective language learning approaches at the classroom level.

Much of the discussion among researchers on the prospects of reversing language shift remains speculative. Often "case studies" of both successful and unsuccessful attempts at language revitalization reveal one or another seemingly exceptional aspect that discourages generalization, for example, Spolsky (1989) and Bratt Paulston *et al.* (1993) on the revival of Hebrew. In the fledgling science of language planning, laboratory experiments are not possible, and never will be. Thus, indigenous communities and educators should, after examining the evidence and comparing experiences, take the measures that seem appropriate and necessary for the situation that corresponds to their language. Proposals and solutions that are simply intuitively appealing will deserve serious considerations as well, and studying their outcomes will further contribute to our understanding of the complex processes involved. As a general rule of thumb, we should remember that concepts and theories must always be applied to particular contexts that sometimes present special circumstances; however, no situation of bilingualism and language contact is completely exceptional.

Chapter 3

Language Policy and Language Planning: The Role of the School and Indigenous Language Literacy

Historical Perspectives: The First Experiments in Bilingual Education

Thirty years ago the renowned Mexican literary historian, Miguel León-Portilla, presented a series of lectures at the then newly established Navajo Community College (NCC), now Diné College. Entitled *Identidad cultural o asimilación en la corriente de la sociedad mayoritaria* ("Cultural identity or assimilation in the current of the majority society"), the encounter represented an important early attempt at initiating an ongoing dialogue between Latin American educators and researchers in the area of indigenous languages and their counterparts in the United States. One of the central themes of León-Portilla's presentation focused on the dynamics of cultural change and cultural conflict, the tension between the expansion of the national culture, and the corresponding resistance on the part of the indigenous communities.

León-Portilla's (1976) concept of *nepantla* (from Náhuatl, "in between") captures the essence underlying many of the problems of language contact under conditions of the extreme inequality that the teacher of an indigenous language would face. Both in school and in the community as a whole, it often seems that the national language has at its disposal all of the advantages (in the first place, the print and electronic media), while the indigenous language struggles to maintain the few functions that the national language has not yet taken over. Indeed, investigations of indigenous students' language development have made reference variously to concepts such as ambivalence, semilingualism, subordinate bilingualism, and language conflict, all attempting to describe one or another "in transition" phenomenon, being "in-between." To these we could add the contrasts and tensions that seem to oppose: orality and literacy, traditionalism and modernity, maintaining proficiency in the indigenous language and attaining full proficiency in the national language (NL).

Unfortunately, this discussion has never prospered, despite important advances in the field of bilingual indigenous education on both sides, parallel in various aspects, but developing for the most part independently. On occasions educators have shared experiences at international conferences, and some published reports of research make their way across the borders. However, the perception that the indigenous cultures of Latin America and North America occupy separate terrain, and face fundamentally different problems, has inhibited the exchange of ideas. For North American educators, access to information has been limited because most reports from the south are published in Spanish. On the other hand, for Latin American educators, not all the pertinent research findings from the United States and Canada are readily available. Comparing North and South, the distinct histories of contact between Europeans and Native Americans have left their mark in many ways; but today, especially in the area of bilingual education and language teaching, the respective indigenous communities have more in common than ever before.

The history of the contact between the European and Amerindian languages has from the beginning been closely tied to the history of indigenous education, and to the evolution of indigenous language literacy. In both Mexico and the US Southwest, the early colonial era use of indigenous languages for academic purposes (centered primarily on religious instruction) was developed by Jesuits, Franciscans and other mendicant orders, in both cases in conflict with the policies of the civil authorities (Reyhner & Eder, 1992; Heath, 1972). Although the respective bilingual and intercultural contacts between missionaries and Native peoples in both regions belong to two distinct historical periods (the former to the first half of the 16th century, the latter to the late 1700s and 1800s) the outcomes parallel each other in a number of ways. In Mexico, by 1570, the bilingual friars, for the most part, had produced over 80 titles in Náhuatl, including dictionaries, grammars, and ethnographic studies. With the introduction of the alphabetic system, native-speaking Náhuatl writers began to participate in what would turn out to be the beginnings of a significant production and distribution of written works in the indigenous languages, mainly Náhuatl (soon to be overturned by the imposition of a Spanish-only policy in all the colonies) (Heath, 1972; León-Portilla, 1992a).

The most illustrious of the various bilingual academies was the Colegio de Santa Cruz de Tlatelolco, established in 1536 by the Franciscans. Classes began with 80 Náhuatl students drawn from families of the former Aztec elite, taught by Náhuatl-speaking bilingual teachers. With the newly published books in Náhuatl, students quickly acquired literacy skills in their first language, skills that were later applied to the Latin religious/philosophical texts. This is hardly surprising given the rigorous training

---

Voices 3 (Náhuatl)

Itlatol temictli
Auh tocnihuane,
tla xoconcaquican yn itlatol temictli:
xoxopantla technemitia,
in teocuitlaxilotl, techonythuitia
tlauhquecholelotl, techoncozcatia.
¡In ticmati ye ontlaneltoca
toyiollo, tocnihuan!

(**The dream of a word**
And, O friends,
hear the dream of a word:
Each spring gives us life,
the golden ear of corn refreshes us,
the tender ear of corn a necklace for us.
We know that the hearts
Of our friends are true!)

Cantares mexicanos (from the pre-Conquest Náhuatl
oral poetry in León-Portilla, 1992b)

---

that the young people had received in the *calmecac*, the traditional Aztec educational institutions where academic-type language proficiency was developed, principally through oral means (León-Portilla, 1996). By 1570, Náhuatl had become a required course of study at the University of Mexico for all seminary students aspiring to be named to positions of responsibility in one of the growing number of missions that were proliferating throughout the central highlands and beyond. At Santa Cruz de Tlatelolco, the indigenous students were also encouraged to learn Spanish in order to be able to assist missionaries who had neglected to learn Náhuatl, or whose proficiency in the *lingua franca* of the Mexican conversion campaign was still deficient. By now the language had received, because of the broad influence of the religious orders, official status by royal decree (Gonzalbo, 1988; Aguirre Beltrán, 1983; Cisneros Paz, 1989).

Under the direction of the great missionary/ethnographer/historian Bernardino de Sahagún, one of the leading members of the Colegio's faculty, a series of graduating classes of erudite indigenous catechists returned to their communities of origin, some of whom became prominent Náhuatl language writers and historians including Fernando Alvarado

Tezozomoc and Chimalpahin Cuatlehuanitzin (León-Portilla, 1992a). However, the experiment was short lived; by 1595 the school, having lost support from Madrid, fell into neglect and decay. Among the principal objections to the project was the opposition, from various quarters, to the teaching of Latin to Indians. The language of science and academia was to be reserved for the new colonial elite: priests, monks, and scholars of European origin (Heath, 1972: 30–31). A letter written to the authorities in Madrid in 1541 by a leading cleric both confirmed the effectiveness of indigenous language instruction, and foreshadowed the fate of all the bilingual academies in New Spain.

> All this has become something to admire, to see what they can write in Latin, letters, colloquia, and what they can say. A priest came to the school a week ago to celebrate mass. He told me that he had to come to see it, and two hundred students gathered around him, and as they were conversing with him they asked questions about the Holy Scriptures and about the faith. He left astonished, covering his ears, saying that it was hell, that they were disciples of Satan. (Joaquín García Icazbalceta, *"La instrucción pública en México durante el siglo XVI"* (1896) cited in Aguirre Beltrán, 1973)

Until the Spanish-only policy became consolidated by the 17th century, the spread of indigenous language literature (both religious and secular) found expression, in addition to Náhuatl, in Zapoteco, Mixteco, and Purépecha, among the other Mexican languages, with Náhuatl continuing, for an extended period, to be recognized in legal documents and official petitions (Lockhart, 1990).

In the United States, long periods of assimilationist English-only policies were punctuated with short periods of interest in bilingual education. Missionaries and traders were most likely to be interested in learning Indian languages, the previously-mentioned 17th century work of John Eliot being among the earliest examples. While the traders who learned to speak Indian languages left little mark on history, missionaries, who sometimes spent their entire lives in efforts to convert Indians to Christianity, left primers, grammars, and dictionaries that attract the attention of scholars and language activists to this day.

A prominent 19th century missionary example is the work of Stephen and Mary Riggs, who began their work in 1837 with the Sioux in Minnesota. In 1839 Stephen Riggs and a fellow missionary G.H. Pond published *The Dakota First Reading Book*, and in 1852 published a *Grammar and Dictionary of the Dakota Language*. Riggs found teaching English "to be very difficult, and not producing much apparent fruit." From his perspective, "it was not the students' lack of ability that prevented them from learning English, but rather their unwillingness; teaching Dakota was a different thing. It was their own language" ([1880] 1969, 61). The Riggs' children carried on their parents' work at Santee Mission, founded in 1870, and a Bible in Dakota was printed in 1880. A successful bilingual school was established at the mission and grew to include a teacher-training department.

The missionaries by and large favored the eradication of tribal traditions; with this purpose in mind, they were more willing than the government agencies to use indigenous languages in the classroom. For example, they cast doubt on some of the exaggerated reports of rapid success at teaching English through English-only immersion. Reverend S.D. Hinman reported "it is a wonder to me how readily they learn to read our language; little fellows will read correctly page after page of their school books, and be able to spell every word, and yet not comprehend the meaning of a single sentence" and he complained about the "monotony and necessary sameness of the school-room duty." (Hinman, 1869: 25, 29)

In 1871 the American Board of Commissioners for Foreign Missions and the Presbyterian Board of Foreign Missions began publishing, in collaboration with the Dakota mission, a monthly newspaper *Iapi Oaye* (*The Word Carrier*) mostly in the Dakota language. An editorial in an early edition of the paper declared:

> It is sheer laziness in the teacher to berate his Indian scholars for not understanding English, when he does not understand enough Indian to tell them the meaning of a single one of the sentences he is trying to make them understand properly, though they have no idea of the sense. The teacher with his superior mind, should be able to learn half a dozen languages while these children of darkness are learning one. Even though the teacher's object were only to have them master English, he had better teach it to them in Indian, so they may understand what they are learning. (*Iapi Oaye*, 1874: 4)

A correspondent who visited schools with Secretary of Interior Schurz reported that the educational facilities of the Santee Sioux in Nebraska "are perhaps better than those of any other of the northern tribes." At the mission Dakota was taught, and all elementary books and the Bible were written in Dakota. After the children learned to read in Dakota, they received a book with illustrations explained in Dakota and English. The correspondent reported:

> Mr Riggs is of the opinion that first teaching the children to read and write in their own language enables them to master English with more

ease when they take up that study; and he thinks, also, that a child beginning a four years' course with the study of Dakota would be further advanced in English at the end of the term than one who had not been instructed in Dakota. (Board of Indian Commissioners, 1880: 77)

Dr Alden testified to the Board of Indian Commissioners:

Our missionaries feel very decidedly on this point, and that is as to their work in the teaching of English. They believe that it can be better done by using Dakota also, and that it will be done by them in their regular educational methods. While it is not true that we teach only English, it is true that by beginning in the Indian tongue and then putting the students into English studies our missionaries say that after three or four years their English is better than it would have been if they had begun entirely with English. So our missionaries say that if this experiment is to be carried out at Hampton and Carlisle, let us have the same opportunity to show at our school at Santee what can be done there. And we think, after so large experience, that the same work can be accomplished at that Santee Agency, and reaching far more in number than can be done by simply transporting them to a distance [to an off-reservation boarding school]. But with the two together we believe that a splendid work will be done both in the way of English education and civilization of the Indian. (Board of Indian Commissioners, 1880: 98)

Again we can take note that including the Dakota language in the classroom was primarily a means of Christianizing and "civilizing" Indian students more rapidly.

Despite the reported success of bilingual methods, the federal government reacted negatively and suppressed programs that included the use of an indigenous language in the 1880s. Nevertheless, the high priority that evangelization continued to hold represented a strong motivation for missionaries to continue to study the languages of the communities they worked in. For example the Franciscan Fathers, who established a mission at St Michael's, Arizona, to convert Navajos, published *An Ethnologic Dictionary of the Navaho language* in 1910. The Smithsonian Institution's Bureau of Ethnology founded in 1879 did some documentation of Indian languages, including the publication by its first director, John Wesley Powell, of an *Introduction to the Study of Indian Languages*. See Shonerd (1990) and Lockhard (1995) on early Navajo writing and official language policy toward indigenous languages during this period.

It was not until the administration of Franklin D. Roosevelt that policies began to shift toward a more inclusionary approach. Willard Beatty, the

Bureau of Indian Affairs Director of Education contacted the Smithsonian Institution ethnologist John Harrington in 1937 to develop a written form of Navajo that could be used in schools. Eventually the work fell upon the linguist Robert W. Young who, working with Navajo informant William Morgan, produced a series of bilingual booklets for use in schools in the 1940's (Iverson, 1994). However, the financial demands of World War II and the conservative reaction of the 1950's brought these initiatives to an end.

Despite important differences, the parallels between Mexico and the United States language policy and early experimentation with bilingual education are noteworthy: (1) successful pilot programs in teaching indigenous languages by missionaries, (2) reaction and suppression by educational authorities and institutions, (3) without, at the same time, offering any comprehensive and broadly accessible alternative for the learning of the national language. As Cifuentes (1992) points out, the official language policy in colonial Mexico did not envision the goal, or result, in practice, in the acquisition of Spanish by the native-born majority. Rather, its objective was the exclusion of the indigenous languages from the domains that they had so rapidly occupied in the wake of the Conquest. By the end of the 18th century, only a minority of the population actually spoke Spanish. With independence, fundamentally the same policy continued, now under the principles of independence, sovereignty, and national unification. Parallel shifts occurred, following the same historical turning points, in the Andean region, in Peru, Ecuador, and Bolivia, with Quechua, initially, fulfilling the role of the indigenous *lingua franca* that Náhuatl played in Mexico (Chiodi, 1990; Llanque Chana, 1992).

In both cases, in Latin America and the United States, it was the period of political and social upheaval of the 1930s that briefly again witnessed a scholarly and scientific interest in American Indian language development, bilingualism, and literacy instruction in the indigenous languages of the continent. Historically significant are the proposals of John Collier (1941 and 1945) and his collaboration with Latin American specialists at the *First Interamerican Indigenist Congress* in Pátzcuaro in 1940, and the work of Maurice Swadesh in the *Proyecto Tarasco* on initial literacy teaching in Purépecha (Tarascan) as a bridge to Spanish literacy (Castillo, 1945).

With the election, in Mexico in 1934, of the reformist General Lázaro Cárdenas, new proposals, based on early research on bilingualism and education, came forward, explicitly alluding to the historical precedents of Sahagún and the Colegio de Tlatelolco. With the founding of the Department of Indian Affairs in 1936, pilot projects in bilingual education and indigenous language literacy began to report encouraging results, culminating in the discussions and declarations at the Pátzcuaro Congress in

1940. However, a period of retrenchment and reaction postponed the implementation of any educational language policy toward indigenous language (IL) speakers for more than 30 years. Meanwhile, isolated projects managed to survive, maintaining a certain minimum level of visibility of the issues before the scientific community. Following the historic UNESCO declaration (see Appendix D) on vernacular languages in education in 1953, prominent Mexican anthropologists and linguists reiterated their support for the use of the indigenous languages in school and for initial literacy (Comás, 1956; Castro, 1956).

Today, north of the Mexican border, American[7] Indian education and the study of American Indian languages, largely, are still conceived as being limited by the political boundaries of the United States. Thus, one of our objectives in this chapter is to draw together some of the common threads from research and practice in indigenous language pedagogy that educators in the field can, in turn, draw from in implementing the new generation of language revitalization and bilingual development programs that have emerged in recent years. For this purpose we need a broader, inter-American, perspective.

In a recent article, the Peruvian linguist Rodolfo Cerrón-Palomino (1993) calls attention to the need for a new approach to indigenous language revitalization, one that would look beyond the static and localist tendencies of previous research. He argues that we must expand our perspective beyond the mere description of individual languages and local cultures in order to draw the lessons from the general problems and opportunities that are common to all situations of language contact between the indigenous and national languages. This view implicitly accepts as a given the increasingly accelerated nature of cultural and linguistic change in our time. It emphasizes the opportunities for the development of new, amalgamated, forms in contrast to both traditional preservationist and assimilationist points of view. The former is "backward-looking": looking to an idealized world in which the influence of the European languages could, by some means, be limited. The latter is "forward-looking," but in a way that denies communities the right to self-determination, the right to participate in planning for change. Although Cerrón-Palomino is addressing the debate on the problems of language planning in Quechua and Aymara, his critique is of interest to educators working in all contexts of indigenous language bilingualism.

The Case of Navajo

For historical reasons, the current status of the Navajo language presents the most favorable set of conditions for indigenous language preservation in the United States. With the largest number of child speakers, more school-age children participate in bilingual school programs than in any other American Indian tribe or nation.

Nevertheless, language displacement has continued its course, gradually but steadily, tipping the balance toward English monolingualism in virtually all reservation communities. As recently as one or two generations ago, the absolute number of speakers had reached an all-time historic high point, but evidence suggests that even this demographic advantage has begun to slip. During the same 30-year period since León-Portilla's lectures at NCC, a major shift has occurred in school-age children's language proficiency and use. In 1970 it was estimated that only 5% of six-year-olds were monolingual in English. Recent surveys place the figure at over 50% (Crawford, 1995). In a study based on actual language dominance interview data (Holm and Holm, 1995), 4% of kindergarten children in the Fort Defiance area were identified as competent speakers, with 38% as passive bilinguals. In a reservation-wide survey by Holm (1993), 87% of five-year-olds were considered to possess at least passive knowledge of Navajo (level 1), 52% were categorized as "speakers" (level 2), with 31% rated as fluent speakers of the language (level 3).

Slate has argued that Navajo is, in many ways, a test case for the viability of all American Indian languages, where conscious language planning and concerted community action still hold out the possibility of reversing the shift toward English monolingualism: "if this cannot be done for Navajo, perhaps it cannot be done for any Native American language" (Slate, 1993: 35).

In this regard the circumstances that define the sociolinguistic relationship between Navajo and the national language[8] closely resemble that of most indigenous languages in Latin America. As we shall see in the following sections, the practical issues facing educators are similar. In all cases, communities that have expressed an interest in language revitalization face a wide disparity between official policy and practice. Declarations and goal statements in favor of the teaching of indigenous languages are not difficult to find among the resolutions and educational policy statements of many countries today. Drawing together, examining, and comparing the initial results of indigenous language teaching represents the first step in formulating a workable plan of action.

Research evidence from reservation communities

Commenting on the discussion on the viability of indigenous language literacy in a study by Spolsky and Irvine (1982), McLaughlin (1990) questions the applicability of the standard model of diglossia[9] in the case of Navajo. In regard to the issue of language choice and literacy, the "standard model" would seek to describe the different roles or functions that the two languages fulfill in society. It would try to identify a functional distribution of sorts in which English, for example, is the "normal" or "expected" language for communication between Navajos and outsiders. Navajo, on the other hand, would correspond to internal communication networks within the indigenous community itself. Literacy (in general), being associated with the "alien culture," would correspond to English. English is used for writing, even, for example, when recording the minutes of meetings held exclusively in Navajo. Literacy in the indigenous language would be accepted if and when domains and functions for writing are present prior to its introduction and promotion. In other words, there exists a kind of dilemma: opposition exists to using Navajo in the written domains given the perceived necessity to maintain a separation of the languages according to social function (indigenous language-oral, English-written); Navajo writing remains undeveloped and actually appears to be inappropriate for functions associated with writing. If, in general terms, such a language separation represents a norm, or expectation, on the part of speakers themselves, that would, in theory, explain community opposition to bilingual education programs that include IL literacy. Written Navajo would remain marginal since the institutions with which it is associated (churches and schools primarily) represent a kind of outside "imposition" upon traditional Navajo communities.

McLaughlin proposes examining the concepts of language function and language domain from the point of view of the individual's interactions with power relations in society. The tension between the national and indigenous languages represents one aspect of the "struggle for voice within institutional and ideological contexts in which forms of oral and written communication are embedded" (McLaughlin, 1990: 28). In his ethnographic study of the sociolinguistics of writing in one small Navajo community with a recent history of bilingual education, the results indicated that uses for Navajo literacy were identified with ideas about self-determination and self-empowerment. In a survey of bilingual secondary students attending a school that actually promoted these values, 50% of the younger respondents claimed to use Navajo when writing letters and lists, and 25% of junior and senior high school students reported writing notes in Navajo. Some 75% of all informants reported reading articles in Navajo (in the school newspaper); half reported reading the Navajo Bible. However, most noteworthy was the finding that, the higher the grade level of both students and teachers, the greater was the likelihood that Navajo literacy was viewed as a means for self-empowerment and enhanced ethnic identity.[10]

As McLaughlin points out, even if, historically, both Christianity and the academic institutions are not indigenous to Navajo culture, under the influence of broader community-wide resistance to the forces of language shift, "non-traditional" or "alien" institutions become arenas for the "struggle for voice," to the point where, under certain favorable circumstances, they become transformed to serve the objectives of community and linguistic self-affirmation.

To this point, in his assessment of language use and literacy in Rock Point, Spolsky touches on the inherent instability of the distribution of language functions, as in the case of Navajo/English bilingualism, where intercultural communication has been far from harmonious:

> As time goes on, and as the old group changes to accommodate and accept the newly introduced values, literacy too may slowly become integrated. Tension continues between old and new values, between a tendency to integrate the new function by having literacy in the vernacular and one to continue to mark its external associations by having literacy in the standardized outgroup language. (Spolsky, 1981: 483)

Destabilizing tendencies lead to tension and conflict, which in turn drive cultural change forward. Internally, within the speech community itself, *nepantla* (the "in-between-ness" that is always associated with a certain measure of tension and disagreement) would preclude consensus on such matters as bilingual education and IL literacy.[11] As Cerrón-Palomino points out, the relationship between Navajo and English is no longer stable, if it ever was. In a very real sense, it is *in transition*, "in between." Within the community itself, disagreement on the role of literacy and bilingual education should be expected.

Three bilingual programs on the Navajo reservation merit a closer examination, thanks to the availability of evaluation data on actual student achievement. As a whole, the published reports shed important light on the discussion of school language policy and language choice in literacy teaching.

Rock Point

Within the framework of its ESL program, limited Navajo literacy instruction was initiated in the mid-1960s. In what came to be called a *coordinate bilingual program*, academic language activities alternate among classroom centers where teachers are assigned teaching time and space to either Navajo or English. Holm and Holm (1995) report that standardized test results have shifted the relative standing of Rock Point elementary students from the "lowest scoring school in the lowest scoring BIA agency" to a position of favorable comparison with area schools. The margin of advantage for Rock Point students increases with grade level. This shift has occurred in parallel with the transformation of the composition of the teaching staff to majority indigenous, especially at the elementary level. Overall averages remain below national norms, but according to the authors, not on all subtests.

In general, written Navajo pervades all levels of the local school system, including student texts, a quarterly bilingual high school newspaper, public announcements and signs, as well as in interpersonal communication among students and teachers (notes, letters, graffiti). Perceptions and attitudes toward written Navajo are largely positive but as the "in transition" model would predict, far from unanimous.

Rough Rock

Similar patterns are reported for bilingual K-3 classes for the Rough Rock Community School on recent national assessments; a doubling of median percentile scores in reading vocabulary, for example. Summarizing the findings from a study of literacy development in two languages, McCarty (1993: 26) concludes that: "bilingual students who have the benefit of cumulative, uninterrupted initial biliteracy experiences in Navajo make the greatest gains on local and national measures of achievement". The introduction of Navajo literacy implies creating new school-based contexts for the production of texts of indigenous origin and the development of oral and written Navajo for academic purposes (Dick & McCarty, 1994; Dick *et al.*, 1994).[12]

The very concept of creating institutional school functions for the indigenous language implies reclaiming and revitalizing traditional discourses. Traditional discourses (the more highly structured and abstract uses of language of the oral tradition) develop higher-order discourse abilities and cognitive proficiencies which children can apply to academic tasks in any language they learn (see Figure 1, in Chapter 1). All indigenous communities have over the course of history developed a body of oral history, narrative, poetry and song, pedagogical speech, and ceremonial language. In many cases, these language functions have been neglected by the younger generations, but where these formal discourses have survived, they represent an important store of language learning material. For example, traditional, orally transmitted, narratives can be integrated into the reading and language arts program (a proposal that we will examine in detail in Chapters 4, 5, and 6). At the same time, the school, along with other community institutions, will expand the use of the indigenous language beyond conversational, familiar, every day, interpersonal communication. For many young people, especially among the majority of English-dominant bilinguals, Navajo language use is restricted to these kinds of informal, face-to-face situations. Unless their parents and grandparents have maintained the traditional formal discourses at home, young people are often no longer skilled in this domain of language use, even passively, as listeners. Community institutions also can play an important role in revitalizing traditional discourse practices, which in fact would contribute to the development of literacy-related, academic-type, discourse proficiencies.

Directly related to our theme of inter-American dialogue is the report of the collaboration between Rough Rock and the Kamehameha Early Education Program in Hawaii (Jordan, 1995, and McCarty, 1999, for a recent assessment of the Rough Rock program). As the Hawaiian researchers have demonstrated, when discourse patterns that correspond to the children's experience with indigenous oral forms are recognized and incorporated into the school-based literacy program, discontinuities between community and classroom begin to break down.

Fort Defiance

The circumstances of the Navajo language *immersion** program at Fort Defiance differ in many ways from that of both Rock Point and Rough Rock, most notably, as was indicated above, the fact that only a small minority (less than 5%) of five-year-olds were considered fluent speakers of Navajo in preliminary assessments of bilingual ability. Somewhat less than one third demonstrated any knowledge of Navajo. The same series of assessments suggested that the English language abilities of majority of K-2 students', while evidencing age-appropriate conversational skills, were not "adequate for school purposes" (Arviso & Holm, 1990).

Modeled on the Canadian immersion programs (see Chapters 4 and 5), where the *target language** is learned through sheltered subject-matter teaching, a select group of kindergarten and first grade students received all instruction in Navajo, except for daily 40 minute English classes. These children were primarily English-dominant bilinguals with only passive or perhaps beginning-level expressive skills in Navajo. By second and third grade, Navajo and English are distributed equally across the subject areas. Significantly, comparisons between Navajo Immersion (NI) and Monolingual English (ME) programs closely parallel the research findings from second language immersion in Canada and the United States. By third and fourth grade, NI students performed as well as ME students on tests of *English* language ability. On local assessments of writing-in-English NI students outperformed ME students. On standardized measures of reading, NI students initially fell behind, but began to close the gap at the upper grades (see Genesee, 1987; Harley *et al.*, 1990; Baker, 1996 for a review of research on Canadian immersion). As would be expected, while the Navajo language skills of ME fourth graders had declined in comparison to their entry level in kindergarten, the NI group improved in this area (Holm & Holm, 1995).

Applying one of the key features of the *coordinate bilingual model* (Rock Point), planned classroom language distribution maintains a separation between English and Navajo: first language (L1) does not mediate second language (L2) instruction by means of *concurrent translation**. Teachers, subject areas, topics and activities, and even classroom time and space, are allocated according to the respective L1 and L2 instructional domains. Instructional methods and materials are separate, and designed to maximize access to academic language proficiencies (Arviso & Holm, 1990). A skill related to reading comprehension, for example, learned through Navajo is subsequently available to the student when reading in English, and vice versa. For a complete discussion of the concept of Planned Alternation of Languages (PAL), consult Romero and Parrino (1994), for a discussion of language distribution issues in general, Jacobson and Faltis (1990), and in reference to early childhood Navajo language teaching, Holm (1993), and Holm *et al.* (1996). In Chapters 4 and 5, we will examine these concepts and how to apply them in the classroom.

Additive bilingualism and Navajo for academic purposes

More and more educators who work with Navajo students are coming to the conclusion that their ancestral language has an important role to play in the classroom. Nine out of the eleven public school districts in the Arizona portion of the reservation offer some Navajo language instruction. In large off-reservation "border" towns such as Flagstaff, the language can be studied as an academic course at high school, community college, and university levels, in addition to Navajo immersion at the elementary level. Seen as a conscious reversal of the previous exclusionary English-only policy, indigenous language instruction in schools represents one of the few opportunities available to language-preservation advocates to stem the tendency toward English monolingualism. And, as Holm (1993) points out, such educational language policy decisions often are made short of complete community consensus on the role of the indigenous language in school. A school represents a community level domain that *is* subject to some degree of planning and, under optimal conditions, can have a "reciprocal impact on the language and culture of public life" (Dick & McCarty, 1994). As the authors imply, the direction of increased Navajo use is two-way between school and community. School-based IL revitalization initiatives cannot but have a positive impact on language use in the individual family units where, ideally, the language transmission mechanisms work most effectively. These, in turn, will replenish the limited language teaching resources available to the school.

Inclusion of the indigenous language in the school curriculum, however, implies or sets into motion new tendencies. If the objective of bilingual education is one form or another of additive bilingual development, Navajo use in school begins to shift toward more formal usage. The IL begins to function as a school language and takes on features associated with academic discourse. Not only do children develop oral and written proficiency in Navajo, but Navajo itself continues to evolve as students and teachers use the language for academic purposes, both in writing and orally.

McLaughlin (1992) speculates on a different application of the concept of *diglossia** that would be compatible with the above extension of Navajo in the academic setting. If trading post and chapterhouse functions of writing are oriented toward the economic and political structures of the broader English-speaking society, access to the cultural resources of the community are facilitated by the development of written Navajo in school (and the church). New functions for indigenous language literacy are "grounded in ideologies of self-determination" (McLaughlin, 1992: 163), and this new specifically educational function implies, necessarily, its extension to written forms and *text** types previously reserved for English.

Arviso and Holm (1990) suggest a more basic, or immediate, rational for promoting early biliterate development. Arguments for language preservation (in the abstract) aside, early, sustained, reading and writing in Navajo, in coordination with English language and literacy, represents the most favorable condition for reaping the academic and cognitive benefits of additive bilingualism. "Ultimately, it's not a question of what [Navajo] children can do for the language, it's a question of what the language can do for [Navajo] children" (Arviso & Holm, 1990: 47). Precisely, this seems to be one of the central conclusions to be drawn from the evaluation data (preliminary and partial as it may be) from Rough Rock, Rock Point and Fort Defiance.

The Hopi Language Survey

Recent findings from language use research on the Hopi reservation suggest that an important shift within the speech community itself may be occurring in regard to the role of school and literacy in language preservation. What seems to be involved is a different perception or appreciation of the concept of diglossia and how it may be applied to the intergenerational transmission of the Hopi language. In a 1995 document, the Hopit

Pötskwaniat (the Hopi Tribal Consolidated Strategic Plan), outlined a series of language planning measures including a bilingual language curriculum for all reservation schools, and the development of language teaching methods and materials for village-based and off-reservation immersion programs. In an effort to establish a kind of "baseline of language fluency" the Cultural Preservation Office was directed to survey the villages – thirteen in all were included in the study (Joseph, 1997).

The results from the 1,293 adult informants are particularly relevant to the discussion in this chapter. Regarding reported language proficiency, a generational shift toward English monolingualism is evident in the data. While the "elder" category (60 years and above) indicated 100% conversational ability, "adults" (40–59) reported approximately 80%, with "young adults" (20–39) slightly higher than half. The most dramatic contrast, however, corresponds to the 2–19 age range. Almost 50% were identified as passive bilinguals, "understand, cannot speak," with approximately 20% who "speak a little," and an equal percentage "none." The remainder, a small minority, command full conversational ability. Perhaps the most important finding, however, reflects a possible major rethinking of questions regarding appropriate language teaching domains: 98% of all respondents answered "very important" to the question: "how important is it for children/grandchildren to speak Hopi?" To the item: "where should the Hopi language be taught [check all that apply (community classes, home, religious societies, school, other)]" *school* was second only to *home* (approximately 70%, and over 90%, respectively). Significantly, 46% answered "yes" to the difficult question of whether classes on Hopi language and culture should be a graduation requirement at the local high school, and a full 78% expressed the desire to be able to read and write Hopi (Hopi Cultural Preservation Office, The Hopi Tribe, 1997).

In 1997, in an interview punctuated by the front-page headline: "Language assessment sets off alarms" in the *Navajo-Hopi Observer*, Stan Lomakama, Executive Assistant to the Vice-Chairman, alludes to the change in expectations and perceptions:

> There was an effort in the 1980s to survey the state of the Hopi language. It was observed then that there was a language drift occurring. It was asked if the Hopi language could be taught in the schools. The message then was that the language belonged at home, in the kiva with the clans, not in the classrooms. Since then there has been a 70% reversal on that feeling, without the loss of emphasis on home education. (Lomakama, 1997)

The 1997 Hopi language survey results are noteworthy in regard to two key points:

(1) erosion of proficiency in the indigenous language apparently has proceeded at a faster pace than previously estimated;

(2) in the past, observers have made a distinction between the apparently more "traditional" perspective of the Hopis and the "less restrictive" posture of the neighboring Navajo communities on the question of the role of formal instruction and educational institutions in language teaching.

As formal schooling continues to occupy an increasingly central social space in all indigenous communities, views on the appropriateness of indigenous language use in different domains will most likely shift as well.

Research from Latin America

The experience of bilingual education in Mexico

One year after León-Portilla's lectures at NCC, Nancy Modiano's (1972) study of reading and bilingual education in Chiapas was published in English. Her findings, that initial bilingual literacy instruction that includes the first language (Tzotzil or Tzeltal) was more effective in developing *second language* literacy skills than all-Spanish monolingual instruction, had an important impact on the discussion on bilingualism and bilingual education in the United States (initially more so than in Mexico itself). Within a year, the US Supreme Court would rule on the historic Lau vs. Nichols case.

Over the next ten years, in Mexico, under the aegis of the Dirección General de Educación Indígena (DGEI) 30,000 new bilingual indigenous teachers would enter the school system. Qualifications include bilingual proficiency (Spanish and the community language), the equivalent of a high school diploma, plus normal school training at one of the branches of the National Pedagogical University (UPN). In recent years, in-service teachers are being encouraged to continue working toward their *licenciatura* (a four-year degree). Although the material resources available to indigenous education have been extremely limited (representing a small fraction of the national education budget), during the same period an impressive body of research and pedagogical material has been produced: reading primers in 36 of Mexico's 56 languages, linguistic studies covering approximately 50% of the language groups (grammars, dictionaries, etc.), bilingual teaching guides, and official curriculum plans that outline a form of developmental bilingual education (DGEI, 1990b; Varese, 1990).

Actual program implementation, however, has lagged far behind, meeting concerted resistance on many fronts (Coronado, 1992; Nahmad Sittón, 1999). Powerful interests within the various state and local educational bureaucracies (reflecting the fears and prejudices of monolingual Spanish-speaking teachers) often stand in the way. Inexperienced DGEI administrators sometimes neglect the difficult task of prior consultation with IL communities; and in many cases, even under the best conditions, parents vigorously object to any suggestion that teachers use the indigenous language in the classroom for instruction.

The same discussion on the role of bilingual education and vernacular literacy occupies center stage among Latin American educators and researchers, the concept of diglossia again framing the issues at hand. Hidalgo (1994) argues forcefully that the fundamental perspective of bilingual education in Mexico has been, historically, and continues to be, that of assimilation of the indigenous peoples. Pointedly, the author suggests that there exists no correlation between language maintenance and bilingual education, and that resources would be more profitably utilized in domains other than those of formal education. However, as Hidalgo notes in regard to reversing language shift, the broader dilemma resides in the absence of conditions that insure a diglossic situation in which Spanish and the indigenous languages maintain a functional distribution. There is an absence of self-imposed or externally enforced boundaries specifying purposes and domains for each language. According to the author, when the indigenous and national languages "compete" for space, and where the "boundaries" between using one or the other are not clear, this imbalance puts the indigenous language at a disadvantage.

The experiment in bilingual education in Peru

In Peru, the PEEB-Puno envisioned a dual language program that explicitly went beyond the narrow framework of short-term transitional approaches. This is particularly noteworthy given the strong community pressure in favor of early all-Spanish instruction that would militate against any extended use of the IL in school.

The program description and critical assessment by Jung (1992) and her colleagues merits a close examination by all educators working in the field. The section devoted to language teaching, initially Quechua and Aymara, is of particular interest to us. The goal of *developing first language proficiency*, for example, forecasts building on the native speaker fluency of the students, to extend their skills beyond the basic communicative functions to the use of language in extra-familial, academic-type discourses. Students would extend the use of Quechua and Aymara to topics, themes, and discourse patterns that require degrees of abstraction and independence from *situational** and interpersonal context (of the direct face-to-face variety) to which the indigenous languages have been restricted in large part.

Consequently, the use of language will become more conscious (attaining higher levels of what the researchers term *reflexividad* – the ability to reflect upon and be conscious of language itself). Self-monitoring and language awareness on many levels leads to a kind of linguistic consciousness that forms the foundation of all subsequent development in the areas of second language learning and literacy. Here, the role of indigenous language literacy contributes to the development of bilingual children as autonomous language learners, more and more capable of reflecting upon their own language use, and directing learning processes that previously were largely outside of their conscious control.

The introduction into the classroom of texts originating in the oral tradition plays a central role. Again, students' own extensive knowledge of this particular *genre,** now having become an *object of study*, can contribute to greater learner autonomy (Jung 1992: 85), and a more analytic posture toward their own language use. The actual workings of the language itself become important to the student. The Puno project educator's confidence in IL literacy, and literacy-related academic language in the IL, is based on the general principle (which should apply in all its essentials to all IL contexts) that this cognitive academic language proficiency will be available to bilingual students in both languages when they attain a certain minimum threshold of grammatical competence in their second language.

An extensive external evaluation of the PEEB schools was carried out by a team of researchers from the Departamento de Investigaciones Educativas (DIE) from the National Polytechnic Institute in Mexico (Rockwell *et al.*, 1989), focusing on a comparison of achievement measures with local monolingual Spanish (MS) elementary schools. Reflecting the general pattern regarding these kinds of inter-program comparison, the bilingual school students' Spanish skills (L2) were on par with their peers in the MS program, but evidently not superior. Predictably again, on all assessments in Quechua and Aymara, PEEB students scored significantly higher. And, as would be expected as well, for those children with limited extracurricular access to Spanish, the benefits of the bilingual program were especially notable in comparison with their IL-dominant peers in MS schools on measures of *Spanish* language proficiency. See also the report by Pellicer and Rockwell (1991). As other program evaluations have pointed out, the acceptance of the use of the indigenous language in school depends on the ability of teachers to demonstrate that, despite the fact that fewer hours per week are devoted to second language literacy activities, bilingual program students maintain comparative gains in L2. In other words, allowing students to build academic language proficiency in both languages will not only benefit development of the indigenous language, but apparently also represents the best way to maximize the learning of the national language. Surely the finding that PEEB students' reading and writing scores, by fourth grade, had not *surpassed* those of the MS program students, weakened the argument for school-based IL literacy from the community's perspective. Again, on the issue of second language learning and national language literacy, the Puno findings are consistent with previous studies. On balance they indicate either superior L2 learning or comparable achievement in L2 learning for bilingual programs, but not weaker or less effective second language learning in comparison to exclusive L2 instruction.

Based on an extensive sociolinguistic investigation of bilingual schools in the department of Puno, Hornberger (1989) approaches the dilemma of IL domains in a manner that seems at first to echo Hidalgo's note of caution on the value of bilingual education as a resource for language preservation. Calling attention to the fact that the Quechua-speaking community had rejected the government-sponsored bilingual education project, the author suggests that "the exclusion of the vernacular from school does not necessarily work against Quechua language maintenance" (Hornberger, 1989: 155). Maintaining the school as an exclusively Spanish language institution might (contrary certainly to the logic of most proponents of bilingual education) enhance community-wide tendencies for language preservation. Here again, overlap or confusion between traditional-vernacular and institutional-national language domains would represent an unfavorable condition for reversing language shift. In any case, Hornberger suggested that the use of Quechua in school is not an unambiguously positive factor in favor of language preservation.

The general findings from the study demonstrated that the bilingual teachers were able to achieve greater communication with both parents and students, and deliver the educational content more successfully. As Modiano had demonstrated in Chiapas, initial language and literacy instruction in the indigenous language would facilitate subsequent Spanish literacy learning. Consequently ("paradoxically" as the author noted), the greater the success in integrating the school-age, Quechua-speaking, population into the educational system by means of a linguistically more inclusionary policy, the more likely it may contribute (in the long run) to the shift toward Spanish monolingualism.

On the other hand, in a more recent assessment of the Puno study's findings, Hornberger makes the following observation:

It is the community members' perception that Quechua is the language for *ayllu* "community, family, home" and Spanish the language for everything outside the community, home and family. However, such a characterization, though probably true in the past, no longer adequately describes language use in the community. There is today, to a greater or lesser degree from community to community, some use of Spanish within the physical confines of the communities. There are, first of all, domains within the community in which Spanish is either the usual or accepted language. Furthermore, there is both code-switching into Spanish in the midst of Quechua discourse in Quechua domains, and strong lexical borrowing from Spanish into Quechua. Similarly, while the use of Spanish is making inroads into the informal functions, home and community domains, and oral channels for which Quechua has traditionally been valued, Quechua, in turn, is increasingly finding use in formal functions, educational and employment domains, and written channels, former exclusive domains of Spanish. (Hornberger, 1997: 96)

Summing Up the Discussion: Common Threads

Different researchers have emphasized the various contradictory aspects of the cultural and linguistic conflict that always accompany the process of indigenous language loss. Pardo (1993) applies the concept of boundary maintenance of language use domains to the question of the viability of indigenous language literacy in a study of bilingualism in Oaxaca. Taking note of the interest on the part of bilingual teachers and language activists in IL literacy, she suggests that the role that writing can play in revitalization efforts is entirely overstated. Along the same lines, Díaz-Couder (1990) points out that any cultural innovation, such as writing, will not produce the same effects, or perform the same functions, in speech communities that differ radically in their fundamental social organization. In such circumstances one would perhaps question the viability of programs whose aims include the development of standardized forms tied to the promotion of indigenous language literacy.

On the other hand, various authors propose what appears to be an alternative model of diglossia and the role of IL literacy. Summarizing the findings from the Mezquital Valley in Mexico (Hñahñú) and the experience of Zapotec in Oaxaca, Hamel (1995) seems to take issue with the standard theory of functional distribution of languages. Here, exclusive Spanish literacy within the indigenous speech community is viewed as reinforcing a "diglossic ideology" that contributes to devaluing the indigenous language (as a mere "dialect" unfit for the higher written functions associated with the national language, especially in school). The example of linking indigenous language literary production with initiatives toward greater autonomy in Zapotec communities is consistent, for example, with McLaughlin's description of the role that Navajo literacy plays in the *indigenization** of local institutions in "Mesa Valley." In fact the possibility of reestablishing the kind of stable allocation of language use domains that characterized language contact in the early decades of the past century is categorically excluded for the major ethnolinguistic groups in Latin America, for whom integration into Spanish-speaking socioeconomic networks (locally, regionally, and on a national level) is highly advanced. In some ways, entertaining this possibility corresponds to the "backward-looking preservationist" perspective on language maintenance mentioned earlier in this chapter. Given the relations of sharp inequality and ethnic conflict, the practical consequences of attempting to circumscribe "traditional" and "national" domains in the area of language would be to deepen the perception of the superiority of Spanish and its unrivaled ascendancy in *all* language use contexts. Thus, for example, an alternate explanation for a community's rejection of IL literacy in school would point to the generalized resignation toward, or conscious acceptance (as inevitable) of, the displacement of the indigenous language. From this perspective would flow the necessity to shift as effectively and decisively as possible toward exclusive use of Spanish, especially in the classroom.

Research in indigenous schools has revealed that, even among the most ethnolinguistically conscious bilingual teachers, language attitudes are marked by conflicting perceptions and ambiguity, driven by the same mechanisms of cultural and linguistic denigration that operate at the institutional, community-wide, and regional levels (Chiodi, 1993). Teachers' own preferences (for example, Spanish for written language functions), uneven proficiency levels, and ambivalent postures contribute to the implicit view that the indigenous language's oral, "dialectically fragmented" condition is evidence of its inherent deficiency as a language for academic purposes, particularly for reading and writing.

The notion that language revitalization, enrichment bilingual education, and the development of an indigenous literature are necessarily linked implies, for these authors, a *transcending* of the standard diglossic framework. In one way or another, communities would need to find ways of *extending* the use of the indigenous language beyond its traditionally conceived boundaries. Exploring the possibilities of a transition of sorts from oral tradition to written forms then becomes an explicit planning objective (Cerrón-Palomino & López, 1990). Ideally, the "transition" from oral to written would be *additive*: literacy develops thanks to the infusion of new material from oral narrative, oral poetry, etc. At the same time, the traditional oral discourse practices are affirmed and reinforced. Literacy need not, in principle, replace them. Regarding the actual viability of such an undertaking, the point made by Holm and Holm (1995) concerning the use of Navajo in the school is especially pertinent. Although it perhaps represents a somewhat less than optimistic perspective for the majority of indigenous languages, the authors point out that no other successful language revitalization effort in the 20th century has been able to circumvent the educational institutions of the community.

In Ecuador, the Proyecto Educación Bilingüe Intercultural (PEBI) began operations during the 1986-87 school year, serving 74 public schools in eight highland provinces. While the total student population represented only a small fraction of IL school-age children, the dual language instruction model closely parallels that of the Proyecto Puno. The project is significant for its ambitious projections: the development of a Quechua for academic purposes (Chiodi, 1990). In first grade, the more highly context-embedded mathematics concepts, for example, allow for the early introduction of Spanish. At the same time, the indigenous language becomes both the vehicle for the relatively less contextualized subjects, and the object of linguistic development. Quechua expands into new language use contexts. The development of academic language skills in second grade and beyond continues through the medium of both Spanish and Quechua. Chiodi (1993), who has studied extensively the experiments in bilingual education in South America, insists that systematic language planning measures are necessary. He goes on to argue that the indigenous languages themselves must undergo changes (e.g. standardization and modernization) to be able to adapt to the new circumstances of interethnic communication and the ever-expanding market economy.

On the surface, there appears to be a fundamental difference of approach between two distinct perspectives regarding the scope of the language revitalization program and the contexts in which promotion of the indigenous language would yield tangible benefits. On the one hand, a kind of "stable" diglossia becomes a goal: preservation of the vernacular will be favored by identifying the linguistic space where the national language has not penetrated or from which it can, in some way, be separated out. The boundaries that mark off indigenous language domains would be preserved, in part, by avoiding situations of "competition" with the language of wider communication. On the other hand, for those researchers who view diglossia in terms of the conflict between hegemonic and subordinate speech communities, the perceived or existing language distribution is a condition that, as far as possible, should be overcome or undermined. In the case of indigenous languages the distribution can never be stable, implying that a competition for, or struggle to recover, language-use domains cannot be avoided.

However, on some level, the notion of the separation of language functions must be valid, and specifying the circumstances and the manner in which this concept can be applied will contribute greatly to reframing the debate. Returning for the moment to the discussion of the classroom applications of language alternation in the Navajo bilingual programs, the consensus today among language educators on the most effective learning strategies involves maximizing the communicative aspects of L2 teaching. Information that is transmitted or exchanged in the second language should be new and authentic in some significant way (Holm, 1993). In other words, the use of the second language by both teachers and students should not be totally contrived and artificial (the practicing of isolated phrases and patterns without any reference to meaning). The language learner seems to profit most from L2 comprehensible input when a separation is maintained, no repetition of content in L1, no concurrent translation. Having separate instructors for L1 and L2 (or separate times when the same instructor teaches in L1 or L2) facilitates learning the target language, whether this is the socially subordinate language or the national language. A similar positive effect is produced by the separation of languages in the classroom by subject matter, topic, or the degree of access to content-related schemas and culturally shared knowledge.

Creating an academic space (Spolsky, 1989) where, for example, indigenous language writing is somehow logically or naturally required allows novice bilingual writers to consciously direct their attention to specific writing skills and other language abilities in their "weaker" language. The instructional situation itself would require the use of the indigenous language, even though students may be more proficient in the national language. Such an opportunity would not present itself in a situation where national language and indigenous language "compete," or are equally available, for the writing task. Often, bilingual students are perfectly fluent speakers of both, but have always engaged in literacy tasks in the customary language of school and books, sometimes referred to as the "unmarked" language of the academic domain. Their reaction to a request to read or write in the IL may vary from surprise, negation or confusion, to avid curiosity.

Variable language ability grouping (Romero & Parrino, 1994) for the purpose of manipulating the sociolinguistic and contextual constraints that determine language choice among students is another example of *distributing* languages by *function* in the classroom. For example, during a lesson involving high-context support (a "hands-on" activity related to a science project or math game) grouping monolingual *IL speakers* with NL-dominant *IL learners* would encourage the latter to use the indigenous language, even among themselves. Other examples of conscious language choice within the curriculum, and day-to-day school management situations (using the IL for administrative functions, parent-community/school communication, non-academic routines, teacher/student, teacher/teacher interaction outside of the classroom) represent standard features of any successful additive-developmental bilingual program. The same principle should apply beyond the boundaries of the educational institution, especially to domains where custom, the particular context, or cultural expectations, have historically favored use of the indigenous language.

Again, questions of language shift and preservation aside, if it is true that indigenous language literacy instruction and bilingual methods contribute significantly to literacy development in English or Spanish, then the dilemma regarding the effects of bilingual education on language shift must be posed in different terms. The most effective and complete learning of reading and writing skills in the national language (today something virtually all American Indian parents expect from school) cannot be an optional program feature or negotiable issue. And if, as Holm and Holm suggest, enrichment IL bilingual education offers academic and cognitive benefits for young American Indian bilinguals (similar to those reported for bilingual children elsewhere), educators are in effect presented with pedagogical considerations that would clearly override other, less immediate, priorities. Most probably, the authors would argue in favor of the possibility that we can have our bilingual education program and promote IL revitalization at the community level too. The attentive reader will note that the preceding is not a variation on the hypothesis that one can both have and eat a cake.

The tensions and conflicts that León-Portilla referred to, more often than not, are viewed in negative terms regarding the consequences of the rapid cultural change experienced by all indigenous communities today. However, in taking up again Cerrón-Palomino's critique, in regard to IL development at least, educators should consider *embracing* the dynamics of change in order to take advantage of the opportunities, for example, that recent advances in the technology of communication and information processing have to offer. Indigenous languages need not retrace the same stages that today's languages of wider communication passed through in their development in the areas of written expression, standardization, and the expansion into new media. Stages and transitions can be conceived of in a way such that the relevant and culturally appropriate resources of both "traditional" and "national/modern" cultures are critically reexamined, interwoven and/or fused.

Part 2

Curriculum and Materials, Classroom Strategies

Chapter 4

Promoting Additive Bilingual Development

Constraints and Opportunities, Situational Factors and Universals

In the next three chapters we will present a sample of possible language and literacy activities for indigenous languages in school and other community-based language revitalization programs. As second language learners, indigenous children face the same challenges that all bilingual students encounter when learning a new language. The same principles of language learning and language teaching that have emerged from research and practice internationally apply to indigenous communities as well. For a survey of teaching strategies for the second language learner we refer the reader to the many recently published comprehensive overviews that are available. To this end, at the end of this chapter a brief review is provided of additional readings on second language teaching that we recommend both for their concise treatment of the theory and practice in the field, and for the numerous suggested learning activities that together represent a complete teacher's handbook. Our purpose is not to recapitulate or review the existing material on second language and literacy curriculum, but rather to propose directions and explore ideas for the indigenous language (IL) teacher that are specific to his or her situation of language contact.

The particular circumstances of IL teaching call for approaches that correspond, at times, to special opportunities and, at other times, to specific limitations. On this point, a note of caution is in order. There exists a broad consensus regarding the social and historical circumstances in which bilingual indigenous children learn second languages and learn how to read and write. These *situational factors** have a direct bearing on language curriculum, on teaching strategies, and materials. Indeed, this set of circumstances could be considered the point of departure for this book: how teachers can take advantage of opportunities and work around limitations. On the other hand, theories concerning the "exceptionality" of Indian children (peculiar cognitive or learning styles, culturally determined thought patterns, etc.) remain speculative and controversial. Aside from the obvious danger in generalizing purported learning characteristics to the wide diversity of indigenous peoples, teachers should approach with a healthy measure of skepticism sweeping claims about: global-holistic learning styles, non-analytical thought, field-dependency, fatalistic world views, and fundamental differences (in contrast to "Western norms") in perception and cognition. None of the above idiosyncratic traits, which have from time to time been attributed to Indian children, have been reliably shown by research to be inherent characteristics of any ethnic group, indigenous or otherwise. For a critical assessment of the different claims regarding "learning styles" of bilingual indigenous language speakers, readers should consult McCarty *et al.* (1991).

In designing and planning the curriculum of a school whose students come from a bilingual community, educators must concern themselves with the language development of children who speak or are in regular contact with two languages. In relation to the school's educational plan, and actual classroom instruction, it is important to distinguish between two kinds (among others) of childhood bilingualism: additive and subtractive.

As the term itself implies, subtractive bilingualism involves the loss, sometimes gradual, of the child's first, or primary, language. If the indigenous language community has made the decision to work toward the revitalization of their ancestral language, its widespread and early erosion among children represents a clear danger signal. If not reversed, the permanent and irreversible loss of the language is simply a matter time.

However, subtractive bilingualism often involves other consequences aside from the displacement of one language system by another, the stronger language simply occupying the vacated space left by the weaker. Rather, for many bilingual children, the process of language loss is accompanied by negative consequences in the area of academic achievement, and even perhaps in some cases, cognitive development.

For example, the bilingual child may, over a period of years that coincides with the primary elementary grades, suffer a total loss of his or her first language. Whatever temporary imbalances in fluency may occur, normally the now-dominant second language will eventually replace the first language completely and become, in effect, the child's new "primary language." In situations of face-to-face peer interaction, conversation concerning familiar topics, where the situational context coincides with the topic, the child will be able to express him or herself fluently and understand messages in a way that does not distinguish him or her from other native speakers of the language.

However, aside from the erosion of the indigenous language itself, the issue that concerns teachers and parents is the possible effect of language loss on the student's ability to perform in academic situations, to be able to use language for the higher-order, literacy-related school tasks that with each grade become more and more challenging. For many bilingual children who undergo subtractive language loss, this very process may affect their ability to fully develop these kinds of literacy-related language skills, the broad category of discourse competencies that Cummins and Swain (1987) have termed Cognitive Academic Language Proficiency (*CALP**). This may occur because of a combination of a number of factors, some of which could include the following:

(1) Lack of expressive ability and incomplete comprehension in the language used in the classroom for instruction. This isolates and marginalizes the student, for example during language development activities such as "show and tell," sharing time, story telling, and beginning reading instruction.

(2) Reading material that is at the instructional level for the average native-speaking student turns out to be at a frustrational level for the second language reader. Consequently, the child has a diminished access to this primary source of academic discourse in addition to other indispensable sources of CALP, during a critical period of literacy-related language development.

(3) As the first language is losing ground, the acquisition of the second may be delayed. If this occurs during especially critical periods of academic language development, the student may not profit from or take full advantage of classroom verbal interaction (direct instruction in particular), most of which may not be comprehensible (McLaughlin *et al.*, 1995)

(4) In situations of unequal contact between the indigenous language and the national language (NL), the tension and conflict surrounding the process of learning the NL and, at the same time, feeling ashamed of still speaking the IL, could impact negatively on students' participation in class, attention to school tasks, and interaction with peers. For many Native American students, shame and inhibition extends to situations in which they are speaking the national language (students may not even be fluent speakers of their first language and rarely use it outside of the home). The Indian "accent," "tone," choice of words, speaking style, etc., mark an individual's identity. When children are ashamed of, or are overly self-conscious about, how they sound when they speak in their second language they tend to prefer passive interactions with teachers and other students. Inhibited from speaking and using their second language for other purposes (especially academic),

the opportunities for developing higher-order language skills through the second language become more and more limited.

To be more specific, we could conceive of two types of subtractive bilingualism:

(1) Loss of a first language under conditions in which the L2 comes to replace it in such a way that academic proficiencies are not negatively affected. While perhaps this kind of replacement of the L1, first by a dominant L2, subsequently becoming the sole primary language, might limit the child's movement in certain social-communicative networks, the actual language displacement transpires during those stages of development, or under certain favorable circumstances such that initial literacy and early academic discourse abilities are able to benefit from adequate comprehension levels. This variant of subtractive bilingualism is in fact quite common.

(2) Loss of a first language under circumstances in which the teaching of literacy and academic discourse (through the L2) are imposed without regard to adequate levels of comprehension (see Note 16). The new primary language (the former L2 that replaced the now-eroded L1) comes to fulfill all basic interpersonal communicative functions of the every day conversational kind, but literacy and academic discourse proficiency lag far behind (often permanently) in comparison to the average student.

Additive bilingual development involves, as the term implies, the maintenance and "growth" of two languages, a positive development, by itself of interest to IL speech communities. But evidence from research on childhood bilingualism suggests that there are general academic benefits for students who have maintained a balanced, or rather "positive" bilingual development,[13] and who can take full advantage of all classroom opportunities to build skills and competencies associated with academic uses of language (Cummins, 1989). Examples of these kinds of academic use of language include: reading textbook material involving new concepts (working mentally with concepts of increasing levels of abstraction), understanding complex narratives, writing essays and other expository-type compositions, comprehension of teacher expositions of unfamiliar topics, understanding complex directions, organizing one's own expositions and narratives in a logical and coherent manner, and development of expressive abilities in the esthetic genres.

The proposals and suggestions for effective language teaching that the reader will consider in Chapters 4, 5, and 6 have as their starting point the goal of additive bilingualism outlined above. For Native American communities, and their schools, the concept has a special significance, a kind of double benefit: avoiding the negative consequences of subtractive bilingualism and promoting dual language proficiency in children will not only contribute to the historical continuity of the community's language, but will provide for children the most favorable conditions for success in school. Among these favorable conditions are those that provide for effective learning of a second language and for using it as a tool for cognitively demanding, higher-order, thinking.

A Second Language Teaching Model for the Indigenous Language and the National Language

Let us return for the moment to the distinction that was made in Chapter 1 between indigenous students who are dominant in the national language and those who are learning English or Spanish as a second language (the IL-dominant bilingual). In the first place it is important to note that these two categories do not represent clearly distinct, closed, and separate groups of bilingual children, but rather represent end points on a continuum between which we will find a series of intermediate categories (e.g. the balanced bilingual with complete conversational fluency in both languages). However, keeping in mind the different set of circumstances that each of the contrasting categories presents will help us to design the appropriate language learning program for each student. While each group will share certain common needs, each, in turn, relies on a different set of resources and supports. Clearly, it will serve the language learning objectives of all students to maintain a constant and fluid interaction among groups of learners of different levels of IL and NL proficiency; and cooperative, heterogeneous group learning activities should be a prominent feature of each day's teaching plan. But it is important to emphasize from the beginning that providing the Indian student whose *dominant language** is English, for example, with only incipient proficiency in the IL, with the same language instruction program that the ESL student receives is neither pedagogically sound nor, we believe, ethically justified.

The language-learning situation is different in certain (not all) critical areas for each student, as are his or her particular individual learning needs. For example, in Arizona and New Mexico, Navajo as a Second Language (NSL) students and their ESL peers share the same classroom, and teachers, and, depending on the language learning situation and teaching objectives, participate together in many classroom activities. They should, and in real life before and after school they actually do, have the opportunity to work together on common projects. However, the teacher must plan and be conscious at all times of:

(1) opportunities for necessary context support for each subject or content area; and most importantly, when the specially designed context support for second language tasks becomes progressively less necessary, begin (incrementally, little by little) to withdraw it;
(2) the level of comprehensible language *input** that each student will receive;
(3) the opportunity that each student will have not only for meaningful oral and written expression, but for the opportunity to work with cognitively demanding language tasks beyond his or her present independent level.

In second language teaching, indiscriminate and unplanned integration, in the hope that casual and spontaneous interaction among students will meet the educational needs of all concerned, is a recipe for mediocrity.

For the Indian student, dominant or monolingual in the national language, the program model that we will take as our point of reference is Second Language Immersion, developed originally in Canada for majority English-speaking children learning French. Both in the United States and Canada, the immersion model has been creatively applied to Native American language teaching situations. Today, in the United States, we could point to the Fort Defiance Navajo Immersion school and some aspects of the Hawaiian Language Immersion (HLI) model as potentially the most promising program options for indigenous language teaching (Arviso & Holm, 1990; Slaughter, 1997). Also see the brief report of Mohawk immersion in Quebec by Genesee (1991).

For Indian children entering school, dominant or monolingual in their Native,[14] indigenous, language, the program model that appears to have produced the most consistently positive results is that described by Krashen and Biber (1988) and Krashen (1991, 1996): the "Gradual exit, variable threshold" approach. ESL students are mainstreamed early in activities where language comprehension is virtually guaranteed because of the complete context support in academically less demanding situations (art, music, and physical education). In school subjects, where context support is high (e.g. primary level mathematics), ESL students receive early immersion in the second language, reserving (in the early grades) the subjects that are more language-dependent and abstract (e.g. reading, language arts, social studies) primarily for the dominant, primary, language. As we will see in Chapter 5, key elements of the "variable threshold" approach can be incorporated into the IL immersion model for NL-dominant children.

As students' second language (L2) proficiency improves, more and more lessons are taught through Sheltered L2-type teaching, and eventually they are taught in mainstreamed situations together with peers whose proficiency level in the NL is native or near-native. For enrichment purposes, for example, the indigenous language would continue to be the medium of instruction in subjects where further development of the IL becomes an integral part of the development of CALP-type, higher-order literacy-related skills, again through the study of academic content. The principal merits of the "variable threshold" model are: (1) second language learning is integrated into the content curriculum (in Chapter 5 this will be described in more detail under the heading of L2 immersion teaching): (2) this content-based language teaching approach, which research has indicated is appropriate and effective in IL communities (Holm & Holm, 1995; Holm *et al.*, 1996; Kamaná and Wilson, 1996; King, 1999), is implemented in such a way that it matches the current level of L2 proficiency of the child to the level of context support that content instruction will, by design, incorporate. In other words, as L2 proficiency increases, context-support for the purpose of making L2 input comprehensible diminishes, as it must. At the same time, subject matter that is more language-dependent will exploit the full primary language *competence** of the child's L1 by ensuring that some significant component of this less-contextualized content is available to the learner in the language he or she understands best. This coupling of language and context (which in turn is continually shifting in response to the learner's progress in L2) is particularly useful during critical initial stages of literacy learning, when young children must get a jump start on strong and efficient text processing strategies.

For both groups of students (NL-dominant and IL-dominant), however, the same general principles of language learning apply – early immersion in the second language in subjects and classroom activities where:

(1) the children's world knowledge, cultural expectations, schemas regarding procedures, etc. serve as a support;
(2 appropriate context support can be provided, accompanying all second language instruction, thus making the second language input that students receive highly comprehensible, regardless of the their level of proficiency;
(3) During instruction in the L2, the necessary modifications in speech and teaching style are applied to maximize comprehension. Researchers call these kinds of modification in teacher talk "characteristics of language addressed to learners" or "L2 learner talk" (Hatch, 1983; Gass, 1997). Teachers can refer to Table 2 as a kind of check list for Language Learner Sensitive Discourse (LLSD).

Table 2 Language Learner Sensitive Discourse

Phonology and sound patterns
(a) slightly reduced rate of speech and slightly increased volume
(b) clearer enunciation, e.g. pronounce final consonants that tend to drop off in normal speech
(c) contractions can be expanded (e.g. "They're" to "They are")
(d) extra emphasis on intonation cues (e.g. the intonation pattern that marks questions)
Grammar
(e) simplify grammar by avoiding unnecessarily complex constructions
(f) use more standard sentence patterns (what linguists term "canonical word order")
(g) make referents (e.g. what pronouns refer to) easier to identify
Vocabulary
(h) special emphasis on content words and high-frequency words, and avoidance of particular regional expressions, slang, and idioms that are difficult to interpret, until they become explicit language learning objective themselves
(i) use generic terms more often ("hat" instead of "derby", "bowler" or "coif")
Communication devices and discourse strategies
(j) more repetition and rephrasing (in its many forms: e.g. providing multiple examples, positive and negative, of an abstract concept, synchronizing speech more closely with visual context support)
(k) more explicit questioning techniques – making it easier for students to respond using the language knowledge they possess at that moment
(l) modeling the answer in the question, as in "tag questions," narrowing the options for appropriate response (e.g. converting open-ended questions to limited-response or closed ended questions, or "choice" questions)
(m) sentence fill-ins that take advantage of highly predicable sequences: "Coyote's wife would sit on one side of the fire and he on the _____. Her form appeared clearer and _____."
(n) "negotiating meaning," for example, by directing learners' attention to language structures that should be corrected by asking clarification questions.

As students' proficiency in the IL or the NL improves, context support is gradually removed to focus the learner's attention on the language itself. At the same time, the above speech and discourse modifications are relaxed to gradually allow learners to follow and comprehend normal, native-like, oral language input. Remember that the additional context support and the special LLSD modifications that second language learners benefit from are not necessary and appropriate in the abstract and across the board. Rather, they are always, and in all situations, transitional adaptations that are continually fine-tuned downward as L2 learners progressively master the grammar and vocabulary of the target language. As with all teaching approaches that may be helpful at one stage of learning, they become obstacles at another, as in the case of an excess of "hands-on" context support when children are capable of processing information in a more context-reduced way. For an eloquent contrast to all this, see the testimony of Condori Mamani in *Voices 4* (later this chapter).

In situations of second language teaching, these procedures apply just as well to English and Spanish as they do to the Indian language. On principle alone there is no reason to doubt that the model of a *bilingual* approach combined with variable thresholds for context support plus LLSD, corresponding to different levels of L2 proficiency, would not apply to IL children learning the NL as a second language. We propose that the converse applies as well: for indigenous children learning their IL as a second language, a total early immersion in the IL (a variant of immersion that we do not recommend) runs the risk of either:

(1) not providing access to abstract, context-reduced content through the language in which the child has sufficient linguistic competence (since the NL is the primary language); in this case adequate comprehension is not assured;

(2) diluting instruction as a result of having to provide an excess of content support and other kinds of simplification because all instruction is given in the child's L2 (especially in the case of beginning language learners); here adequate comprehension is assured at the price of instruction that can turn out to be cognitively and academically unchallenging.

While students work in content areas in which they receive highly comprehensible language input in L2, they can develop literacy skills primarily through their dominant language.[15] Each of the two language learning groups would learn CALP-type proficiency, utilizing the language they understand fully and completely. This seemingly common sense principle of teaching does not imply that CALP-type skills must be taught *exclusively* in children's primary language. However, the converse, exclusive literacy instruction in a language that children do not fully understand, surely represents a less than optimal condition for developing CALP for many, if not most, beginner L2 learners. In situations where, for whatever reason, the indigenous language cannot be used as the primary vehicle for teaching reading and writing (e.g. community opposition, unavailability of materials, teachers' lack of IL proficiency) some *significant quality time should be reserved for indigenous language learning activities related to the acquisition of literacy-related skills* (for specific lesson ideas also see Chapters 5 and 6).

So far in our discussion of program models that correspond to different language learning situations, for clarity's sake, we have emphasized the more obvious differences: the child who is clearly dominant or monolingual in the NL, as compared to the monolingual or Indian language- dominant speaker. But, in the real world, just as children do not come to school in discrete categories of bilingual language proficiency (the combinations of IL and NL dominance and balanced bilingualism are typically quite varied), so too the program design that will meet *all* children's needs will be flexible in the same proportion.

For any one language activity in IL and/or NL, a whole range of variations in ability grouping, peer tutoring, whole class direct teaching, and individualized instruction will be available to the teacher. This is precisely what makes bilingual education and Indian education more demanding, but at the same time more interesting, when all the possibilities begin to unfold. In the field of education, and in language teaching in particular, "problems" are *circumstances* that the creative teacher turns into *opportunities*.

Oral Language Development as Preparation for Literacy

Let us return to the issue of developing literacy-related skills through the IL. This is related to one of the circumstances of teaching in the IL that traditionally has been viewed in terms of limitations and constraints, but we propose to approach it as an opportunity. To restate the dilemma that teachers face: on the one hand CALP-type, literacy-related, language proficiencies are most effectively developed in the language in which children do not have to also struggle with basic grammar patterns, all new vocabulary, and a new sound system. On the other hand, for IL-dominant children, whose community does not have at its disposal written materials in the language, the only alternative would appear to be that of literacy teaching in the second language. Depending on the child's actual level of L2 proficiency, among other factors, this can represent a major obstacle to

Voices 4 (Quechua)

Chhaynallataq mana simiyoq haykunki, mana simillayoqtaq lloqsimunki, apenas castellanoman simi t'okhashaq. Cuartelpin chay tenientekuna, capitankuna, mana munaqkuchu runa simi rimanaykuta. "¡Indios, carajo! ¡castellano!" – neqkun. Chhaynatan a pura patada castellanota rimacheq kasunkiku clasekuna.

(Up until that time [entering the army] I didn't speak Spanish and I scarcely left there speaking Spanish; I almost spoke some Spanish at the end. The lieutenants and the captains didn't want us to speak Quechua. "Indians, dammit! Spanish!" they used to say. With that, they make you speak Spanish in classes.)

Condori Mamani (1977), quoted in Harrison (1989:15)

learning how to read and write, in particular using written language for higher-order academic functions.

Today in the great majority of Indian community schools the view that prevails is that given the scarcity of written materials and the lack of a *literary** tradition, there exists no practical alternative to exclusive literacy instruction in the L2. Teachers generally are resigned to this view despite the difficulties that literacy instruction in a language children do no understand implies. One must do the best one can, work around this limitation, and teach literacy skills in the L2 applying a series of modifications that may facilitate the task, especially for IL-dominant students who are just beginning to learn the NL[16]

In the first place it is important to remember that academic language skills, that are typically associated with literacy begin to develop before children are formally introduced to reading and writing. These language abilities develop to a large extent through verbal interaction that is not strictly dependent on written forms. See Faltis' (2001) review of the research on discourse patterns that preschool children from "literacy oriented" families begin to learn patterns and networks of knowledge that in turn form the foundation of school-based academic literacy:

(1) exchanges that take the perspective of the child, that assume his or her capacity for "intentional and *representational speech**" and a capacity to represent ideas symbolically (Faltis, 2001: 17);
(2) "richly interpreting" children's utterances (Faltis, 2001: 18);
(3) linguistic play that focuses on interpretation of meaning;

(4)   verbal exchanges involving greater and greater degrees of abstract-
      ness; and most importantly
(5)   the wide variety of narrative types that children spontaneously begin
      to produce, and that language conscious caregivers extend and elabo-
      rate upon, what the author terms recounts, accounts, and event casts
      (Faltis, 2001: 20–21).

The most formal, or structured, category is at the same time the most
familiar type of narrative: the story (from the more elementary, concrete,
and conventionally organized plots to the more difficult and abstract narrative types involving complex sequencing, not strictly temporal, requiring
advanced levels of inference on the part of the listener, etc.). It is necessary
to emphasize the point, however, that the ability to comprehend, produce,
and elaborate upon these discourse patterns (beyond a minimal rudimentary level) is not universal among all sectors of a given speech community
or culture. Unlike the acquisition of the linguistic structure of a language
(i.e. its syntax and morphology, phonology,* and basic vocabulary), sustained exposure to oral narrative forms, for example, varies widely from
person to person, as does the ability to incorporate this set of discourse
patterns into one's overall language proficiency. In fact, relatively few
persons in any given culture reach the advanced stages associated with the
higher levels of creative production of poems, narratives, and songs
(typically, in turn, receiving a special social designation: poet, novelist,
storyteller, chronicler, griot, bard, jongleur, etc.).

As is suggested by the above list, CALP-type language proficiencies
develop (again to various degrees from individual to individual) in *both*
modern "literate" societies, and traditional cultures where oral means
correspond to the functions of transmission of knowledge, artistic expression, ceremony, and other situations that require some degree of formality.
For students of folklore, oral poetry, and traditional narrative, this notion is
neither original nor controversial. It is in the area of public education
(particularly regarding learners from minority cultures and IL language
communities) where the relevant principles from the fields of linguistics
and anthropology remain to be applied.

In a given indigenous community that has maintained a degree of
cultural and linguistic continuity in relation to its traditional discourse
practices, children are likely to come into contact with a range of oral forms
that go beyond, and rise above, face-to-face conversational speech embedded in the immediate concrete situation. Both functions and stylistic
features overlap among the different categories. But, depending on the
level of language and discourse maintenance, the variety of oral genres

extends beyond the prototypical legend or story that is usually associated with the oral tradition of indigenous communities. It would also be a mistake to assign exclusively utilitarian motives (e.g. transmission of cultural knowledge) to the oral tradition. As in non-indigenous societies, the esthetic and expressive functions play a prominent (if not predominant) role; the select group of oral *genre** specialists perform many of the same duties as their counterparts who work in the written domains. The range of oral discourse forms would include the following categories (among others):

(1) **Narrative** in all its different forms and sub-varieties, including the significant number of stories "borrowed" and readapted from the European oral tradition. Its predictable structure, among other features, makes narrative accessible to all age groups and levels of language proficiency.

(2) **Oral history:** accounts and recounts of events from the past. Memories of childhood and critical moments of the narrator's life history are shared with children. Versions of the collective history of the community, remembrances of important turning points, struggles, crises and conflicts evolve and are recreated crossing the boundary, back and forth, between history and legend – as in the account of the monster hog that a local landowner kept on the *hacienda* at Rancho de Jesús in the municipality of San Pablo del Monte en Tlaxcala, fattened to giant proportions from all the Indian farm hands that were secretly thrown into the pen to be devoured. The Mexican Revolution that swept the region in 1918 sent the *hacendado* back to Spain, not before his voracious pig had engorged upon many a local revolutionary. The sacrifices continued until the narrator's grandfather, aided by his wife who concealed a scalpel-sharp blade in his daily ration of tortillas, liberated the ranch hands from the four-hoofed Mexican Minotaur (recorded in San Pablo del Monte from a Náhuatl-speaking informant).

(3) Often sharing purposes with (1) and (2) are the **pedagogical discourses** (Garibay, 1963): here referring to more specific, instructional, objectives; for example, the pre-wedding admonition to the daughter regarding her duties and responsibilities as wife, daughter-in-law, and mother, and other types of formal counsel. To these can be added the broader category of shorter proverbial sayings, precepts and maxims. Under the heading of pedagogical discourses we should include the important category of religious teaching, representing for many indigenous language communities the primary source of academic-type language use.

(4) **Ceremonial speech:** also tied to religious and spiritual expression,

including enchantments, incantations, and conjurations where these are still current in some communities. In this case attention to the form (e.g. the exact wording) of the discourse is often paramount. On important occasions, functions that have become routine and almost unconscious, reduced to their minimal expression in non-indigenous societies (e.g. greetings and leave-taking) require special discourses of a highly formal style (see example of ritual kinship discourse below).

(5) **Poetry and song**: from the aesthetic point of view, perhaps the highest form of literature in modern society, it is probably also the first attempt by speaking humans to use language, or the voice, for artistic ends (Bowra, 1963). Along with narrative, poetic forms can be counted among the great literary universals shared by all cultures. Of special interest to educators, the musical aspects of language and voice are an important component of early language development in the preschool years. Again, unlike ordinary conversation, special attention is directed to *how* words go together, the manner in which they are expressed beyond and apart from the requirements of communication and negotiating meaning (van Dijk, 1990). Traditional narrative and ceremonial speech, especially, exploit the poetic resources of language (e.g. repetition and *parallelism,** rhythmic patterns); and *metaphoric** language permeates all genres, by no means restricted only to non-conversational discourse.

(6) **Language play**: riddles, guessing games, jokes of the double-entendre variety require the participants to consciously reflect upon the relationship among word meanings, and the structure of the utterance in some of the more sophisticated types of linguistic recreation. Even at this level the activity of *recreating* requires the application of certain higher-order mental resources on the part of the language learner. Typically this occurs without the benefit of any kind of *extralinguistic** context support.

(7) The particular style of **formal reconciliation** represents a kind of equivalent or analogy to legal discourse of the courtroom, although its objective is different in many ways (Sierra, 1992). Oratorical styles in general combine verbal art and political speech (Rosaldo, 1984; Feldman, 1991).

To illustrate some of the concepts outlined above, we offer examples of (6), (4) and (5) in the following excerpts; see Appendix A and B for full texts of two examples of (1) the traditional oral narrative.

Riddles (language play)

See tosaasaanil, see tosaasaanil.
Maske mas tikitasneki, xwel tikitas.
(It's necessary to guess, you can't see it,
although without any effort, you feel it go by.)

See tosaasanil, see tosaasaanil.
Se totlaakatsiin, nochipa kwak kiawi, notlakenpatla.
An old man very much alive,
every time it rains, he changes his clothes.)

See tosaasaanil, see tosaasaanil. See tootlaakatsiin,
Tlaakati istak, nemi xooxowki, waalmiki chichiltik.
(White was it's birth, green it's life.
Red it becomes when it gets ready to die.)

Náhuatl riddles from *Adivinanzas nahuas*, Flores Farfán (1996)
(Answers: wind, mountain, chili)

Cognitively, young children must reach a certain level of development,
somewhere during Piaget's pre-operational stage where symbolic thought
begins to emerge, to be able to find interest in such sport as "I spy" and
other guessing and word games. The manipulation of symbols, and being
able to mentally compare word meanings, begins to emerge early, long
before first grade. However, the continued development of this critical
literacy-related capability requires sustained and conscious attention,
especially in regard to the more complex and abstract kinds of conceptual
play by verbal means (answers to the riddles: wind, mountain, chili).

In the following *agradecimiento* [formal offering of thanks] to the newly
initiated co-father of her granddaughter, doña Eusebia Rojas of San Miguel
Canoa, Puebla, offers an example of what many in this indigenous community recognize as a dying verbal art form.

Ritual kinship ceremony closing: *agradecimiento*
[giving thanks] (ceremonial speech)

Coza timotlazocamati otmochihuilitzino in
We give much thanks that you have made the
obligacion mo compadrito mo comaletzin.
commitment thy cofather thy comother.
Ocpixque gusto de metzinotiez compadrito.
They have the pleasure that you are cofather.
pues yoc mochihuili ni obligacion compadrito.

The cofather has already made the commitment.
Coza timotlazocamati. Amoc pia tanto mitz
We give much thanks to him. They do not have much
momaquilitzi nozque mitz mo tetemilitzinozque.
to give you to fill you.
Dios oquin mo tlacolili. To Huey Tatzin amo quin
God has given them... The Great Father has not given them
motlacolili pero mas ica tlen hueliti
many things but with that which they have been able
ocmomazehuitzino itech tzinco. Ocoman mas ce
to offer you have enjoyed together with them. They offered but a
pedazo tlaxcaltzintli, mas ce iztatzintli.
morsel of (venerable) tortilla, but some (venerable) mole.
Amo opoli inahuactzintli, coza timo tlazocamati to
Your person was not wanting, very much we give thanks to our
vompaletzin, tlazocamatitzin ocmochihuilitzino
cofather, thanks that he made
in obligacion. Huiquilitzinoz cotzin chilayotzintli
the commitment. Take home some (venerable) chili
para in comaletzin. Itechtzinco aziz?
for the comother. Will her person arrive?

Underscoring the significance of the ritual kinship ceremony and the gravity of the co-father ties themselves, no seemingly trivial detail of the ritual is referred to in less than the most reverential terms (to the last *venerable* fritter of tortilla). Again, note that oral genres are salient not primarily for their content (doña Eusebia, in many words, is actually transmitting little information) but rather for the manner in which the words are pronounced, and the way the discourse is organized.

Lastly, we offer the following excerpt from the oral poem *Los vaqueros vasarios*, performed as part of a traditional dance of the same name every May 15 (Day of Saint Isidro) in the indigenous town of San Isidro Buensuceso, Tlaxcala. The stanzas (seventeen in all) are committed to memory and pronounced by the lead reciter, with the *refrain "¿Y qué les parece amigos y compañeros?"* ("And what do you think, friends and companions?") Corresponding to the dance line which responds in chorus.

Dance of the *Vaqueros vasarios* (poetry)

Abre la puerta Jacinto
Open the gate Jacinto
que entre mi caballo repinto con mi capa de gala.

that my painted horse enter with my full-dress cape.
Con una mano la garrocha, con otra mano la bandera.
With one hand the spear, with the other hand the flag.
Que este torito de pontal que sale por donde quiera.
This (...) bull that comes out from every which way
Ponte en cuidado mi caporal,
Be careful my foreman,
primero con este torito de pontal,
first with this (...) bull
que lo sacamos del corral que no nos vaya a largar.
that we take him from the corral that he does not escape.

¿Y que les parece amigos y compañeros?
And what do you think my friends and companions?
Muy lindamente mi señor caporal.
Very nicely my foreman sir.
Trabajan bien espuelas y botines.
Work [them] well spurs and boots.
Como ninguno mi señor caporal.
Like no other my foreman sir.

De las encumbradas nubes me informaron de los ángeles,
From the clouds on high they told me about the angels,
que los vieron con una
that they saw them with a
corona de flores, con su arco de colores.
crown of flowers, with its arch of colors.
Yo no sé para quien será.
I don't know for whom it will be.
¿Será para mí?
Will it be for me?
¿Será para el hijo de Dios que enterramos en su Campo Santo?
Will it be for the son of God that we laid to rest in His holy burial ground?
¿Qué santo llamaremos?
Which saint will we call?
Solamente a nuestro Santo San Isidro Labarador
None other than our Saint Isidro the ploughman.
que está en su primoroso altar.
who is in his exquisite altar.

Y qué les parece amigos y compañeros.
Muy lindamente mi señor caporal.

Trabajan bien espuelas y botines.
Como ninguno mi señor caporal.

Amigos y compañeros vengan por detrás de mí.
Friends and companions come follow me.
Si acaso me mata el toro rayado, no me entierren en tierra sagrada.
If by chance the striped bull kills me, do not bury me in holy ground.
Me entierran debajo de un piñón verde y un durazno colorado,
Bury me under a green piñon and a red peach tree,
Mi sepultura de caliacate, mis labradas espuelillas de campanillas.
My tomb of quicklime, my crafted little bell spurs.
Si de casualidad pasa una muchacha bonita preguntando por mí,
If by chance a pretty maiden passes by asking for me,
de qué se murió este pobre triste vaquero, no le digan con que se murió
how did this poor unhappy cowboy die, don't tell her that he died
nomás, con un cuerno de toro y dolor de costado, deseperado,
just like that, with a bull's horn and with pain in his side, despairing,
y tampoco fue enamorado.
and that neither was he in love.

Y que les parece amigos y compañeros.
Muy lindamente mi señor caporal.
Trabajan bien espuelas y botines.
Como ninguno mi señor caporal.

Aztazti (1991)[17]

In the absence of writing, extensive oral poems exploit special techniques and stylistic features: formulaic* structures, rhythmic patterns and other kinds of *redundancy** (Ong, 1982), as well as organizing the verse along narrative lines (Ong, 1992). These aspects of oral poetry, which distinguish it from written literature, are of special interest to teachers who look to this material as an instructional resource. Feldman (1991) sums up the critical attributes of traditional oral discourses[18] in general that are particularly relevant for the language teacher: students' attention is directed to the pertinent aspects of language structure as an integral part of learning about comprehension and expression.

> Whether a genre is written or spoken, it works much the same way, by fixing a form for expression...Within a genre the words themselves and not just their meaning can acquire a certain salience ... and only when words are fixed in this way as text can they invite interpretation and reflection. (Feldman, 1991: 50)

Students' comprehension and expression skills, especially in their L2, develop not only as a result of *engaging in* language activities that involve comprehension and expression, but also depend on *learning about* how language works. Thinking about words, as in the "dream of a word" in *Voices 3* (Chapter 3) underlies both esthetic, narrative, and expository genres. Language proficiencies are used, applied to authentic purposes, and also should become an object of reflection when, ultimately, the language learner will be able to monitor his or her own learning.

How First Language and Second Language are Related

One obvious way in which second language learning is different from acquiring one's first language is the fact that the second language learner already possesses extensive knowledge of another language system, at a certain age so complete that he or she is considered a native speaker of the language. The young child commands a high degree of fluency in the mother tongue, one that most learners do not attain in their second language, even after many years of study. This linguistic knowledge will, in turn, exercise an important influence on learning the second language, a phenomenon that some researchers refer to as transfer, or *cross-linguistic influence*. Knowledge of the L1 interacts and combines with other kinds of knowledge and other kinds of learning in the progressive construction of second language competence.

The well-informed teacher will be able to apply these basic concepts to facilitate language learning in both of the cases we have mentioned in this chapter; where: (1) the target language is the NL, and (2) the target language is the IL. Fundamentally, the same learning processes are involved; however in the case of indigenous languages, the special *social* circumstances related to the sharp inequalities between IL and NL will affect how students and teachers work through the challenges and opportunities that L2 learning will pose.

How L2 learners utilize first language knowledge and other learning strategies

In the past, for the purpose of guiding instruction, language teachers would point out the many predictable errors that second language learners commit that are directly or indirectly traceable to their first language. This category of errors, termed *interference*, would form the basis of an important part of the language teaching syllabus: first, an analysis would be made of the contrasting features that correspond respectively to L1 and L2, then instruction would focus on "weakening" the habits (originating in the

L1) that continue to cause errors in the second language. According to this point of view, new, second language, habits replace old habits. As the term interference implies, the influence of L1 was viewed as generally negative across the board when the transfer in question resulted in errors. On the other hand *positive* transfer would refer to influences from the L1 that involve patterns that both languages perhaps "share," resulting in grammatical structures that are correct or native-like.

For example, errors in marking nouns for plural may be related to Lakota speakers' first language rules:

> Sometimes it's almost five hundred dancers, man and women together. There's two way of talking. (quoted in Leap, 1993: 53)

A stronger candidate for L1 transfer would be the incorrect deletion of pronouns by a Mohave learner of English:

> I didn't know it either [   ] was playing, playing 'til the bell rung, [   ] open my book and felt my pocket; [   ] wasn't in there. (Leap, 1993: 61)

And perhaps we might find something in Isletan grammatical patterns that may explain persistent errors in verb agreement for a particular ESL student.

> All the dances that goes on like that occur in the Spring. Some peoples from the outside comes in. (Leap, 1993: 73)

Of course, transfer from the NL grammatical system to the IL works the same way. For example, the influence of Spanish grammar appears in the widespread use of "de" [of] in Náhuatl story telling, generating sequences that seem to depart from Náhuatl *syntax,** approximating that of Spanish. However, bilingual informants from the community in which the following language sample was taken point out that Náhuatl has been able to incorporate this grammatical item from Spanish in a way that is compatible with the patterns of the indigenous language.

> *Luego oyaya Puebla. Ocalaquia can quinnamaca pipiloltin de patioque....* *Oyeccocotozque, yeccocotozque, nochi, nochi, nochi, de miec pedazos. Huan* *ocrepartiroque de huehca, pues nonque pedazos huehca ocrepartiroque para* *ahco mololoa.*

> Then he went to Puebla, he went in where they sell expensive earings {pipiloltin de patioque} (earings of the expensive kind) ...They cut him up, they cut him up really well, everything, everything, everything in small pieces {nochi de miec pedazos} (everything of, or in, lots of pieces)

and they spread him far and wide {*de* hueca} (far away, in the sense of scattered). Then these pieces they spread far so that they do not reintegrate again.

In the following excerpt from another Náhuatl traditional story, the narrator (parenthetically, a young man who recently had spent a number of years working outside the community) seems to switch to Spanish with greater difficulty. Unlike in the previous example, the grammatical patterns between the two languages appear to be in conflict; or in other words, switching is less fluent (see Note 21, and the section in this chapter on "Borrowing and codeswitching"):

In tlacame huehca yoyahque tla hasta ocachi onenenque que todo mero.

The men went far away if (or but) to (or even) walked further that everything just like that (or that everything right here)

On the level of vocabulary knowledge, a second language learner of Navajo, whose L1 is English, may persist in committing errors regarding correct kinship terms related to distinctions that are explicitly marked in Navajo but not normally indicated in English (e.g. the distinction between maternal and paternal grandparents).[19]

However, the experienced second language teacher will notice that while some errors can be clearly attributed to first language influences (the Spanish-L1 to Náhuatl-L2, and the Mohave-L1 to English-L2 transfers, for example) other *error** patterns are common among second language learners from very different L1 backgrounds (for example, perhaps the verb agreement errors of the Lakota speaker). In fact, many of the errors that teachers notice in the production of their L2 students are strikingly similar to patterns that correspond to certain developmental stages in first language acquisition in young children.

Thus, the intermediate stages that L2 learners pass through (stages of *learner language**), and the error patterns that characterize them, are the result of complex processes. First language transfer is only one factor that interacts with others – factors that are not directly related to the grammatical patterns of the learner's primary language. This conclusion that researchers have arrived at has important implications for the language teacher, especially in IL teaching contexts.

Depending on the particular indigenous language in question, the region, other sociocultural and even political factors, what appear to be examples of transfer of IL linguistic features when speaking or writing in the NL are often highly stigmatized. Teachers may emphatically call students' attention to them and place an inordinate emphasis in the daily teaching program on eradicating what NL speakers point to as an Indian accent. Sometimes stemming from benevolent intentions, for example, the bilingual teacher, himself perhaps a speaker of the community's language, will insist upon this approach, to spare his students the effects of discrimination that their parents' generation suffered in school, and continues to experience in their day-to-day contact with speakers of the majority language.

Aside from the obvious effect of intensifying negative feelings of self-consciousness, and inhibiting expression, two serious errors are involved in focusing second language teaching on identifying their "source" in the IL, and then proceeding to head off, divert, or frustrate their emergence in the L2:

(1) As was pointed out earlier, the "origin" of the error may not be in the first language system at all, even in cases where, superficially, this may appear to be the case. Or the nonnative structure (the error) in question may be the product of a number of interacting factors (a developmental stage of the learner language, hypotheses that learners construct from a combination of their partial knowledge of the L2, their perceptions of what is applicable from their L1, etc.) (see Schachter, 1992);

(2) Transfer of language structures from the L1, even when they result in errors (together with the errors that originate elsewhere), form a part of the present stage of the student's evolving learner language. Not only are such errors both inevitable, and often impervious to correction at the early stages, but they are *necessary*.

Second language learners, whenever they engage in communication, or use the L2 for comprehension, apply whatever partial knowledge happens to be at their disposal at that moment. Language educators, today, see this application of the learner's knowledge system in authentic, ongoing, communication not as reinforcing "incorrect habits," but rather as indispensable for developing this same partial knowledge in the direction of complete knowledge of the L2 system. Thus, the "erroneous" hypotheses (drawn from the L1 and other sources) that are put to use permit learners to continue building and perfecting their second language knowledge; in the absence of opportunities to use the L2, learning will cease.

Language learners also need to reflect upon their partial knowledge (e.g. comparing their usage to that of more advanced learners and native speakers of the L2), but this is only possible if they are also producing language, and are engaged with other speakers. Here again, the stigma associated with the low prestige IL, and the resulting over-sensitivity to, and preoccupation with superficial errors (sometimes called "local errors") creates an obstacle to the necessary process of extensive use and interaction, coupled with selective reflection. Active and frequent use of the learner language also provides for the opportunity to receive helpful kinds of corrective feedback, another vital source of evidence about how the L2 system is structured and how it works, allowing learners, in turn, to compare and contrast the target forms with their own learner language patterns. This kind of judicious self-monitoring is only possible if the students can view their indigenous language in a more "objective" way, that is, free of perceptions of inferiority and feelings of shame. Teachers, in fact, can openly discuss these affective issues in order to promote higher levels of consciousness about why speakers of the IL may continue to perceive their language (and the "interference" that induces silence in situations of L2 language use) in abnegative terms.

At this point an important distinction should be made among different categories of error, particularly those aspects of learner language that may be attributed to transfer. Broadly speaking, for teaching purposes, researchers distinguish between:

(1) Global errors – rule violations that involve larger grammatical patterns that, in turn, lead to significant problems of comprehension or misunderstanding. In the example "They started to learn English as childrens, because they speak very good" (Faltis, 2001:139), the incorrect usage of the causal conjunction "because," is the global error;

(2) Local errors (in the above example, "childrens" and "speak good") generally occur at the word or phrase level, and are easily interpretable by native speakers and learners alike. Following proper teaching approaches, error patterns of both categories will be surmounted by the student, and the correct structures, in both cases, form part of the teacher's learning objectives (although the intervention strategies will differ; see "error correction" later in this chapter and in Chapter 5).

However, within the second category (local errors), there exists a truly superficial level, corresponding to the phonological patterns of L1 and L2, that should be treated differently from the above examples. Transfer of sound patterns from the L1 that actually impede comprehension on the part of the listener will be the object of self-correction and sometimes conscious effort on the learner's part. However, the evidence is unclear regarding the efficacy of active intervention strategies on the part of the teacher, with pronunciation almost always improving spontaneously with sufficient opportunities for active communicative use of the L2.

Especially in the case of bilingual indigenous students, educators and parents often go one step further in an attempt to remediate what, by extension, we could call the "local phonological errors." Strictly speaking, examples of non-native "accent" are "errors" in the sense that they represent patterns that are clearly non-native in the target language. Also, socially, they single out the speaker as Indian. Nevertheless, they are errors of no practical consequence in communication, language prejudice aside. More importantly, they present no obstacle in the area of academic language use. If remediation of this kind of transfer, or error, is viewed as a high language learning priority by parents, perhaps for understandable subjective reasons (e.g. deep-rooted linguistic prejudices on the part of the majority culture persist, despite many positive changes in both attitudes and official language policy), educators must be conscious that any such efforts in the classroom have no pedagogical value of any kind. If anything, they become impediments to improving the receptive and expressive skills in the L2; and ironically, may prolong the process of improving pronunciation.

This commonsense approach to learner errors (for example, in interactive exchanges, teachers should be sensitive to the disruptive effect of direct correction) does not mean that errors should be ignored. If in most situations of student oral expression, direct correction shifts the speaker's attention away from the content of the discourse toward what often turns out to be an unsuccessful search for the correct pattern or rule, appropriate corrective feedback can sometimes be timed just right to coincide with breaks in the discourse when the learner will be able to process the teacher's observation and reflect. In addition, there are a number of indirect correction techniques of the "negotiation of meaning" type that maintain the focus of corrective feedback on meaning. Secondly, learner reflection should be directed toward the "higher level" grammatical patterns: word structure, sentence-level patterns, and meaning relationships, as opposed to pronunciation (the subsystem of language least susceptible to conscious reflection, and most removed from meaning). Corrective feedback, as a rule, is more effective when the patterns in question can be examined, with time to actually mentally compare errors and target language forms. For example, after taking note of recurring error patterns in speech and writing, teachers can collect actual examples from students' production and develop focused activities in which the class as a whole, or in small groups, contrasts error patterns with their target form counterparts. A number of other reflective, noticing-the-gap type activities can be organized (Ellis, 1997; Gass, 1997; Loschky & Bley-Vroman, 1993), following the same principle: time and opportunity to examine and contemplate pertinent contrasts, and avoidance of counterproductive kinds of direct correction that impede communication and expression. Logically, when learners are given the opportunity to work with examples in written form, all this is greatly facilitated. Bottom line: there is no contradiction between communicative-comprehensible input approaches and systematic and ongoing focus on form. In the next chapter, we will return to this point: how to integrate grammar learning into a content-based L2 immersion program.

Access to a common underlying academic discourse proficiency

Textbooks and teacher's guides for bilingual educators refer to another kind of "transfer": aspects of academic language proficiency that are not *language specific*. For example, under this category we would find:

(1) literacy-related skills directly related to decoding and print awareness (letters and words represent language in a systematic way), directionality, etc.;

(2) comprehension strategies – readers' and listeners' ability to follow extended texts (or orally presented lectures), link one idea with another, and mentally keep the important components together and form a coherent understanding of the message;

(3) analytical abilities that allow the student to examine different aspects of a text (an argument for example), one against another, one in relation to another, and if necessary, integrate the ideas and concepts in accord with the intentions of the author, or, in a new way;

(4) the ability to apply logical operations to texts and discourses;

(5) knowledge of different text types and genres – how content or information is organized in each type, and the patterns that one can expect when reading or listening;

(6) critical thinking and evaluation.

These aspects of language proficiency are not language-specific in the sense that:

(1) they are not peculiar to any one language, and they are part of what we referred to at the beginning of this chapter as CALP, competencies that "underlie," so to speak, the bilingual's knowledge of his or her first and second languages (i.e. strictly linguistic knowledge refers to the grammar, vocabulary, and sound systems);

(2) when students learn how to apply a given CALP skill, it will not be necessary to relearn it in a second language; it is still available for application. Second language learners will have access to the underlying language use abilities regardless of whether they were learned through the medium of L1 or L2, through oral means or written means.

A common error in thinking about CALP and how academic-type language skills are available for use in an L2 is related to the learning contexts of indigenous languages. Since they have, to date, generally been excluded from school, there may appear to be little in terms of "academic" language ability that ILs have to contribute to the development of CALP. However, as our survey of the oral genres demonstrated, languages that are not taught in school, or even languages without a writing system, can also be the vehicle of discourses that share many of the characteristics of academic language ability. Children who have had the benefit of extensive contact with these oral genres will have acquired and stored CALP-type language proficiencies and, given the opportunity, will be able to apply them to school and literacy-related language tasks: (1) applying these proficiencies, learned through the oral medium, to *literacy* in the indigenous language, (2) applying the *same* proficiencies (because they are not language specific) to higher-order language tasks in general, both oral and written, in both IL and NL.

The obvious example would be the oral narrative tradition, where we could say that prediction strategies, inference, analyzing and contrasting character traits, knowledge of story structure, etc. "transfer" (or as we prefer to describe the process: knowledge and skills that are learned are stored and reorganized, and subsequently made available for similar language tasks). Perhaps less evident would be the benefit of exposure to ceremonial language or religious ritual. Here, children learn to direct their attention to how *language forms themselves* are important. In metaphoric language (common in ceremonies and rituals) specific wordings and patterns stand for ideas and concepts. The words themselves are important, and not any wording that might mean the same thing would be sufficient or appropriate, prompting the child to consciously attend to language itself. This ability, together with other kinds of reflective language use, is one of the building blocks of academic language use.

Unlike in the transfer of grammatical or phonological patterns from L1 to L2, which sometimes result in errors and at other times result in target language forms, selecting from the storehouse of CALP-type language skills does not result in errors. Perhaps an L2 learner may gain access to the wrong schema or processing strategy for a given purpose, but this is a different matter. Rather, the challenge that bilingual students face here is: (1) finding a way to make readily available to themselves this stored knowledge, and (2) choosing the appropriate tools for the task at hand. The educator's role consists in facilitating (1) and (2), in the first place, recognizing that the IL speech community is indeed a resource for these higher-level language proficiencies, and helping students make the connections so that they too perceive this knowledge as applicable.[20]

If a portion of each teaching day were set aside for listening to, reflecting upon, and exploring representative examples of the IL oral tradition, bilingual students will not only begin to ascribe to these genres a more positive cultural value, but will begin to view them as belonging to the same universal literary tradition that is taught in every school Language Arts program. Again, to facilitate access to the knowledge base of higher-order discourses, students need to become aware that they do indeed possess it, and that this knowledge base is not unrelated to the academic language of the classroom. From this awareness will follow the ability to select the most adequate schemas, and then apply them to new tasks, which in reality are not new in all respects.

Interactions between L1 and L2 when learning the indigenous language

Historically, in bilingual education for Indian students, transfer (of grammatical patterns from L1 to L2) was considered as a phenomenon that affected only the learning of the national language. In the first decades of the 20th century, most students spoke the IL fluently, and a minority spoke English or Spanish. The national language was always the second language learned in school. Today, with significant numbers of Indian children whose primary language is not the ancestral language of the community, what appears to be the transfer of language patterns in the opposite direction, so to speak, from NL to IL, has become an object of study and interest on the part of bilingual teachers. Also, remember that our earlier point about the "origin" of errors is pertinent here as well: what may appear to be transfer from the NL to a learner language stage of IL competence may be the result of a combination of factors, often having little direct relation to the student's first language.

Ever since the first contacts with the European languages in the 16th century, elements of Spanish, English, and French began to enter into the speech and writing of speakers of indigenous languages (Lockhart, 1990). However, as an aspect of second language learning (that is, learning the IL as an L2), the field is very new, with scarcely the beginnings of any research at all to refer to.

At this point it is important to emphasize that all the basic concepts and pedagogical principles discussed earlier in relation to how second languages are learned apply to the new situation of teaching and learning of indigenous languages. Learners will call upon their knowledge of English grammar, for example, to form sentences and communicate messages in the IL; and together with the influence of other factors, they will produce utterances that range from grammatically correct, near-native, structures containing local errors, all the way to responses that are incorrect and incomprehensible. IL learner languages evolve in fundamentally the same way as all others; and the very same understanding of the role of errors and the use of partial knowledge in communication should be applied. Being a relatively recent development, the phenomenon of child or adult learners speaking an IL with an English or Spanish "accent" may sound strange or even disconcerting to many elders and other fully proficient speakers. However, the stages of language learning that are reflected in the persistent errors of pronunciation, grammar, word choice, etc. cannot be avoided, skipped over, or suppressed. The recommendations regarding error correction apply to the development of the IL as a second language in the same way as they apply to the development of a second language when this is an NL. For example, Hinton and Ahlers (1999) and Wong (1999) report on aspects of IL learner language, and how this is different from how children in the past developed grammatical competence in the indigenous language. Competent adult speakers of the IL may need to adjust their expectations and assessments of this new language-learning phenomenon.

Borrowing and codeswitching

Probably one of the most visible manifestations of cross-linguistic influence in the speech of fluent speakers and IL learners alike is the prolific use of language elements originating in the NL. The attitude that bilinguals should take toward borrowing and *codeswitching** is also one of the more contentious debates among indigenous language teachers and community language activists. The controversy aside for now, from the linguistic point of view alone, note the complex patterns of alternation between Náhuatl and Spanish in fifth grader Constantino's story of *Tetsitsilintlan* [The sounding rock] (switches to Spanish underlined):

... *tlakco octli in pipiltontlin obajaro in silla en el tlali in papan*
half way down the road the boy lowered the chair to the ground the father

y in pipiltontlin omodescansaroki y luego omolebantaro in pipiltontlin
and the boy rested and then the boy picked him up

y omik in tlacatl umukedaro para siempre en el tetl.
... and the man died he stayed forever on the rock

Some older or more experienced narrators, perhaps more proficient in the language, or more conscious of the language structures themselves, may tend to avoid switching as frequently, as in Reyes Arce's version of *In tlacuatl uan in coyotl (The Opossum and the Coyote)*:

... intla quincuaz pero ti mozahuaz
yes you will eat them but you must fast.

[God to opossum]
Mozahuaz in coyotl nenchihuili chihuili miec cosas
Coyote will fast, you will do lots of mischief to him, many things.

nimozahuaz para cualiz niccuaz ni pilhuatzitlin
I'll fast so as to be able to eat his children...

Como yonenamiquia quitoa bueno ma niconi.
Since he was already thirty, he says OK, I'll drink.

Quicacati cuicacati ocmomacac cuenta que amo melahuac.
He starts to let it go. He realizes that it's not true.

Nevertheless, as evidenced in the above transcription, the presence of elements from the NL is an almost universal feature; especially noteworthy is the frequency of "borrowed" function words and discourse connecting words.

Regarding the teacher's approach to borrowing and codeswitching in their students' language use, there are two separate categories to consider, the IL learner with partial knowledge of the target language systems, and the fluent bilingual speaker:

The influence of the national language on second language learners of the indigenous language

For NL-dominant students at one or another stage in the evolution of their learner language, the same principles of second language learning discussed in the previous sections apply. Learners will put their L1 knowledge to good use in situations where a vocabulary item or grammatical pattern has not yet been learned. If the listener is known to be bilingual (as is always the case with his or her teacher), NL switches will be more frequent. In addressing a monolingual speaker, the learner may attempt to apply other strategies, try harder to search his or her mental dictionary for the appropriate word, or simply avoid certain topics. As in the case of errors (although we would hesitate to categorize codeswitches in this way) many NL elements in IL discourse will gradually be replaced by their Native counterparts as the learner's L2 proficiency marks progress toward native-speaker norms.

Teacher feedback should always emphasize the communicative aspects of learner's utterances, i.e. respond to the meaning that is being expressed. At the same time, the IL teacher is monitoring and taking note of all the evidence of partial knowledge, analyzing the present stage of students' learner language, and then proceeding to organize learning tasks that will help them advance to the next stage. When students appear to be ready to substitute a borrowed item with the appropriate IL term, direct instruction involving conscious attention to the word(s) or pattern may be helpful (for example, when learners show evidence of knowledge of the item in comprehension, but do not use it themselves in production).

For all practical purposes, we can consider the case of the student who perhaps once spoke the indigenous language fluently, but who has lost proficiency, as similar to the learner of the IL as a second language. Under normal circumstances, in both cases, the national language will be the dominant or primary language, with competence in the IL being incomplete. Respectively, codeswitching and borrowing will show similar patterns. From the pedagogical point of view, the approach is also similar: the teacher who wishes to promote the development of the indigenous language has no interest in discouraging codeswitching among learners, since this kind of expressive use of the language is necessary. To reiterate, the continuous and sustained use in communication of the learner language is the only condition under which it will develop. One can imagine, for example, what the consequence of a prohibition or negative attitude toward codeswitching would be. Learners would simply avoid the IL, and be less likely to make the special effort to use it in communicative situations; if their attempts are devalued or minimized, exclusive use of their dominant language, the NL, is inadvertently being encouraged.

This approach corresponds to the general framework for teaching second languages:

(1) students are immersed in communicative language use of all kinds centered around content learning objectives;

(2) teachers thus provide significant amounts of comprehensible input in the L2, interacting with and responding to learner's messages (i.e. to the content, the meaning, or the intention in their attempts at communication);

(3) within the context of using the second language for authentic purposes, promote conscious reflection upon language itself (*how* meaning is expressed);

(4) based on a systematic and ongoing monitoring of learner's progress, select the language patterns where errors are ready to be corrected, and where partial knowledge, of a rule for example, can be restructured to approach more closely the target language form;

(5) design learning activities that specifically focus on these points, and

provide the opportunity to practice and reflect upon the new language structures that are ready to be mastered.

Especially regarding points (3), (4), and (5), see Hedge (2001).

The influence of the national language on fluent speakers of the indigenous language

Codeswitching and borrowing is a practice that is, in fact, just as common in the general population of bilingual speakers of the indigenous language. One particular characteristic that will distinguish the fluent bilinguals, however, is their tendency, when switching from one language to the other, to do so at points in the sentence where the grammatical patterns of both languages can be synchronized, to switch where they would "naturally" concur.[21] The alternation sounds fluent and actually does flow, unimpeded by awkward shifts from one grammatical system to another. Researchers point to this interesting phenomenon as evidence of high levels of competence in both languages. This kind of codeswitching represents an ability, based on the bilingual's knowledge of both systems, to interweave words and phrases from both languages in a systematic way, very often for the purpose of expressing particular meanings by way of this complex skill that only fluent bilingual speakers possess. The story excerpts above from Constantino and Mr Arce are both examples of how switches respect the grammatical patterns of both Náhuatl and Spanish. In fact, both of our subjects are indeed balanced bilinguals, and unlike many learners (i.e. non-native, beginner speakers of one or the other language) they tend to either switch grammatically or avoid switching at points where the languages do not "permit" it.

Contrary to past beliefs, codeswitching of this kind does not reflect or, much less, promote confusion and unruly mixing of languages. Indeed, as should be apparent from our description above of how the grammatical systems work together, this kind of language choice that bilinguals make is evidence of the ability to mentally keep the language systems separate, and to be able to manipulate them in a systematic way. More importantly, by itself, codeswitching does not weaken the indigenous language, nor foster its erosion.

However among the proficient speakers of the language, especially the most conscious members of the community who are also the most active in preservation efforts, what we could call the "purist" position remains predominant, simply stated, the "intrusion" of words and phases from the national language corrupts the ancestral language and hastens its decline. While in general we can see where the purists go wrong, and how in concrete language learning situations their approach can actually be counterproductive, they have called our attention to one particular aspect of the codeswitching phenomenon that teachers should be mindful of. Our own research has highlighted the purists' observation that the interactions and transfers between IL and NL are hardly based on anything even approaching equitable terms of language contact. For example, when speaking, and especially writing in the national language, codeswitching is rare. In the sample of children's language use from our study of Náhuatl speaking bilinguals, both in students' oral and written stories in Spanish, codeswitching or borrowing was virtually non-existent (Francis, 1997; Francis & Nieto Andrade, 1996). In the case of Náhuatl, on the other hand, switching to Spanish was universal and frequent. The purists point out that in all language contact situations: (1) it is never the NL that is losing ground; and (2) indigenous languages do not normally disappear from one generation to the next, but rather are eroded gradually from one domain to another. Likewise, in the case of individual bilinguals experiencing language erosion, it is more accurate to say that grammatical structures and vocabulary items are not *lost*, but rather *displaced* by the other system, which gradually occupies the mental space in which the now-weaker language was once secure. During this process, the new expanding language system imposes itself, with greater and greater frequency, even when the old system must be used for communication. Even fluent bilinguals reflect the erosion of the language itself where, over the years, IL vocabulary items are *replaced*, and dissipate almost completely from the community's collective memory (e.g. kinship terms). However in these cases, the concept that is important to keep in mind is that under some circumstances codeswitching and borrowing *reflect* language loss, not cause it (Francis & Navarrete Gómez, 2000).

The informed bilingual teacher/IL promoter will always value the students' attempts at expression, at the same time taking note and recording the wide range of items that originate in the national language. Any effort to positively promote the substitution of borrowed NL items with the appropriate IL terms must begin by carefully categorizing them, distinguishing among the different classes to which they correspond, and respectively, applying different teaching approaches. The following categories serve as a first approximation:

(1) words that historically entered the IL vocabulary during the first years of contact; often these are now archaic terms that are no longer in current usage among monolingual speakers of the NL;

(2) terms for new concepts, objects, animals and plants not native to the

Americas, technologies, etc., that are commonly "borrowed" by all languages (in English: *al-jabr* from Arabic – algebra, *xoco-atl* [bitter-water] from Náhuatl – chocolate);

(3) new terms that actually did replace indigenous words or expressions that are now so common in IL discourse that most speakers, monolingual and bilingual alike, are either unaware of the existence of the original, view it as archaic, or would consider it inappropriate because it sounds too formal, snobbish, exotic, etc.;

(4) more recent entries that are not universally recognized, where the usage varies, for example by generation, but the items are common among fluent bilinguals;

(5) "on the spot" spontaneous, borrowing for a particular purpose or occasion, which does not form part of common everyday usage of any group in the speech community; and

(6) switching between grammatical patterns and borrowing vocabulary items by learners, or language "unlearners," that actually indicates a lack of knowledge, or beginning stage of acquisition (one reliable indicator being switches that are not grammatical and would not normally be heard in the speech of fluent bilinguals).

Teaching approaches include:

(1) modeling the IL equivalents, e.g. consistently referring to a kinship relationship with the correct term;

(2) organizing open-ended discussions about bilingualism and code-switching with the class, encouraging students to reflect upon some of the pertinent language learning aspects discussed in this section, social issues, language attitudes, and perceptions. Even young bilinguals are curious about these linguistic phenomena and often surprise adults with a precocious awareness of concepts and categories of language and language use;

(3) designing group language awareness tasks where students try to identify the origin (IL or NL) of terms used in everyday conversation, place names and proper names, and critically examine the criteria they used to make their decisions;

(4) translating short passages from stories or other types of texts. Present students with the hypothetical situation of a monolingual speaker of the IL who would be unfamiliar even with commonly used loan words. How would the translator solve the problem using only the lexical* resources of the indigenous language?

(5) if the language has at its disposal a body of literature, of its "classic"

works, reading passages to the students and talking about how the language has evolved;

(6)   identifying loan words in the *NL* of *indigenous* origin;

(7)   as a regular activity, e.g. once a week, writing a short paragraph on the chalkboard containing switches that are more amenable to correction (categories 4, 5, and 6 in the previous list), and ask students to consult with each other in small groups on how they would rewrite the sample;

(8)   in correcting students own work, using written samples, and avoiding the correction of speech if the teacher's observation interrupts the student's discourse; "on-line" correction of oral language is rarely effective. The advantage of correcting written samples lies primarily in the opportunity that the writer has to examine and deliberate on the language forms in question, free of "communicative pressure" and time constraints. Students should find their own examples for potential revision; this spares the teacher from this task, but even more importantly students are more likely to take ownership of the activity. In fact, the benefits of thinking about language and how it works are realized to the greatest degree when the learner directs the reflective process.

As a rule, any attempt at revitalizing the actual structure and use of the language must proceed selectively, following all the effective language teaching principles that apply in other domains; above all, and at all times, respecting the actual language use of the community itself is the fundamental point of departure. Attempting to modify students' speech patterns against the current of community language norms comes as close to the very definition of futile as any educator can get. Purists can rest a little easier knowing that switching and borrowing, of the fluent and non-fluent varieties, are systematic, and contribute neither to cognitive confusion or language loss. On the other hand, any serious language revitalization movement will surely have on its agenda, in reasonable proportion to other planning objectives, the recovery of ancestral language forms that have fallen into decline.

Additional reading

Second Language Acquisition by Rod Ellis (1998) is a concise survey of the research on the key characteristics and the development of learner language (also known as "interlanguage"). Useful sections for teachers can be found on L1 transfer, the role of *Universal Grammar**, individual differences in L2 learning, and especially on the role that form-focused instruction can play in advancing students' L2 development as far as is possible.

Input, Interaction and the Second Language Learner by Susan Gass (1997) presents an "input-interaction perspective," and reviews the research on how teachers modify their speech for the purpose of maximizing comprehensibility, and what pitfalls to watch out for (e.g. ungrammatical "baby-talk" type simplification). A good follow-up to Ellis on the role of corrective feedback (also known as "negative evidence"), and how this can foster L2 learning when properly applied.

Foundations of Bilingual Education and Bilingualism by Colin Baker (2001), has strong chapters (5–9) on the cognitive aspects of bilingualism and second language learning, for example on the role of metalinguistic awareness.

Cummins' recent *Language, Power and Pedagogy: Bilingual Children in the Crossfire* (2000) is a must-read basic text on the nature of bilingual proficiency as it is related to the school context and academic achievement. How language interactions in the classroom can be transformed: from coercive to collaborative.

Chapter 5
The Bilingual Classroom

In this chapter we will discuss how teachers might be able to put the traditional indigenous language (IL) discourse practices to good use in the classroom for developing language and literacy skills in general, and how L2 immersion methods can be pressed into service for the task of teaching the indigenous language as a second language. Chapter 6, on biliteracy, will return to this theme: how IL narrative in particular might be applied to the teaching of reading and writing. A final note to this chapter will take up issues of language use in the bilingual classroom as they might be related to intercultural communication.

Working with Oral Genres: Teaching Higher Order Discourse Abilities

The obvious starting point for tapping the vast underutilized reservoir of traditional oral genres, and applying it to the task of language development, is to set aside classroom time and resources for listening to and working with these genres (Francis 1991). The first salutary effect of focusing students' attention on *sustained and continuous oral discourses*, on a daily basis, will be to begin to reverse the trend today in many classrooms toward a virtually exclusive emphasis on individual seatwork-type assignments. With the justification of individualizing instruction, and promoting peer teaching and small-group cooperative learning (all proper and necessary strategies for the increasingly heterogeneous classroom), often students have little or no opportunity to engage in extended, higher-order, oral comprehension tasks. In fact, teachers tend to increasingly avoid these opportunities when students become inattentive, shifting their role more and more toward that of a manager of one series of individual and small group projects after another. Teacher discourse directed to the whole class gradually becomes reduced to the essential sound-byte type of instructions for the next assignment. In the majority of cases where children seem incapable of listening (and behaving properly during story-time, lectures, extended demonstrations, etc.), we suspect that the reasons have little to do with purported "attention deficits" or peculiar non-oral "learning styles."[22]

The ability to "follow a story," for example, and maintain one's attention, is directly related to the ability to mentally reconstruct the events and scenes (which, in turn, form episodes), to distinguish the different voices (that of the narrator, the characters), to tie one aspect of the plot to another, and to discern the overall theme. These are comprehension strategies that are learned by most children, at least in their rudimentary form, long before they come into contact with these strategies in kindergarten and first grade. Clearly, in any given IL community, some children will have benefited from a rich and extensive experience in this area of language learning, others less so. Perhaps for many, kindergarten will be the first contact they will have with this kind of more cognitively demanding oral discourse.

Hypothetically, at least, indigenous children from communities that have maintained the oral tradition should be able to count on certain advantages in this important domain of academic language. For communities that have lost this oral heritage, the task of language revitalization will require conscious language planning efforts on two fronts: the language itself, and its traditional discourse practices. Young preschool children from "book-oriented" cultures, for example, enjoy listening to stories from parents and siblings. Typically these narratives are read from attractive, colorfully illustrated books, with the listener's attention maintained both by the actual words and by the very explicit and concrete visual support available on the page. Withdrawal of this immediate context embedding is also typically met at first with resistance by the listener who has developed such a "dependence," and who still must pass to a higher level of language processing to be able to comprehend complex narratives by verbal means alone.

Access to illustrations in early narrative development is certainly not an impediment to literacy learning. However, in the case of exclusively oral storytelling practices, it is entirely plausible that children in these situations benefit from contact with a kind of discourse that challenges their developing capacity to process information to an even greater degree, and at an earlier age. At the very least, listening to traditional oral narratives is as cognitively demanding as listening to stories from any variety of published children's literature. Precisely, the development of academic language proficiency involves the ability to comprehend extended and continuous passages of speech or writing with progressively fewer and fewer cues that the situation may provide. In the more abstract academic language of lectures, and explanations of content-area concepts, even "previous knowledge" context support must be partially suspended or put aside to one degree or another (Widdowson, 1984).

The narrative is the most logical beginning for daily oral language comprehension activities, for no other reason than for the broad selection that is readily available. Especially in the case of second language learners of the indigenous language, students will profit from numerous repetitions of the same story. This is because, for each telling, there still remain various aspects of the plot, and this or that vocabulary item or grammatical structure, which are beyond their current level of L2 proficiency. With each retelling, new aspects of the narrative are revealed; something different emerges, and new language structures are either assimilated outright, or come to the foreground to be examined by the learner. The teacher-as-storyteller will be sensitive to this movement: what is comprehensible "as is," without any special modifications; which aspects are within the "instructional level" (comprehensible with additional context support); and which are beyond the learner's level, even with assistance. This makes the actual presentation of each retelling different and new, in some important way, for both reciter and listener. As long as children voluntarily maintain their attention focused on the narrative, there must be some significantly novel language experience involved, hence learning. Of course the task of compiling the broadest collection of narratives becomes one of the primary responsibilities of the indigenous language teacher.

In contrast to the performance of traditional oral narrative in the non-academic setting, the language teacher has an interest in the material beyond the telling/listening act itself. In fact, it would be a mistake, a missed opportunity of major proportions, not to take advantage of the language learning potential of the stories. Consciously and systematically reflecting upon the narrative's theme, for example, is an extension of the activity mainly associated with school and schooling. For children, engaging in the act of listening (to oral *genres*, not just conversational language) is the beginning of academic language development; but it represents only the beginning, a foundation upon which the higher-level competencies can be built. As children listen, they mentally reconstruct the narratives. However, only through retrospection, looking back and thinking about what they understood, can children reorganize and re-elaborate these mental representations to form part of a complex of proficiencies that they can later apply to more sophisticated language tasks. For many reasons the narrative is the most appropriate point of departure on the long road to academic, CALP-type, language ability. For beginners and young children especially, it is the most accessible of the different school *registers** or discourses. However, to ensure that development continues, retrospection and reflection are necessary. This kind of language activity is necessary for building the literacy-related comprehension skills associated with subject area *expository text**, and especially the ability to compose one's own texts (Wenden, 1998; Garner, 1994).

Cummins (2000) urges educators to recognize and incorporate into the curriculum the vernacular discourses of language minority students, and at the same time to guard against romanticizing the role they can play in the full development of academic language proficiency. This caution pertains to our discussion of the oral tradition as well. Firstly, for historical reasons, the richness and productivity of the oral tradition varies from one indigenous language community to another. And even in the case of a language with millions of speakers, and a long and extensive development of its oral genres, language learners need to go beyond the traditional discourses. The complexity of expository texts, for example, in the content areas of science, mathematics, history, etc., developed along with the development of writing systems. The material from the oral tradition narrative will help children travel a good distance down the road toward building the necessary foundation of CALP and higher-order literacy abilities. But nothing in Chapters 4, 5, and 6 should be taken to imply that it can substitute for also working with the kinds of text that the oral tradition could not have given impulse to much beyond a certain limited threshold; see Note 33, and Ong (1992) and Olson (1994).

So far we have emphasized the development of oral discourse abilities as a preparation for higher-order literacy learning. In fact this hypothetical connection between traditional IL genres and traditional discourse practices on the one hand, and literacy on the other should confer a clear advantage to children who have been exposed to these more sophisticated ways of using language. If in practice, it does not, the deficiency surely lies not in the discourse practices, but rather in the school's inability to avail itself of them in preparing children for literacy. At the same time, it is important not to conceive of this connection as a simple one-way relationship. Rather, it is reciprocal and interactive: early literacy learning helps develop the same discourse abilities outlined above, and helps children become more reflective about their own language use. Thus, sustained exposure to and reflection upon written stories contributes to the development of oral discourse abilities as well (Horowitz, 1990; Olson, 1991). Teachers should remember, however, that children can begin to perform complex operations on higher-order discourses long before they are skilled in the orthographic system of their language. This conclusion follows from the evidence of such mastery among indigenous children and adults alike, monolingual in an IL, which may have little or no published literature of any kind.

Reflection upon the structure and form of the narratives is the complement of comprehension activities focused on meaning (not something that is postponed for the more "advanced stages"). As we will see shortly, written language facilitates this objective in peculiar and unique ways. In Chapter 6 we will examine in more detail the special contribution of *literacy* to language learning.

The Immersion Approach to Teaching Indigenous Languages

As a method of teaching a second or foreign language to majority language speaking children, immersion programs have demonstrated their superiority over all other elementary-level language programs. In North America, for the most part, English-speaking children are engaged in learning a second national language or foreign language (French in Canada, various "foreign" languages in the United States). However, the few experiments that have explored the possibilities of immersion for the teaching of indigenous languages strongly suggest that the overall approach is applicable, despite the important differences between the respective language learning situations. Its primary feature resides in the complete integration of language and content teaching for significant blocks of instructional time, during which learners receive substantial amounts of comprehensible input in the second language ("substantial" being, in fact, an understatement: in an early immersion program, L2-medium instruction for kindergarten and first grade could take up as much as 60–70% of the school day, decreasing to perhaps 30% by sixth grade). Teaching the second language is never divorced from its sustained use in subject-area learning activities and daily classroom language routines of all kinds. Second language students should also learn *about* the language, study its rules and patterns, and think about *how* it works; in any case, language study itself is integrated into the content curriculum. In reality, "Language Arts" is also a content area and, as such, can be taught applying immersion methods. And the idea of integrating the traditional oral genres into the language program will find in the immersion approach the ideal framework for both IL development and content-related academic language development. As we will see in the next chapter, traditional narratives such as the *"Coyote and Opossum"* are just the kind of material that L2 learners need. They lend themselves well to immersion teaching because even beginner L2 learners can follow the broad outlines of the story with appropriate context support provided. As L2 vocabulary and grammar knowledge develop, reliance on context clues is diminished. Students are impelled toward focusing greater and greater attention on the language itself; and this progression is accomplished without recourse to translation.

In regard to the general applicability of the model and to the issue of student learning outcomes, bilingual teachers may be familiar with some of the points of contention in the discussion on immersion teaching:

(1)   the extension of early total-L2 immersion for ESL students in the United States as an alternative to bilingual instruction;
(2)   the effectiveness of communicative language teaching based on the content-based approach, given the finding from the Canadian studies that, even after six to eight years of French immersion, students evidence conspicuously non-native grammar knowledge in their performance.

In applying immersion to IL teaching, let us consider (2) first. The research to date has shown impressive results in all four language skill areas: reading, writing, oral comprehension, and speaking. In reference to native speakers of the target language, immersion students' levels of reading comprehension are comparable, with oral comprehension and *coherence** in writing approaching levels that are also comparable to native speakers. In the area of speaking, immersion students demonstrate considerable fluency and ease of communication. However, they continue to commit frequent and glaring errors in grammar and in other linguistic aspects of language proficiency (evident in their writing as well, even though in the area of coherence and organization their composition skills are not significantly inferior to those of native speakers).

Regarding this persistent deficiency of majority language speaking immersion students, which in fact seems impervious to remediation, there is reason to believe that *indigenous language immersion students* would be more successful in approaching native-speaker norms. The key variable here, again, would be sociolinguistic, but in this case, a variable that would work in the IL learner's favor. Unlike most other immersion situations (e.g. French in Canada, Spanish in the United States), the IL student returns from school to a speech community where the target language may be spoken at home or in the extended family, or may be important for interpersonal communication in certain community contexts. At least for some sectors of the population the language may be the primary means of communication. Clearly, the degree of extracurricular language support for in-school immersion will depend upon the level of actual IL use in the local domains of communication (see Table 1 and Figure 1). Nevertheless, IL immersion, even in situations of advanced language erosion (e.g. the Hawaiian language) involves the teaching of a *heritage language*, intimately linked to a culture and an oral history, spoken for centuries often in the same geographical region where the present-day community continues to reside.

Immersion is a bilingual approach where language one and language two are compartmentalized (review Chapter 3) throughout the school day and across the various domains of language use in the classroom. The relative weight, or distribution, given to the IL can vary widely depending on the circumstances:

(1) the importance of the national language (NL) and how this issue is perceived by families;
(2) availability of fluent IL-speaking teachers and learning materials;
(3) the degrees and variation in IL proficiency among children;
(4) the access that children have to the NL outside of school.

The Hawaiian Language Immersion (HLI) model probably represents the most intensive and sweeping application. HLI provides total immersion in the IL through grade four; only in fifth grade is English introduced – for one hour or less per day as a part of a literature-based language arts and social studies program. Hawaiian Language Immersion is projected to continue through the high school grades with approval from the state Department of Education where English-medium instruction will be limited to two hours daily (Slaughter, 1997). On the other hand, Navajo Immersion at Fort Defiance sets aside a block of time from Kindergarten for English: K and first grade – 20 minutes, second grade – 50% English and 50% Navajo, and by fourth grade, English increasing to 80%. Navajo remains the medium of instruction in Social Studies-based language arts in the upper grades.

While from the point of view of language revitalization, HLI would appear to be the stronger program, the research evidence on the relationship between number of hours in immersion and ultimate proficiency levels in the second language is still inconclusive. However we should point out that probably no other immersion program studied in Canada or the United States has ever shifted the balance so far in favor of L2 medium instruction as in the case of HLI. Perhaps the critical variable may turn out to be not quantitative in nature (amount of instructional time) but rather a combination of: (1) uninterrupted, sustained, IL-medium content teaching, and (2) (especially in the case where by fifth or sixth grade the IL is reserved a smaller fraction of time), the indigenous language is the vehicle for the development of higher-order academic proficiencies. Subject area content that is taught through the IL is *cognitively engaging* (Met, 1994), motivating, and linguistically challenging.

Nevertheless, researchers and educators alike will closely observe the HLI experiment. Granted that special circumstances allow for such a minimal presence of English in the curriculum: students are English-dominant speakers, their families represent a self-selected, highly motivated, and ethnically conscious sector of the community, all served by an equally conscious and dedicated teaching staff in active partnership with the

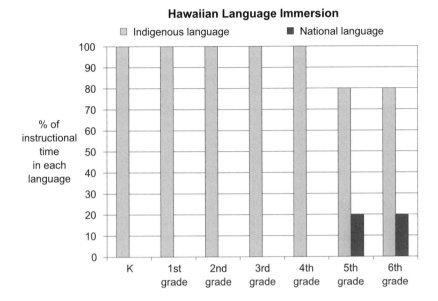

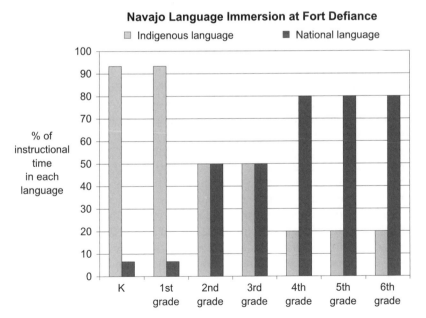

Figure 3 Two contrasting indigenous language immersion programs

University of Hawaii. But independent of the favorable conditions under which HLI has prospered, two research questions will come to the forefront of the discussion regarding the efficacy of this immersion model:

(1) perhaps other immersion programs have not been able to reap the full benefits of content-based language teaching because the threshold for the amount of comprehensible input, in fact, must be higher, and there must be continuity through the secondary level, and active participation of families in second language learning;

(2) how much English-medium instruction is necessary to maintain achievement levels, in all subject areas, including English language arts, that are comparable to students in the mainstream all-English programs? Initial results from state-wide standardized testing show that sixth grade HLI students are below average in some areas (such as vocabulary knowledge), at least average in others (reading comprehension), and overall, keeping pace (Slaughter, 1997). This finding is surely cause for reflection if one considers the fact that through sixth grade, children receive only 7% of their instruction in English.

Our own proposal regarding the optimal program model is neutral on the precise, quantitative, distribution of languages across the grade levels. However, we do not recommend the early total-IL immersion approach (exemplified in HLI) as a universal model for NL-dominant indigenous children learning the IL as a second language, for the reasons outlined earlier in Chapter 4. In any case, the actual time allotted to IL-medium instruction (not an unimportant consideration) cannot be determined ahead of time. In the first place, a broad consultation with parents is necessary not only to secure their support, but also to integrate the most conscious language activists among them into planning and implementing the second language curriculum. In all situations, in our view, the least effective program design for the purpose of IL revitalization would be "late immersion." Postponing the introduction of the indigenous language to the middle elementary years would represent a significant interruption in children's IL linguistic development, a break in continuity that languages facing the pressures of erosion and replacement are particularly vulnerable to. In fact, in situations where language shift has already made headway among the entering generations of Kindergartners and first graders, the only school-based programs that will prove to be successful will be those that have made provision for *preschool* IL immersion. While the innate language acquisition mechanisms are still available to children, even if the NL has taken center stage, sustained, daily, contact with the IL may serve to "set the parameters bilingually," so to speak. The young bilingual (e.g.

dominant in the NL) may have received sufficient input in the IL during his or her "critical period" of linguistic development, such that subsequent opportunities to consolidate the indigenous language will be greatly facilitated. Here again, the relevant variable is probably sustained, continuous, contact with the language (not necessarily exclusive, or perhaps not even predominant contact).

How does IL immersion work?

Let us consider the example of indigenous language immersion where the national language is the dominant language of most children. Following Krashen's "Variable threshold model" (see Chapter 4) a significant portion of the day will be devoted to literacy and Language Arts instruction in the students' primary language; and the greater part of the school day is reserved for the indigenous language (as is indicated in Figure 3 for Navajo language immersion). Instead of teaching IL vocabulary and grammar as separate objectives, the academic content that corresponds to the students' grade level is taught through the target language. In addition, all non-academic language use situations (classroom routines, non-academic subjects and activities, etc.) become opportunities to immerse students in the IL. Here, the reader will take note of still another advantage of early preschool IL immersion: through the end of kindergarten, a significant percentage of the school day corresponds to non-academic activities, and the academic language input that children receive is either inherently *context-embedded** or can be easily modified to provide this.

Classroom routines

This aspect of school language use, which actually takes up a significant portion of time, can now be exploited much more productively. In fact, for this aspect of second language immersion no special L2 teaching modifications are necessary. Calling role, collecting homework, library books, etc., lining up in the morning and for dismissal, going to recess and to lunch, distributing materials and supplies, managing movement and reorganizing seating and other routine-type instructions, and greetings and leave-taking, are so completely context-embedded that they are automatically transformed into language learning activities simply by *doing* them in a language that the children are learning. If the verbal message is not clear, or even incomprehensible, one normally only needs to look around for a relevant clue. The aspect of "doing" is the other key ingredient: an appropriate response, and thus the beginnings of authentic language use and meaningful verbal interaction, does not require any kind of expressive language ability. Some language and context support adaptations by the teacher may be helpful at first, but under this category we would recommend rapidly shifting toward normal, native-speaker, speech patterns. Students also need to receive input that is not highly modified for learners and, in all areas of immersion teaching, learner-sensitive discourse must be progressively phased out. The domain of classroom routines would be a good place to start, as soon as possible. It cannot be emphasized enough that Language Learner Sensitive Discourse is not an end in itself, but rather a temporary means toward native-speaker norms of verbal interaction.

Repetitive/predictable language activities

Marking the calendar and days of the week, paying tribute to the national symbols, and singing songs are examples of *expressive* language activities that are the counterparts of the contextualized receptive language tasks listed above. They require a somewhat higher level of second language proficiency, but their collective/choral response nature allows even the level 0 beginners to participate. Remember, not all aspects of language learning depend on comprehension. In their primary language, how many five-year-olds understand all of the abtract and subtle metaphors of their national anthem or that of many traditional children's songs? As children's L2 proficiency develops, songs, rhymes and the different sorts of recitations that are presently beyond their level begin to take on meaning.

Other highly context-embedded activities

The language demands that the learner faces in art class fall under the same broad category of contextualized instruction, as does supervised recreation and the more structured physical education class. While special modifications in the teachers' speech are not necessary for the L2 student to be able to participate successfully, some of the adaptations listed under Language Learner Sensitive Discourse in chapter 4 are advisable to increase the amount of comprehensible input. In this way, students not only perform the tasks in a satisfactory manner (for which LLSD is not required), but are also able to take advantage of the optimal combination of context support plus modified language input for language learning. However, this category of comprehensible input will follow closely behind that of "Classroom routines" in the shift away from second language teacher talk. Remember, even *before scaffolding** is no longer needed for a learning objective, the teacher begins to dismantle it. In this way teachers can scaffold the next learning objective, which before was beyond the students' capabilities even with significant amounts of context support, decreased information load, and LLSD.

Total Physical Response

Total Physical Response or TPR is a beginning second language immersion teaching method popularized in the 1970s by James Asher (2000). TPR takes into account the initial "silent period" in language learning by having learners respond physically to simple requests by the teacher. The physical act of responding to the teacher's instructions as the teacher models the expected behavior helps students learn new vocabulary and even some basic grammatical patterns. Asher's book *Learning Another Language Through Actions*, now in its 6th edition, "demonstrates step-by-step how to apply TPR to help children and adults acquire another language without stress." It has 53 sample lessons beginning with requests like "stand up," "walk," "jump," and so forth, and ending with a skit involving students acting out a trip to the supermarket as they are given verbal instructions. In addition to his book, Asher has several videotapes showing classroom examples of teachers using the method, and these can be purchased on his website at http://www.tpr-world.com/. Richard Littlebear (1992), in a column "TPR Works!," attests to the effectiveness of using TPR to teach the Northern Cheyenne language to college students. This kind of teacher–student interaction (verbal request – physical, non-verbal, response) lends itself especially well to the first L2 lessons. Since at the beginning students are not yet able to produce even simple sentences or phrases in the L2, most if not all the talking in class is dominated by the teacher. Requesting nonverbal responses gets students engaged in meaningful exchanges from the very first day.

The teacher's primary challenge will be getting past the one-sided pattern of teacher command and student nonverbal response. Necessary at first, providing L2 learners with this kind of comprehensible input, even in massive amounts, can take them only part way down the road toward proficiency in all aspects of the second language. To help teachers with more advanced instruction, Ray and Seely (1997) have developed what they call TPR Storytelling (TPR-S) that involves students acting out stories with written scripts. Cantoni specifically recommends the use of TPR-S to teach indigenous languages. She writes that TPR-S lessons "utilize the vocabulary taught in the earlier [TPR] stage by incorporating it into stories that the learners hear, watch, act out, retell, revise, read, write, and rewrite" (Cantoni, 1999: 54). Extending TPR to storytelling raises the overall level of abstraction, requires children to process more complex grammatical patterns (within each sentence), and gets them to work harder to comprehend significantly longer sequences of the second language.

Relatively context-dependent academic subjects

Second language teachers often view mathematics as the one subject area in which their students will experience the greatest success even with beginner-level language proficiency in the L2. In principle this view is correct. Teaching mathematics through the IL again provides the ideal opportunity for combining context and Language Learner Sensitive Discourse. In regard to number concepts, manipulating arithmetical operations, calculations, and solving basic problems, the reason for this is obvious: (1) the L2 learner enjoys access to a wide variety of physical manipulatives, and all kinds of non-linguistic visual representation that allow the student to conceptualize the task at hand; and (2) the basic universal concepts of mathematics are common to all cultures and language communities, embodied so to speak, in the universal notational system that is independent of language ($+ \times \pi \mu = \% \$ - \div \neq > < \Sigma \geq \leq \infty$ 0 1 2 3 4 5 6 7 8 9).

On the other hand, the application of mathematical operations to the solution of complex problem-solving tasks that involve combining intermediate or partial solutions depend to a greater extent on language ability. In this sense it is necessary to make an important distinction within this subject area between: (1) tasks that are largely independent of language ability; and (2) tasks that still afford the same kind of support from non-linguistic previous knowledge and visual context, but that require the previous mastery of specific L2 linguistic structures, or general L2 proficiency above a certain minimal level.

The physical and biological sciences fall into this last category (universality of concepts that are mentally stored independent of language, a non-linguistic notational system that they share with mathematics, and the opportunity to represent abstract concepts visually or schematically, not to mention access to the context-embedded processes of direct experimentation and demonstration). It should be apparent by now that "context-embedded" is not the same as "cognitively undemanding." And in this regard the reader will also have taken note of a kind of hierarchy of Language Learner Sensitive Discourse: the more the task (receptive or expressive) depends on knowledge of the L2 linguistic system and L2 proficiency in general, the more extensive and systematic LLSD modifications should be. Logically, the most "language-dependent" subject areas, such as language arts, will be the last ones to make the "transition" to unmodified, native-speaker, styles of delivery (social studies perhaps here occupies a kind of intermediate level between science and language arts/literacy). The same idea applies to programs where subject areas are integrated into blocks of "thematic units."

In the case of IL immersion, the teaching of mathematics and science represents a special opportunity. Because of the unequal allocation, in society, of language use domains, respectively for IL and NL, the widespread perception that indigenous languages are inherently more compatible with some academic subjects than others remains as a persistent misconception. The use of the IL as a vehicle of the higher-order academic objectives will begin to dispel this false impression. This in fact leads us to an important clarification of the concept of compartmentalization.

For teaching purposes compartmentalizing, or separating, the languages within a bilingual program is an essential aspect of curriculum design. Especially in the case of immersion language teaching, allocating L1 and L2 to separate domains, contexts of use, and even to different teachers, affords a number of advantages:

(1) Separation is inherently incompatible with the counterproductive practice of concurrent translation. During IL-medium instruction, for example, students' attention will be focused on the target language, shifting the mode of listening and comprehension toward a more deliberate application of their own second language learning strategies. Otherwise, students would tend to tune out IL input while they wait for the translation to their dominant language. And perhaps more importantly, since teachers must now rely on making IL input comprehensible (because the opportunity of fall-back on translation is not available), they are more likely to apply the necessary LLSD+context modifications. Second language input becomes more comprehensible, students can actually process more of it, and language learning advances more rapidly and effectively.

(2) Reserving special times for use of the target language makes it easier for students to apply their partial knowledge both to difficult academic tasks and to conversational exchanges with teachers and peers. If no expectation is made explicit regarding language allocation, language choice decisions are shifted to the learners. For example, during a writers' workshop activity, the natural tendency on the part of IL learners to use their *dominant language** will eclipse the IL. This may occur for two reasons: on the one hand, social rules of language choice dictate that members of a group of bilinguals speak in the language that is "most common" in regard to the proficiency levels of the individual members of the group. On the other hand, students' natural predisposition is to favor the language in which verbal expression and writing are more fluid, automatic, and unhampered by incomplete grammar and vocabulary knowledge.

(3)   In the process of allocating subject matter areas to the IL and the NL, school language policy becomes more conscious and deliberate. It allows for planning in a way that concurrent approaches cannot provide for as effectively. This consideration is especially pertinent in the case of indigenous language revitalization. Being the socially subordinate language, the expectations of students, parents, and teachers generally favor use of the NL for many reasons – some perhaps legitimate, and others that are a reflection of the NL-speaking society's linguistic prejudices. Thus, prescribing the use of the IL for certain purposes, for selected academic content instruction, for prominent symbolic functions, and various forms of recognition "protects" it, so to speak, from the pervasive pressure of the forces of language shift. In this way the language separation associated with immersion represents a kind of diglossia applied to the school day (refer back to the discussion of this concept in Chapter 3). The key concepts here are conscious *policy* and deliberate *planning*.[23]

However, as bilingual classroom research (Faltis, 2001; Lessow-Hurley, 2000; Cloud *et al.*, 2000) has shown, separation of the languages, if it is implemented in a way that recapitulates the inequitable allocation of IL and NL in society, will simply reinforce long-standing prejudices and misconceptions. Languages at school can be separated along a number of categories: physical location, time, subject matter, different phases of the same lesson or unit, or by person (some teachers are assigned to teach only the IL, others the NL). Thus, an allocation scheme that reserves mathematics, science and language arts to the NL, and restricts the IL to academic areas that are perceived as less rigorous will only confirm students' preconceptions about the relative prestige and utility of each. The same predictable outcome will result by assigning teachers, for example, to the NL and assistants to the IL. The solution is actually quite simple and straightforward: do not reproduce society's compartmentalization, but rather distribute language functions in a way that challenges language-related stereotypes. Teachers' and assistants' assignments are systematically rotated, subject areas alternate between the languages, subject areas are integrated when possible to form thematic units, even blocks of time and classroom space can be shifted around, if necessary, to avoid transmitting subtle and unintended messages about inequality.

Integrating content and language teaching
Immersion also provides for the ideal opportunity to integrate subject matter teaching with language learning. Here again, indigenous languages in particular will benefit from this important advance in the field of second

language teaching (see Met, 1994; Swain & Johnson, 1997; Snow & Brinton, 1997). Traditional methods that emphasized teaching the structure of language apart from content learning depend on a body of linguistic research describing the subsystems of the language, and pedagogical materials that focus on these descriptions. Most indigenous teachers, for example, will point out that, while they know how to teach the grammar of the NL, they would hesitate to do likewise in the indigenous language, despite the fact that they may be fluent speakers. In addition, pedagogically oriented descriptions of grammar are not even available except among only a small fraction of the indigenous languages of the Americas.

The integration of content and language teaching partially resolves this imbalance as well. With significant amounts of comprehensible input in the IL that students receive through the "medium" of content area learning, many language structures will be learned without direct instruction. That is, conscious learning will not be necessary for "picking up," so to speak, a certain number of grammatical patterns of high frequency where the rule is revealed in a straightforward and transparent way from simple exposure to many positive examples. In other words, some patterns are easy to learn from frequent contact with positive evidence when the student understands messages in the target language.

During the early years of immersion, as well as in some other "communicative" approaches to L2 teaching, this kind of exposure to positive evidence was thought to be sufficient in and of itself for successful language learning. "Acquisition" would depend primarily on large amounts of comprehensible input, with conscious learning and practice playing a secondary role.

Today, after more than 30 years of experience and research evidence, immersion maintains its focus on subject area content and communication of authentic messages. In addition, the immersion approach has been refined to include direct teaching of language structures. Each content lesson offers the teacher the opportunity to design learning activities that call students' attention to specific patterns in the language: (1) some will involve linguistic knowledge that is specific to the lesson and is necessary for comprehension. Without the ability, for example, to recognize language patterns that indicate causality (e.g. If...then...) certain explanations and demonstrations in science class will be impossible to follow; (2) other language structures are not strictly necessary for comprehension, perhaps because the lesson can easily avail itself of sufficient context support (mathematical operations often fall into this category). However, the opportunity that the lesson affords happens to be ideal for teaching the grammatical pattern. For example, to begin a unit of study in history, while the *recogni-*

tion of past tense forms is necessary, being able to *produce* the various past tense forms accurately is not. Thus, the attentive second language/history teacher will take advantage of the opportunity by providing practice specifically focused on the grammatical pattern in question. For example, students can work on distinguishing between two different past tense patterns, both in contrast to appropriate uses of the present tense (Snow *et al.*, 1989, discuss the distinction between content-obligatory and content-compatible language objectives).

Students learning an indigenous language will profit from direct teaching of language patterns to the same degree as other L2 learners, in fact it is just as necessary. Fortunately, the most effective way to teach grammar, integrated as it is now into academic content, is not to teach the rules, but rather from the bottom up, so to speak. Following inductive methods,[24] students' practice patterns focusing their attention on series of positive examples, and reflecting upon negative examples that correspond to errors. Practicing patterns can thus be integrated into the content lesson. Snow *et al.* (1989) give the following example. Teachers monitor their students' written work and identify persistent errors in the use of the conditional. Content activities can then be designed that require the conditional. For example, while asking students to reflect critically about the complex historical issues surrounding the first European/Native American contacts, the following pattern would provide for the opportunity to focus attention on the grammatical form that is also (at the same time) an objective of teaching:

> If Columbus had been from England ...
> If the Aztecs had not initially welcomed Cortés ...
> If the contagious diseases that ...
> If gold and silver ...
> If ...
> (Snow *et al.*, 1989: 207)

From the point of view of the indigenous language teacher, who may not have studied the formal grammar of his or her ancestral language, now all that is necessary to begin to teach grammar is: (1) sufficient (not necessarily complete), IL native-speaker competence and (2) an opportunity to reflect upon the patterns that recur in everyday speech or that are particularly salient in some way. Being able to state, or explain, the rule is not required; however being able to integrate this kind of attention to language forms into the content lesson is necessary for language development in the area of grammar and vocabulary. This approach offers yet another advantage from the perspective of maximizing comprehensible input in the IL. Since highly abstract explanations of how grammatical rules are applied can be largely dispensed with (although at times these also can be useful to learners), so can the temptation to switch to the students' primary language when faced with this kind of context-reduced and cognitively demanding objective. Foreign language teachers, for example, often feel compelled (against their better judgment) to interrupt valuable classroom interaction in the target language to insert grammatical explanations in the language in which students will be able to "understand" them. Consequently, less time is available for comprehensible input and interaction in the L2, and learners' attention is again shifted back to their primary language.

In summary:

(1) maintain high levels of comprehensible input in the IL;
(2) avoid switching to the NL for explanations and clarification when another visual-context clue, example, repetition, or reformulation will suffice;
(3) teach grammatical patterns inductively (without translation); and
(4) language teaching objectives are drawn from the subject matter materials, thus in addition ensuring that these are the most important aspects of the grammar that students need for their academic learning objectives.

A final note on why any variety of concurrent translation should be scrupulously avoided: aside from not retarding progress in second language learning, one of the objectives of the IL teacher is to model the *sufficiency of the indigenous language* in this domain of teaching and learning. For the expression of all kinds of thoughts, and feelings, for the purpose of speculating about hypothetical worlds, and for teaching new concepts, the indigenous language is sufficient. It does not require the intervention of the NL to compensate for any alleged inherent deficiency. Teachers may resort to codeswitching (which, remember, is different from translation) for various reasons. In addition, for one or another content lesson both teachers and students may borrow extensively from their NL lexicon. But again, the use of loan words and switching are not *required* because the IL grammatical system is inadequate. It is for the same reason that during an IL-medium lesson, conversations between colleagues (if they are known to be also bilingual), in the students' presence, should be in the same language. A reverent and "careful" attitude toward the language of instruction (*Voices 5*) is a necessary underpinning of IL immersion.

Voices.5 (Navajo)

Hazaad baa áhojilyá
(Having reverence and care of speech)

From: Hózhoojík'ehgo Nanitin [Blessing way teachings]
(Office of Diné Culture, Language and Community Service, 2000)

The Bilingual Teacher, the Non-Native Speaking Teacher, and Culture

One of the major advances in the field of Indian education in the last 20 years has been the significant increase in the number of teachers in service who are bilingual, who actually speak the indigenous language of their students (see Chapter 2). Whereas in the past the overwhelming majority of teachers were monolingual speakers of the NL, Indian school staffs today reflect a much more diverse composition.

In Chapter 4 we introduced another of the central themes of the book: that teachers with less than native-speaker proficiency in the IL have an important role to play in the development of a truly additive bilingual program in their school. We will even extend this idea to include the non-IL-speaker. In fact, teachers who fall into all three categories (the bilingual, the NL-dominant bilingual, and the NL monolingual) will continue to be part of Indian education programs. One could even argue that for most communities this composition represents a kind of optimal combination, as long as the greater fraction corresponds to the first two categories. By no means should we ever give the impression that development of the IL is the sole responsibility of the teachers who happen to be bilingual themselves. To this point a number of activities outlined in Chapters 4, 5, and 6 can be directed by the non-IL-speaker. Let us consider, separately, some of the circumstances that each of our three educators faces (remembering at all times that all three are an integral part of the bilingual program, and in one way or another directly participate in second language teaching).

The bilingual, native-speaker of the indigenous language

By way of definition, it is important to clarify that a person with native or near-native competence in the IL has not necessarily learned the language from early childhood, nor need, necessarily, be a member of the same ethnic or cultural group as the majority of speakers of the language. By far the most versatile member of the team, the bilingual teacher will not be limited in any way regarding the allocation of languages across the teaching day. At the same time, with this teacher, all children, including monolingual IL speakers, are able to engage, without restrictions, in the full range of typical and normal teacher–student verbal interaction (Hornberger, 1990). This seemingly obvious point is often forgotten in the current enthusiasm for all-English immersion programs for English language learners in the United States. Even in the best all-English programs, which insure high levels of comprehensible input during instruction, unless the teacher also understands the students' primary language, classroom interaction remains completely one-sided for the beginners.

Often, however, bilingual teachers call attention to two apparent obstacles to their full integration into the IL teaching program:

(1) Dialectical differences between the variant of the IL they speak and the variant spoken in the community where they teach. As we suggested earlier in this chapter, shifting language learning activities more toward integrative-type tasks (focusing to a greater extent on comprehension of longer stretches of discourse, whole texts, etc.) helps to partially compensate for these differences. For example, if the language objectives of a lesson revolve around working with a familiar traditional narrative, students' background knowledge of the story will serve as a highly effective compensator for the unfamiliar vocabulary that they hear in their teacher's version. On the other hand, exposure to different language patterns from other dialects is an important learning objective in its own right. It teaches students new comprehension strategies – how to apply previous knowledge-context information, as well as the contextual information that is to be found within the narrative itself. The very presence of new vocabulary terms and new grammatical patterns compels the listener to work harder to be able to understand. In the process, more advanced comprehension strategies are developed. On another level, as interdialectical communication becomes more frequent, the different speech communities begin to view their language in broader terms: basically as one language with variations, as opposed to a family of different languages that are similar and sometimes comprehensible.

(2) lack of explicit knowledge about the formal structure of the indigenous language. On this point we want to re-emphasize that teaching students about the language should proceed not from an analysis of its *rules*, but rather from activities that promote reflection upon its *patterns* (i.e. learning inductively). If a published grammar of the IL is available, bilingual teachers should begin to study it because this will deepen their understanding of the structure of the language, an

important objective for their own professional development. But such texts generally are less helpful as guides for organizing a language teaching syllabus. The same general principle applies to teaching the NL as a second language, with the obvious exception that a wide range of language learning texts (including valuable grammar study materials) are available.

The NL-dominant bilingual teacher

Points (1) and (2) above apply equally well to the teacher with partial knowledge of the IL. For example, if in addition to speaking a different dialect, he or she is frequently in doubt about the basic grammatical patterns of the language, more reason exists to focus instruction on global comprehension and integrative expressive tasks. This teacher may have to prepare class presentations in more detail, shift some of the whole-class interaction toward the more capable speakers among the students (if this is possible), and rely more on reading aloud from prepared materials such as story anthologies (if they exist).

For both the bilingual and the NL-dominant teacher, often a legacy of language discrimination continues to weigh heavily on their own perceptions. In many cases this discrimination results in perceived inadequacies in their own language proficiency, rather than an objective self-assessment of the actual abilities in question. For example, purist and grammar-translation type approaches to studying the NL that teachers internalized from their own second language learning experiences in school are frequently carried over to the way they view learning and teaching the indigenous language. There is a tendency toward seeing mainly limitations and deficiencies (some real, but largely surmountable, others apparently real but irrelevant). The very notion of teaching an indigenous language at times seems to be plagued by unresolvable obstacles and unnecessary risks. Among the risks, teachers may perceive themselves as vulnerable in the eyes of their students because they are not able to provide a given grammatical explanation, or worse yet because they may commit errors that some of the more competent speakers in the room will immediately recognize as such. In short, approaches to teaching that emphasize accuracy (taking a negative "error-eradication" view of learners' errors), language purism, and linguistic structures over meaning will tend to deepen the ambivalence both teachers and students will feel toward the IL.

The monolingual teacher

The resources available to the non-IL-speaker will become more apparent in the next chapter. Working with literacy in the indigenous language holds out special opportunities for the teacher who speaks only the NL, and this is yet another reason why the activities of reading and writing are not in any way incompatible with what are often termed "languages of oral tradition."

While clearly the limitations of the monolingual teacher place certain unavoidable obstacles in his or her way, with a little imagination and a willingness to relinquish some control over classroom discourse, options and resources become more and more apparent, basically in two areas. These are: (1) the more obvious opportunity that exists among bilingual colleagues and students' families, and (2) the presentation to students of materials in the IL, with which the students themselves take the initiative, in order to develop language learning activities. In this case it is entirely appropriate to provide direction, explain procedures, and clarify objectives in the teacher's primary language, and supervise and even mediate some aspects of the activity as students work in the IL. Often, NL-dominant students will do the same in writer's workshops, problem-solving groups, and discussion circles.

Pretexts abound for keeping the IL out of the classroom.[25] The teacher's less than native-speaker competence in the language certainly ranks toward the bottom of the list of acceptable justifications.

Culture and miscommunication

Among the many interesting topics related to language learning and culture, we have chosen to briefly discuss only one: intercultural communication, understanding and misunderstanding. In this case our interest will de directed toward problems of interpretation and misinterpretation that are not related to teachers', students' and parents' linguistic competence per se (that is grammar, vocabulary, and accent). Rather, we will examine the phenomenon of misunderstanding as it occurs between speakers of the same language, or where superficial differences (e.g. dialect) by themselves are not the source of the misunderstanding. As such, this kind of problem of miscommunication is universally familiar to monolinguals and bilinguals alike, even within a monocultural community. What is important to examine from the teacher's point of view is how patterns of misunderstanding are systematically related to cultural differences.[26]

If we step back to consider our discussion of the composition of the typical Indian community school, we can see that both native IL-speaking teachers and monolingual NL speakers may find themselves in situations of verbal interaction where culturally related misunderstanding causes tension, conflict, and even offense. Research on intercultural communication has shown that these outcomes are more often than not the result of each party to the interchange actually attempting to avoid misunder-standing and conflict by applying appropriate rules of discourse. Thus we will put aside that category of culturally-related tension that arises from deliberate transgressions of cultural norms and expectations (these are in fact the least interesting from the point of view of the educator who has managed to get through the first five chapters of this book, and still finds this material relevant his or her work).

Likewise, in the case of conscious violations of teacher–student verbal interaction norms on the part of the student we would be considering a different kind of problem as well; perhaps more related to a straightfor-ward classroom management issue. Or another possibility would be a combination of: (1) a conflict or offense that arises from a true misunder-standing that leads to (2) a series of responses that deepen the conflict, in turn, terminating in a conscious breach of communication and social norms. Of course, the difficult task for the teacher is to devise a plan for distinguishing between the two categories, and being cognizant of the wide margin of error that plagues all interpretations of this kind.

It is also important not to fall into the common error of thinking that the solution to cultural misunderstanding can be found in learning about the differences in rules and patterns that students from different cultures apply to communication. While greater familiarity about student cultural expec-tations should be a permanent objective of all teachers, let us consider some of the limitations involved specifically in the case of verbal interaction:

(1) How or from whom would one learn? Generally the discourse rules are revealed in very subtle ways, not subject to conscious reflection by the native speakers themselves.
(2) The number and variety of rules is extensive, in addition to being of a rather abstract nature (that is, difficult to describe).
(3) They will vary even within a culturally homogeneous classroom; the "learning problem" is further compounded when students come from different communities, even if they all speak the same IL.

After examining a few examples from research, we will see that not only is it exceedingly difficult to learn the culture/discourse patterns of a speech community that is different from one's own; but more importantly, this kind of misunderstanding in the classroom is not something that should always be avoided in the first place (this turns out to be easy because it is, in fact, inevitable).

In one of the early more significant studies in this field, Scollon and Scollon (1981) examined patterns of interethnic communication between two groups of English speakers, Native Americans whose indigenous language belongs to the Athabaskan family, and non-indigenous English speakers of the majority culture. Two examples from their findings will suffice to illustrate our point: problems related to turn taking, and what the authors refer to as "relationships of dominance, display, and dependence."

Turn-taking

The general rule in the exchange of speaking turns can be stated in simple terms: after one speaker (speaker A) has completed transmitting the message, the other speaker (B) can take a turn. Often there is a pause that signals this exchange. If B does not take the turn after a certain amount of time has elapsed, this, in turn, signals to A that he or she can or should continue talking. If B comes in too soon, it may be interpreted as interruption. It happens to be that the variation in the expectation regarding pauses is related to culture. For example, *overlapping speech* is characteristic of some cultures as an indication (depending on the circumstances, as always) of intimacy and conversational engagement (Tannen, 1985); here the pause is reduced to zero and in fact is now "measured" in negative values (too much overlapping being inappropriate). Along the same lines, the duration of pauses between turns that exceeds expectations tends to also signal that something is wrong.

In the Athabaskan study, the researchers found that the Native American conversants expected a slightly longer pause than the non-indigenous speakers (a difference of approximately 0.5 seconds), a time lapse that is difficult to detect as such and thus equally difficult to identify as the source of potential problems. In a conversation, for example, between a monolingual NL-speaking teacher and an indigenous student the outcome would be predictable: "The Athabaskan feels he has been interrupted and the English speaker feels the Athabaskan never makes sense, never says a whole coherent idea" (Scollon & Scollon, 1981: 25). In the long run, consequences include: stereotypes (Indians are "quiet," majority culture teachers are "arrogant"), reluctance to participate, students' negative perceptions about the relevance of anything they may have to say, etc.

As the authors summarize:

> True dialogue rarely occurs. The exchange of turns works toward the English speaker's continually regaining the floor and against the Athabaskan's being able to hold the floor for more than brief speaking turns. (Scollon & Scollon, 1981: 26)

The key concept, however, to keep in mind here is that neither discourse system is more inclusive, or participatory, or respectful, and neither of the speakers intends either to monopolize the conversation or be taciturn and unfriendly. In this case A wanted to keep the interaction going, and avoid an unnecessary termination of the conversation; B was trying to be polite; A was not being impolite, and B in fact also wanted to keep the conversation going.

Relationships of dominance, display and dependence

Scollon and Scollon identified a common source of confusion in interethnic communication that is particularly relevant to classroom verbal interaction. For example, for U.S. English speakers of the majority culture, the teacher (representing the "superordinate" or authority figure) regularly calls upon students to display knowledge of abilities. A well documented variant of this cultural pattern is the display question or *known-information question*: a kind of query that is different from everyday "authentic" questions that genuinely seek information from the other speaker (Pease-Alvarez & Vázquez, 1994). We could say that the function of display questions is to seek a different *kind* of information. The researchers found that among Athabaskan children the "spectator-knowledge display" expectation is generally reversed. It is the person in the superordinate position, the parent, elder, or teacher who is expected to demonstrate, instruct, and display knowledge for the child. The child, in turn, carefully observes; and only on a later occasion begins to experiment with, practice upon, and perfect the skill that is being taught, for example.

The authors make an interesting observation:

> For the English-speaking teacher an Athabaskan child will either seem unduly reserved because he is spectating, or unduly aggressive if the child has assumed the superordinate role that he feels is consistent with display of exhibitionism. For the Athabaskan child the teacher will seem either incompetent because he is not exhibiting his abilities, or unduly bossy because in spite of not exhibiting he is taking the superordinate role. (Scollon & Scollon, 1981: 17)

Again we see that, in the abstract, neither teaching style is more interactive or exploratory; and the distinction between "direct instruction" and "discovery learning" appears less clear cut. Thus, we can add another factor to take into account when students seem to be confused about the language task placed before them.

Returning to our seemingly contradictory recommendation, in both examples of intercultural misunderstanding, we would hesitate to portray the problem in the usual simplistic terms of "being more sensitive to cultural differences" or "modifying teaching styles to be culturally compatible" (the reader will take special note here that the authors of this book do not recommend that teachers be insensitive, or that they should tenaciously hold to all their preconceived notions about how children learn).

Before concluding this discussion, we invite the reader to critically examine the findings of the Athabaskan study. The first admonition that we all must keep in the foreground when studying culture is to be especially skeptical of all, and all kinds of, generalization. It may turn out that some of the authors' claims are overstated, that the observation of some patterns should be qualified even in the case where we might recognize them, intuitively, to be valid. Their interpretations may even be far off the mark in regard to the specific categories described. But at the same time it should be evident that these are the *kinds* of "out of synchrony" exchanges that lie under the surface of intercultural miscommunication. Some of the facts may be called into question, but the method is sound.

The dilemmas of intercultural communication are complex; but at the same time this complexity (including the tension that it generates) presents an ideal opportunity for exploring the themes of multicultural education in a way that goes beyond the superficial "learning about other cultures" fare that students often find quite bland and predictable. On the one hand, the misunderstandings and conflicts that arise can be turned into objects of reflection (see Glossary for *metalinguistic awareness,* and also Note 13); this is facilitated now by dispensing with the necessity for "placing blame." Clearly, the responsibility for misunderstanding does not lie with children; and since our teachers are subject to similar kinds of confusion, the issues become much more accessible to examination and scrutiny. When we *distance* ourselves from a source of contention, it becomes easier to objectify. In fact teaching children about misinterpretation (e.g. knowing when they are not responsible for the ambiguity in a message) is an important language learning objective that is tied to literacy (Torrence & Olson, 1987).

On the other hand, referring specifically to our second example of expectations in conflict, we can conclude that not all discourse or learning styles that may be unfamiliar to our students should be avoided because they cause confusion. Within the proper proportions, without imbalances, frustrations, and contradictions, learning stagnates – see the writings of Piaget (1952) on "the origins of intelligence in children," especially the concepts of *assimilation* and *accommodation.* The reason for studying cultural patterns is not for the purpose of purging methods and curriculum of "non-indigenous" influences that children may find unfamiliar or even disconcerting, but rather to speculate about their origin, and to no longer take them for granted. Students should have contact with and become skilled at manipulating different kinds of teaching and learning style. This is similar to the development in school-age children away from a dependence on narrative genres toward proficiency in processing other kinds of discourse not necessarily autochthonous, or native, to their local culture. Additive bilingualism also implies degrees of biculturalism.

Understanding the dynamics of intercultural communication will make teachers more attentive, will give reason to pause more often and reflect before interpreting prematurely, and ultimately, after developing skill in this area, will help us to convert misunderstandings into teachable moments.

Additional reading

The Cross-cultural, Language, and Academic Development Handbook by Díaz-Rico and Weed (1995) is one of the most complete foundations texts in the field. It is in two Parts: (1) an overview of the theory and practice in second language learning with a concise review of the basic concepts in linguistics; (2) principles of second language teaching with helpful guidelines for integrating language and content instruction. Chapter 12 and the Appendix present models of successful programs.

Joinfostering: Adapting Teaching for the Multicultural Classroom by Faltis (2001) is the most concise of the four books we recommend here. Chapter 1 introduces the important discussion on Language and Literacy Socialization, key concepts for understanding how children begin to develop proficiency in school-related discourses. Chapters 3, 4, and 5 offer examples of Language Sensitive Content Teaching, and suggestions for organizing second language teaching in classrooms with a wide range of language proficiency levels (with an emphasis on how to organize small group and cooperative learning). For those readers so inclined, Chapter 4 (on pp. 100–106) summarizes the debate on Cummins' concept of CALP (refer to Note 20). Giving both sides their due, Faltis' portrayal is fair, even though (as the reader will see) we don't share his inclination toward the detractors of the CALP model.

Bilingual and ESL Classrooms by Ovando and Collier (1998) outlines basic second language teaching principles with more helpful suggestions on forming cooperative learning groups (e.g. ensuring a balance between homogeneity and heterogeneity in team formation), along with sections on Art, Technology, and Music. Chapter 4 on Language would be a good follow-up to Díaz-Rico and Weed's shorter review of linguistic concepts. Two separate chapters are devoted to second language teaching methods in Mathematics, Science, and Social Studies.

Making it Happen: Interaction in the Second Language Classroom by Richard-Amato (1996) complements our methods and materials resource guide with chapters especially devoted to Music and Poetry, Storytelling and Drama, three areas we emphasized as particularly relevant to IL teaching. In addition, the author's Part II on "Exploring methods and activities" is probably the most extensive of all four of our recommended texts.

Chapter 6

Biliteracy: Teaching Reading and Writing in the Indigenous Language

The concept of biliteracy implies the development of abilities that go beyond the mere decoding of texts in a student's first and second language. In fact, on one level, the term itself is somewhat redundant. People learn about literacy and learn how to read and write once (typically in L1, but often in the case of indigenous language speakers, in the second language), and apply the various reading and writing skills to another language in which they are proficient or become proficient. Depending on the circumstances, and one's definition of biliteracy, bilingual individuals may be able to read with greater fluency in one language than in the language they use for predominantly oral purposes. They may read fairly well in both, but possess incipient writing skills in both or only one language, or they may be simply preliterate or illiterate. For indigenous language speech communities, these categories involve special circumstances. Bilingual Indian children learning to read and write encounter challenges and opportunities that are different in some significant ways from both their monolingual and bilingual peers who speak a "language of wider communication."

A strong literacy component, involving sustained indigenous (IL) literacy development, should be an integral part of any additive bilingual program.[27] Independent of the degree of social prestige and utility of writing in a particular indigenous language, bilingual children's academic and cognitive development is tied to opportunities that they will have in school to learn about, and be proficient in, reading and writing in the two languages they speak or understand.

Indigenous Language Reading Materials

Soon after the initial boom of publishing works in Native American languages that was promoted by the various religious orders (in Latin America in the 16th century, on a more limited scale in North America during the 1800s), indigenous languages began to be viewed as unworthy of writing, or any other academic function. This view has held sway until recent times. Today, with the renewed interest in bilingual education, linguists and educators have attempted to design and edit series of reading primers and other textbook material for the elementary grades.

For example, in Mexico the Department of Indian Education has, in the last 30 years, produced first grade beginning reading texts in 36 of the country's indigenous languages (Modiano, 1988). By all accounts, the project should still be considered as being in its pilot stage; however, two guiding principles in this effort are noteworthy from the point of view of biliteracy development in school:

(1) Alphabets and other word-processing technologies correspond to the practical, classroom settings where children, who actually speak the language, will be learning how to read and write. Practical alphabets are to be designed that avoid unnecessary graphic complexity.[28]

(2) Every attempt should be made to unify criteria among different dialects of each language to arrive at common spelling patterns (DGEI, 1986). A similar policy has guided the ongoing discussion regarding the production of Quechua language school texts in Peru (Jung, 1992).

A typical first grade indigenous language primer from Mexico, for example, is colorfully illustrated with familiar scenes, plants, animals, people, everyday implements and household items that correspond to the students' community and region. Literacy-related activities and texts would include a sequence such as the following (*Noamoch tlen se xiutl tlamachtilistli*, the Náhuatl first grade primer, DGEI, 1988): (1) initial vowels with activities that match words with illustrations, (2) key final consonants combinations as in *atl, elotl, olotl* (water, corn, corn cob), (3) initial consonants, (4) one line cloze-type activities where the students read short phrases and fill in the missing word that corresponds to the picture, (5) short reading texts of two or three sentences, contextualized by an illustration, (6) word analysis exercises, (7) a cultural/historic unit on the Aztec writing system and the modern alphabetic version, together with longer texts, and finally (8) a series of short expository-type texts and stories with accompanying short answer comprehension/response items. See Jung (1992) and Chatry-Komarek (1987) for extensive reviews and critiques of IL school texts in Peru, where a more ambitious materials development project was able to expand its scope beyond reading primers and anthologies to both social studies and science texts, and to grade levels beyond first and second grade.

Clearly, the material in any one language represents only a sample of the kinds of activities that could be generated in local schools. In some of the major languages, story anthologies have been produced; however, their bilingual (with Spanish translation) format reduces significantly the potential for utilizing the material for *indigenous* language instruction.

Criticisms of the inadequacy of the material are well taken considering the need for indigenous language children's literature and texts, but under present conditions, a significant expansion in production for any of the languages appears to be, at best, a distant possibility. The extreme shortage of published materials both reflects the current status of indigenous languages (their exclusion, in practical terms, from the written language domains), and real-life limitations that bilingual schools must be able to work around and creatively compensate for. One response by local educators has been to resign themselves to the inequalities and abandon, in practice, the goal of developing biliterate proficiency. Such a perspective, of course, is hardly unreasonable given the relationship between oral and written language use, both at the community and the regional levels. Literary skills in the national language (NL) are immediately and widely useful and socially prestigious in the broadest sense. For most indigenous languages, reading material is generally unavailable, and social uses of IL literacy are few and far between. In most situations, any significant social function tied to literacy in the indigenous language is virtually non-existent. For communities and schools that do choose to develop biliteracy in the elementary grades, and promote the use of IL literacy, the challenges are of truly formidable proportions: utilizing what may be available in published form, and then proceeding to develop materials and teaching strategies that call upon the linguistic and cultural resources of the children and teachers themselves, and their families.

The following sections of this chapter will outline specific alternatives, methods, and techniques to actually realize the untapped potential of the indigenous language in the area of literacy development. While departments of Indian Education should be encouraged to continue developing professional-quality literacy materials (indeed, such efforts represent a long overdue fulfillment of the official commitment to indigenous education), educators will discover that successful biliteracy programs can be designed and implemented immediately, with the resources at hand, in any IL community.

Oral Tradition in the Literacy Program

Ethnographers and students of folklore have described in detail and extensively analyzed the literary aspects of oral tradition. Given the broad consensus on its artistic merits, the relative under-utilization of this resource in the educational domain represents a major missed opportunity.

Literature-based reading and writing instruction promotes the development of the higher-order discourse abilities discussed in the previous chapters, and is entirely compatible with teaching reading skills and focus on form. For a discussion, see "Language development" and "Reading and literature" in Reyhner (1992: 115–208), Sulzby (1994), Goodman (1992), Adams (1990), Burns *et al.* (1999) and Whitehead (1997). Traditional stories in both oral and written form fulfill all the requirements for high-quality literature that students need to begin the task of building their academic language skills in general and literacy in particular.

All indigenous peoples, regardless of the particular historical, cultural and political circumstances in which they developed, created and preserved, through the oral tradition, an extensive body of narrative, poetry, and other kinds of formal genre. And as we pointed out in Chapter 4, in all cases, the style of language that came to be associated with the performance of these works is different in certain important respects from everyday conversation about everyday matters. For some IL communities, special occasions or times of the year are reserved for telling certain stories. Often, for example, as in the case of other formal genres, the context of the performance is inseparable from the words themselves. Therefore, these restrictions are important to understand when any oral tradition discourse is proposed for classroom use. When teachers are in doubt, competent local community authorities can be consulted. When disagreement arises within the community, the recommended course of action in all cases is consensus building based on the permanent collaboration between families and teachers, community and school.

While authorship and possession of oral narratives have been typically collective, as with all esthetic and formal language use, prescribed conditions, special qualifications for the narrator, and even in some circumstances, strict requirements of execution and replication are observed. For example, in North America, Plains Indians followed set procedures specifically identifying persons for conserving and sharing stories, who, in turn, "owned" and protected individual *story bundles*. When the time was right, transfer of the story bundles would be carefully transacted, a process that involved formal instruction and preparation (Lankford, 1987). As in all cultures, the special language skills of the storyteller are the product of years of training and extensive experience.

Today, oral tradition narrative survives among indigenous communities where the language and the discourse practices associated with the culture have been preserved, although in most communities this tradition is in decline. In fact, one of the signs of language vitality is that young adults and older children can remember and recite the stories. On the other hand, a significant portion of the existing body of narrative has been recorded in writing and published in one form or another, although much of it in translation (and not available in print in the original).

As we suggested in Chapter 2, the question of making use of the resources of the oral tradition should take as its starting point: how these cultural resources can contribute to children's language and academic development. The "stage" of displacement or revitalization, assessments of the long term viability of the language, and the perceived utility of IL literacy, are all interesting questions to consider; but, they should not be the first or overriding consideration in the design of a bilingual curriculum.

Critics of oral tradition transcription have pointed to the differing contexts or circumstances of oral performance, in contrast to writing. Collective and interactive processes intervene between narrator and audience in the case of narrative performance, as opposed to the individual and solitary creative process of the writer. However, despite the modifications that transcription entails (adjusting, for example, for the absence of an immediate and physically present audience, and the loss of certain resources available only to the storyteller), both historical evidence, and our own experience in compilation and transcription, have demonstrated that the alleged discontinuities are greatly overstated. Transcribed and edited versions of oral narrative are not meant to capture the particular interactive features of face-to-face recitation. In the first place the formal oral styles of traditional cultures are more like the planned and structured styles that characterize much written expression, and edited versions, in print, offer the reader a different kind of opportunity to appreciate and learn from oral tradition literature. For children learning to read and write, and who are also trying to recover, relearn, or preserve their indigenous language, oral tradition in written form offers special and unique opportunities for children's language and cognitive development. The extension of the oral tradition to writing implies a "preoccupation with knowing" as Meneses Méndez remarks in *Voices.6*, a profound reflection, as he suggests, that poses new kinds of contradiction. In this regard there need be no opposition between preserving the practices of oral performance and working with this same body of literature in written form in school. In fact, we argue, each narrative form can complement the other. In the classroom, both kinds of language activity are necessary ingredients of children's literacy and academic language development.

Teaching the Elements of Literature

Before discussing the applications of the oral tradition to literacy learning, we want to re-emphasize that no sharp dichotomy exists between school-related academic language development in general and learning how to read and write. Indeed, the reader may consider many of the suggestions and activities outlined in this chapter as a continuation of the previous chapters on language development, and vice versa. This is precisely how teachers should view the task of integrating language and literacy instruction: building a solid foundation of discourse competence, an underlying network of language proficiencies that supports all four academic language skill areas. As was pointed out in the previous chapters, much as developing good listening skills helps students with difficult reading comprehension tasks, skilled second language readers are also developing their oral language proficiencies as they work with texts in their second language.

Teachers should become familiar with the themes, the different styles,

---

Voices 6 (Chol)_

Bajche' mi' ña'tyañ i mel ye'tyel jiñi xts' ibob
Me mi laj käl cha'añ jiñi ts'ijb, jiñach i sujmlel che' mi lak poj ch'äm juñ yik'oty lapís, mahc wokolix yu'bil aja che'jiñi yik'oty ma'ñix i k'äjñi'bal yu'bil je'e. Pero ili e'tyel wal bä lak mel, wali i päs ka'bäl i wokolel cha'añ i na'tyäntyel baki mi lak chok majelel i p'ätyälel o i wenlel laj ke'tyel. Wokoläch ili e'tyel kome wen tsijib tyejchemtyo, jiñ cha'añ ka'bältyo chuki yom ajlel. Jin cha'äñ mi käl yom tsajal mi laj k'el majlel, ku ya'tyi yojlil laj ke'tyel, tyi lak ña'tyi'bal yik'oty tyi lak melbal, yik'oty je'e ya' tyi' pajtyel lak pañämil, jintyak iliyi añ ka'bäl i tyamiel o wokolili i ch'ämbentyel i sujm.

(**The vision of the indigenous writer**
If writing only consists of taking paper and pencil, this is too easy, it wouldn't imply any effort and therefore any effect. But, this isn't the task that we have assumed as writers; as a part of this task a whole preoccupation with knowing is implied, toward where we are projecting our work and our effort. This is because our activity is rather new and there is much that still has to be defined. Particularly I feel that it is necessary to give this matter special attention, because in our work, in our thinking, in our culture, and in the world that surrounds us, all of this suggests many things to discuss, because in all this there are profound contradictions.)

Domingo Meneses Méndez (1992: 21)

and the basic organizational structures of traditional stories. This awareness will be especially useful in guiding students through the process of learning, how different kinds of text are organized. Children will develop awareness not only about stories and their structure, but also about the more complex and abstract patterns of other kinds of text. With this practical knowledge, students will be able to take full advantage of the reading material they work with in school. For our purposes, teaching applications would seem to fall into two broad areas of school-based language learning:

(1) The development of academic discourse proficiencies, the narrative being an "early form" in terms of its acquisition in young children. Teaching language and reading comprehension skills through sustained exposure and direct instruction is realized most effectively in both the indigenous language and the national language. Ideally, students will study the different versions separately, in their respective instructional contexts and classroom domains.

(2) The development of second language proficiency, in the original versions for indigenous language revitalization purposes, and in translation for learning the national language on the part of second language learners of the NL.

As an example (only one example among many that we could analyze), the Coyote story is one of the better known and universally appreciated examples of traditional narrative that can serve these two language teaching objectives. Narratives of this type offer a whole range of opportunities for teachers and students to explore how stories are organized. Aside from a critical examination of the themes, attention will also be directed toward the structure of the text, again, how this (and, by extension) other kinds of text are organized. From this kind of reflection and study, students will begin to develop the kind of reading comprehension strategies that will be applicable to the more abstract narrative patterns in literature, and will contribute to building the broader conceptual base and the more complex discourse-processing strategies necessary for non-narrative texts. Coyote narratives are only one type of story within an extensive range of subcategories; and the following teaching points could be easily applied or adapted to other sub-genres of the oral tradition.

Teachers can focus on the following elements in their guided reading lessons:

(1) The constant play of conflicts and rivalries always leads toward a resolution of one kind or another. Often they are partial or incomplete. Students learn to look for cues, predict, and work to construct a global

mental representation of the story as a whole. As the tension (an important ingredient in all coyote stories) in the story builds, the reader asks, how will it be resolved? The teacher guides students toward being attentive to this pattern, how to ask this kind of question before and during reading. Before reading, the question is asked in hypothetical terms (anticipating some kind of conflict and thinking about resolution), during reading it is posed in more specific terms (how will this particular conflict be resolved).

(2)   Intermediate resolutions and conclusions vary widely, causing readers to *reflect back* on the sequence of events. Students look *forward* to predict, and look back as they confirm or readjust their expectations.

(3)   Coyote stories utilize extensively the literary device of *foreshadowing*.* The skilled reader or listener, again, will set up expectations, and apply them flexibly to the comprehension task.

(4)   The rich use of *metaphor** and word play is closely related to the common themes of deceit, cleverness vs. wisdom, and Coyote's perpetual and hopeless struggle to overreach himself. Students get valuable experience in differentiating between what characters say and what they mean. Focusing on this aspect of language use has been identified as a core competency in literacy, particularly at the higher levels (Torrence & Olson, 1987). Interpreting and reflecting upon metaphoric language calls the reader's attention to linguistic forms, how *language itself* can be manipulated to create meaning, produce effect, or provoke a reaction.

(5)   Closely related to the say/mean distinction is the portrayal of Coyote's complex and ambiguous character. A literary feature usually associated with modern fiction, ambivalence and inner strife is a recurring state of mind for the protagonist here who never seems to be able to get out from under one crisis after another. Research on literacy development has pointed to the reader/listener's focus on and contemplation of characters' *inner psychological states*, thoughts and feelings, as an important milestone toward higher-order comprehension strategies (Torrence & Olson, 1985). Closely related to this line of development is the emergence in children's storytelling of the ability to quote the characters' actual words, and distinguish this *reported speech** from their own narrative voice (Gombert, 1992). These kinds of movement from the narrator's voice to reported speech (the characters' words) are often represented by shifts in verb tense, another discourse feature that teachers can call attention to. These shifts in tense (utilized here as a literary device), in turn, can serve a language teaching objective, focusing in this case on grammar. This is another

example of what we discussed in Chapter 5 under the heading of integrating content and language teaching. Reporting thoughts and feelings, and the different ways the narrator does this, is similarly associated with grammatical forms, again making for a good fit between these two learning objectives.

(6) The use of *dramatic irony** presents another opportunity for the beginning reader to reconcile contradictions and disparities of all sorts.

(7) Sometimes Coyote is foolish, cowardly and selfish. In contrast, on other occasions he can inspire pity or sympathy. He both possesses unnatural powers and is very human-like. In other stories he rises to heroic proportions; and often he combines these traits, presenting young readers with the difficult task of identifying with, or at least trying to make sense of, the *ambiguous* character. When children struggle with *contradictions* their intellectual abilities develop and mature.

(8) The extensive use of *repetition* and different kinds of parallel structure introduces readers to this important narrative and poetic feature.

Starting in kindergarten and first grade, young children should begin to learn about the elements and patterns of literature, especially those that characterize the narrative and poetic tradition of their language community.

A Closer Look at Two Contrasting Examples

Coyote stories vary widely in their themes as well as their complexity. In this variability, precisely, lies their great flexibility as a teaching tool. Two particularly illustrative examples each exemplify features that lend themselves to the two broad language-learning objectives mentioned earlier: (1) the development of literacy-related language abilities that underlie reading comprehension and written expression, and (2) a source of second language comprehensible input; content-based second language reading material that is particularly well suited for beginning level students.

Coyote and the Shadow People: For the development of comprehension skills

For a critique of this Nez Perce Orphic story[29] we refer the reader to Ramsey (1983: 47–59) whose detailed analysis we follow closely, and to the full text version for study and reflection in Appendix A.

Journeying to the Land of the Dead in order to retrieve a loved one is one of the great universal themes of the oral tradition. In this particular version, Coyote rises to truly heroic, and human-like, proportions, making *Coyote and the Shadow People*, according to Ramsey, somewhat unique. The Death

Spirit/Guide offers Coyote (whom we find in the opening episode alone and weeping) the opportunity to be reunited with his wife. Coyote's guide must repeat his admonition too many times (exactly five times, in addition, acknowledged by Coyote twice): "You must do whatever I say, do not disobey." Here, children familiar with this type of narrative will begin to set up expectations, or "sense" that something will not go right, especially following the Death Spirit's last line that "he kept *repeating* to himself," "I hope that he will do everything right and take his wife through to the world beyond." Effective teaching strategies will avoid calling attention explicitly to this cue, but rather, when necessary, will elicit predictions (again, in a way that obliges the student to do the mental work). The teacher's questions encourage the children to make inferences which in turn maximizes their subsequent comprehension.

Guided through a series of images and illusions that Coyote (at first confused) must acknowledge as real, he is rewarded with the arrival at the longhouse, where he greets old friends. Upon being reunited with his wife, and admonished one last time, he sets out on the return journey; the descent of the fifth mountain signaling the triumph over the Underworld. However, by the fourth encampment, the wife's spirit form (that gradually, with each leg of the return journey, began to appear to Coyote more and more touchable) had become too real for Coyote to resist.

> Suddenly a joyous impulse seized him; the joy of having his wife again overwhelmed him. ... His wife cried out, "Stop! Stop! Coyote! Do not touch me! Stop!" Her warning had no effect ... as he touched her body she vanished.

Weeping, he retraces, in vain, his journey, re-enacting the illusions of the first trip to the Lodge of the Shadows. His ritual motions are now useless, and their details evoke in the listener empathy and compassion. Coyote finally arrives at the dusty prairie where the Lodge would again be found. The final episode closes dramatically:

> Darkness fell, and now Coyote listened for the voices, and he looked around. He looked here and there, but nothing appeared. Coyote sat there in the middle of the prairie. He sat there all night but the lodge didn't appear again nor did the ghost ever return to him.

Here, the teacher will take full advantage of the complex interplay between irony and foreshadowing. As Ramsey (1983: 53) points out: "in a sense, everything Coyote does in his quest foreshadows his failure, both for himself and his wife, and for the great precedent of returning from death that he might establish. Specific prefigurements occur at every turn." (1983:

53) Helping students develop an awareness, in the early grades, of literary devises such as dramatic irony will prepare them for the longer and more challenging texts that they will be reading in the upper grades. For example, when Coyote is imagining, or pretending to imagine, his wife during his futile return journey to the lodge, saying to himself: "Now your wife has brought us food; let us eat," we all see it as useless, and even Coyote seems to realize that it is all for naught. Students here (with some help from the teacher) should ask: who is being summoned to this ephemeral meal and by which voice?

Predicting strategies in reading have long been recognized as fundamental to both decoding and comprehension (Smith, 1988). Both specific expectations and generalized anticipations facilitate the decoding and comprehension of texts at all levels. Perhaps at some levels, direct teaching of the patterns may not require a carefully sequenced and highly structured program. However, at the levels of higher order comprehension, direct instruction is necessary for learning the advanced discourse proficiencies that are the mainstay of textbook-type, academic, reading material.

In *Coyote and the Shadow People*, some of the cues are explicit. After insistently advising his fellow traveler against his inclination to do foolish things, and repeating: "You must never, never touch her ... but never touch her," the Spirit, "kept saying to himself, I hope that he will do everything right." Other cues are more subtle. Upon arriving at the Lodge of the Shadows, Coyote suddenly, and in apparent contradiction to his stated desire to take his wife back home, tells the Spirit that he wants to stay with his friends. In this particular episode, the teacher can help students stop and consciously reflect upon what the more attentive readers surely noticed as unusual (perhaps, therefore, representing a signal of some kind). Children with extensive experience with Coyote tales will recognize the request as entirely true to form for the indecisive trickster, always looking to take advantage of one situation or another.

Coyote's futile recapitulation of his failed first journey (pretending to see the wild horses on the prairie, going through the motions of picking and eating the berries, and raising the door flap to the lodge) calls for special attention by the teacher, even perhaps during reading, marking off the critical passage. On the unconscious level the young reader or listener experiences the effect of the different layers of parallelism and symmetry in the narration:

(1) the journeys: one in (to the Lodge of the Shadows), one out (back to the World of the Living);
(2) hoping against hope, trying to do the right thing during the desperate return; and

(3)   the day/night, living-world/shadow-world contrasts. Suffering corresponds to the heat and dust of the *day*, celebration and merriment is associated with the lodge reunion at *night*.

The artful repetition of details evokes images, and provokes empathy for Coyote's plight. But when students begin to *consciously reflect* upon these literary devises, they are learning about another aspect of Cognitive Academic Language Proficiency. In addition to general world knowledge, students' comprehension strategies will need to call upon their knowledge of the different discourse patterns, the way different kinds of text are organized (Carrell, 1989).

The importance of studying the elements of literature and other text types cannot be underestimated; unfortunately, in many elementary reading and language arts programs, it is left for the student to somehow spontaneously develop this knowledge and acquire this ability. These particular comprehension abilities become increasingly more useful as the requirements of academic discourse processing become more exacting. Students in the upper grades will find school texts more "abstract" and less "transparent" because predicting strategies based on shared previous knowledge cannot be relied upon in all situations as they could in the early grades; see McCarthy (1991) on the kinds of demands that different text patterns place on students' comprehension strategies. The reader must rely to a greater extent on the ability to find *in the text itself* the cues, referents, causal relationships, antecedents, etc., that are necessary for constructing meaning, and not rely only on a global appreciation of the story based on personal interpretations based primarily on previous knowledge. Previous knowledge sets up expectations, to be confirmed, only partially confirmed, or even totally overturned as one continues to read and think. The skilled reader is able to manipulate expectations flexibly, not just confirm predictions, predispositions or prejudices. The author's intended meaning, or text meaning, cannot be whatever the reader chooses to interpret, or is capable of interpreting (even in the case of children's stories).[30]

Again, skillful teachers will guide their students in discovering, for themselves, these narrative features and discourse patterns. However, helping students learn these text-processing strategies with the view of learning how to use them in their own writing will require focused *attention to structures and patterns*. It is necessary to do this before introducing the story to the class. In particular, the teacher should take note of the following: (1) the setting, (2) character development, especially of the protagonist when he is cast as an ambiguous figure, (3) the nature of the conflict, the problem, attempts at solution, and final resolution, (4) critical turning points in the narrative, (5) the key repetitive patterns, and (6) the more subtle foreshadowing cues. On a more basic level, before working on a story with students, the teacher should at very least segment the text into episodes.

The Opossum and the Coyote: For second language learning and second language literacy

Our second example comes from the oral tradition of the Náhuatl speaking communities of Central Mexico, where a complete version of *Tlacual uan Coyotl* (The Opossum and the Coyote) was recorded from a bilingual teacher and artisan, native of San Isidro Buensuceso, Tlaxcala (see Appendix B for the full text). Both thematically and structurally, the narrative falls at the opposite end of the spectrum from the Nez Perce Orphic myth, although the particular context of the performance, an audience of young children, surely contributed to the simplification. But in this case, it is the simplification that matches the instructional objective that interests us: second language learning and second language literacy. For native speakers of the language, this story would also be appropriate for initial literacy teaching, for young beginning readers.

Following another common theme, Coyote arrives at what he thinks is an agreement with God to eat all His children (see *Didxaguca' sti' lexu ne gueu*, the Zapoteco version that attempts to account for a different natural phenomenon – why coyotes howl at night; de la Cruz & de la Cruz, 1990). God's confederate, the opossum, submits the (in this case outrageously) foolish coyote to a series of outlandish deceptions and deservingly punishing pranks. If the young listeners had not begun to predict the outcome of the subsequent sequences from the opening frame where the lowly coyote thinks he has actually secured a contract with God, they may take note of Opossum's patent lie, in episode 2, which Coyote wholeheartedly believes, that "God won't see you" drink the pulque (the agreement was for Coyote to fast before he could eat all the Earth's creatures). Seven episodes of Opossum's craftiness and evasion at Coyote's expense end with the latter hungry and alone, waiting forever for Opossum to re-emerge from his burrow.

What *Tlacual uan Coyotl* may lack in complexity, or in the examination of universal themes (as in *Coyote and the Shadow People*), is more than compensated for in the series of repetitive structures in close succession, the ideal kind of sequence for second language learners. Repetitive structures effectively scaffold both L2 listening and L2 reading comprehension. Referents are clearly marked: what or who is being referred to is always obvious, which makes the task of listening comprehension or reading comprehension that much easier for the second language student. Each short episode begins with the same initial event: Coyote comes looking for Opossum, running after him, wandering, and (later) faltering. In each episode he repeats the promise to devour Opossum who, each time, shifts the responsibility for the deception to the "Pulque Opossum," the "Shepherd Opossum," the "Turkey Opossum," etc., etc., nicely recapitulating the sequence of deceptions for the reader or the listener. True to the repetitive pattern, Coyote, pleadingly, demands to know, every time, why Opossum is deceiving him so much, and each time he reminds himself of God's admonition.

The *over*-repetition of key content words (*Toteotatzin* – Our God Father, *niccuaz* – eat up, *amo nimitztelhuiz* – I won't accuse you, *otnechacacaya* – you deceived me), signaled by the appropriate intonation markers, increases the comprehensible input level. This makes the narrative even more accessible to the second language learner, in this case the Spanish-speaking student whose Náhuatl language skills are at a beginner level, or the child who acquired the indigenous language during the preschool years and has lost proficiency in the language.

The singular merit, from the pedagogical standpoint, of the Náhuatl coyote story, and many others like it, consists of the combination of simplified structure and authenticity. Too often authentic texts lack the necessary modifications that second language students depend on to be able to process textual material in their learner language. In fact, with appropriate visual context support (puppets of Opossum and Coyote, and props and displays that depict the seven action sequences) the performance of *Tlacual uan coyotl* would serve as highly effective language and literacy instructional material for level one (or even level zero) beginners in Náhuatl. No concurrent translation to L1 is necessary to get a good approximation of what is going on. The greater part of meaning construction would be carried almost completely by the key content words, the relatively simple concepts involved, the repetitive patterns of each episode, teacher supplied context, and the application of general previous knowledge. This is, in fact, all that the beginner second language student needs to be able to do with the first reading or listening. With each successive reading of the story by the teacher, accompanied by sufficient context support (including gestures, role playing, and graphic displays), the students learn new vocabulary and broaden their base of grammatical knowledge in the second language. At the same time biliteracy develops: CALP-type comprehension skills are being applied in both languages.

For language revitalization purposes, this type of narrative is a central component of comprehensible input that, in turn, represents the raw material for learning new vocabulary and grammar in the indigenous language. Stories being *complete texts* facilitate this learning because language patterns are more predictable. Language structures are embedded in the context of the story itself; the narrative events are embedded in a broader context situated outside the story. Language learning rooted in this kind of two-level context not only contributes to the development of higher-order comprehension skills, but integrates important cultural components into the language arts curriculum. The original IL version of the narrative is always preferred. Recording the most complete and polished exemplar (in audio and then transcribed) will provide for a permanent access to this resource when no published editions are available. In cases of advanced erosion of the oral tradition, IL versions can be reconstructed (retranslated) from published European language translations.

The integration of cultural content adds another dimension to the additive biliteracy program. Geographical features and towns mentioned in the narrative are often concrete cultural referents, tied to important historical moments and turning points. The introduction of non-traditional characters can be tied to historically significant transitions related to interethnic contact: the white man, the priest, and new non-indigenous institutions. An important component of the traditional narrative material traces its origins to the pre-European contact period, the other part to the more recent period after the 16th century; and within the latter category, we can identify narratives influenced by European themes and various syncretic forms. Students should study these different currents that make up the oral tradition of their community, and look for key distinctions, divergent tendencies, as well as universal themes and patterns.

For the monolingual IL speaker, or beginning NL learner, translations into Spanish or English of oral tradition material offer many of the same advantages outlined above. Ironically perhaps, these NL versions are the most widely available, and the most visible, for example in the children's section of local public libraries. Adult level anthologies of indigenous oral tradition represent an almost inexhaustible reservoir of material, most of which can easily be abridged (and translated as required to the IL or the NL) for the child beginning reader. It is no coincidence that the most compelling and enduring children's literature in the European languages traces its origin to the Old World oral tradition. Reading and listening to the traditional stories of one's community insures significant levels of previous knowledge support for the difficult second language decoding and processing tasks. And of course, the straightforward sequence of events, all tied to the recurring pattern of pursuit, confrontation, deception (opossum), and frustration (coyote), makes for a good match for native-level IL-speaking children in the initial stages of literacy development.

The popularity of indigenous oral tradition in translation, especially in regions of sustained intercultural contact, attests to the broad applicability of this literature for language teaching. Integrating indigenous literature into the curriculum beyond the bilingual program can expand non-indigenous students' "narrative awareness" beyond the familiar patterns of their own traditional texts.

The potential of this indigenous literary form for enriching the reading and language arts curriculum has been realized only partially, even in many schools where additive/developmental bilingual education is the stated policy. Our examination of the multitude of applications has focused, so far, on a few examples in the area of reading. Without a doubt, applying the material to the domain of developing writing skills will be equally as productive. Traditional storytellers have learned to manipulate the basic narrative patterns, apply certain formulas that are characteristic of the genre, and introduce variations to produce extensive repertoires of original narrations. The most talented narrators and novice young writers among them will go on to become apprentices in the verbal art of their grandparents. All children learn the rudiments of narrative expression. In school, this common platform can be the basis for building more elaborate and sophisticated narrative schemas – a necessary foundation, in turn, for learning the even-more-abstract patterns of expository text organization.

Here, it is important to emphasize that creativity depends on learning structures and patterns. Developing writers learn to apply them through guided practice. Students need:

(1) significant amounts of exposure to models of well-formed stories; and
(2) to have the opportunity to both reflect upon the stories themselves and receive feedback on their own productions.

Creativity is also expansive and divergent. Coyote stories can take on a virtually unlimited variety of forms, just as Coyote himself does.

Follow-Up Activities for Traditional Stories

The traditional narrative can be applied to a series of classroom literacy lessons and activities. However, the teacher must avoid any tendency toward making the oral narrative/writing connection routine. Just as routinely assigning written comprehension questions after every reading assignment will negatively affect students' disposition toward the passages themselves, following up on each and every narration with a writing task sends the wrong message to students. Remember, traditional stories have stood alone for thousands of years and are complete in and of themselves, requiring no elaboration or transcription for the purpose of perfecting them. However, the complete and integral nature of the narrative makes them ideally suited for literacy instruction, if the teacher exploits this resource judiciously. In the process stories may undergo certain modifications in their structure, some more, some less, but neither, necessarily, for better or for worse.

Graphic representations

Depicting or portraying stories graphically in the form of scenes is a valuable activity that for young children, for example, represents a kind of precursor to composing the stories by means of words alone. Vygotsky (1986/1934), for example, discusses children's artistic expression as an antecedent to literacy. Similar to the ability to summarize, students must transform the narrative that they listened to and understood, reducing it to its essential elements. Far from being an undirected, non-academic type activity, the graphic reconstructions should be actively mediated by teachers. Graphic representations can portray key aspects of narrative structure and the sequence of events: students' illustrations should correspond to an integral representation (in some significant way) of the story. Examples of low-level, cognitively unchallenging, tasks in this category would be illustrations of the student's "favorite character" or the episode that he or she "liked best." In all such cases care must be taken that valuable classroom time is not taken up by non-academic tasks that students can complete independently after school or on weekends – an error that inexperienced teachers, eager to provide themselves with a measure of respite from cognitively demanding instruction, often fall into.

Retelling

With or without visual context support, and depending on the needs of the students, the class can "retell" the narrative, composing their own written versions. This activity lends itself well to small writers' circles, where students collaborate to arrive at: (1) one version, prepared by a recorder, which represents the consensus of the group, or (2) individual products that reflect group discussion and reflection. One particular advantage of the writers' circle would be the way it can facilitate comprehension and expression for students who are dominant in the national language. The teacher, or an IL-speaking student assistant, reads the story in the indigenous language. At this point the cooperative learning group members may choose to: (1) process the story orally in their primary language (in this case the NL) and proceed to compose written versions in the target language, or (2) discuss ideas and write in their primary language, and collectively work on a translation. This approach is an example of a correct way in which students' primary language might mediate a second-language activity (in contrast to incorrect ways of using the L1 during second language teaching, such as *concurrent translation**).

Retelling is not a mechanical, rote-memory type, language task. In the first place, in order to "remember" the listener must be able to understand the story and be able to "analyze" it into its parts, assigning episodes, characters, and voices to components in a structure (slots, so to speak, that correspond to "nodes" in a narrative schema). Students must *actively* listen to the sequence of events and integrate them into a structure that is coherent and complete. This step is precisely what permits the listener to reconstruct and compose an intelligible version of what they heard. Written versions sometimes follow the model closely, often they take their own direction, sometimes even improving on the original. As Harold Rosen suggests, creativity is not unordered and formless.

> [Teachers] are finding that students retelling stories are far more inventive and creative than when they are asked to "make one up." We need to understand this more fully. But it seems that the teller, no longer burdened with the need to invent the basic elements, is free to allow the imagination to play inventively. Surprising dormant resources come into action. A stereotypical character takes on a particular idiom and voice, a new episode is introduced, or an old one elaborated. This is the very opposite of repeating a rote-learned story. Retelling is a creative act. (Rosen, 1992: 6)

This clearly has important implications for how the teacher responds to and evaluates retellings, particularly if students are not explicitly directed to reproduce the original plot. Again the criteria for successful or mature retellings focuses on structure. Was the writer able to apply the basic contours of the model (a scaffolding of the discourse kind) to build a theme and a sequence, and organize details in a coherent way? If anything, reconstructed events that depart from the model would receive extra recognition and a higher grade. And of course, the most advanced writers will begin to manipulate and reorder the model's scaffolding itself. For a report on the application of retelling to IL literacy teaching (the Lushootseed language, Washington state, USA) see Denham *et al.* (2000).

All nature and degrees of context support are valid and recommended as required, always keeping in mind the general rule: the language teacher's medium- and long-term objective is to reduce concrete "hands-on" props, impelling students forward toward greater degrees of independence from extralinguistic, situation-embedded, scaffolding. Refer to discussions of Vygotsky's theory of the Zone of Proximal Development in

Faltis (2001: 130–142), Pérez & Torres-Guzmán (1992: 29–30), and Peregoy & Boyle (2001: 80–87).

Scaffolding student retellings

Students who are beginning readers will vary widely in their awareness of story structure. Our own study of Náhuatl-speaking bilinguals' retellings revealed wide variations at all grade levels in response to oral presentations of traditional narratives (Francis, 1997, 2000c). Providing students with "story stems" (in addition to a complete model, or without a model) helps trigger the pertinent narrative *schema** and gets them started. Simply reproduce the first episode, plus the initiating event of the second in a way that clearly indicates incompleteness, and direct the class to continue the narrative. This procedure happens to be particularly handy for the monolingual teacher not proficient in the students' indigenous language. Worksheets can be prepared easily with a minimum of consultation with a native speaking student assistant.

For more advanced groups (in this case also requiring a certain level of proficiency in the IL on the part of the teacher) scaffolding can take the form of supplying the abstract framework of the narrative and directing students to "fill in" a content. For example, provide guidelines and explore possibilities for each of the following:

(1) opening frame and setting;
(2) appearance of characters;
(3) initiating events;
(4) problem;
(5) attempt and solution;
(6) complications;
(7) second attempt;
(8) crisis;
(9) resolution;
(10) moral (optional).

An alternate narrative scheme of the journey will also be familiar to many students who have extensive contact with their community's oral tradition:

(1) absence from or abandonment of the home;
(2) depravation and want;
(3) search;
(4) appearance of the antagonist;
(5) struggle;

(6)   provision of magical medium or agent (optional);
(7)   reparation/recuperation;
(8)   return.

"Schematic retellings," focused on recurring patterns, direct students' attention to how narratives are structured in different ways. Taking the *Opossum and the Coyote* as an example, the teacher makes reference to the layers of deception:

(1)   Opossum tricks Coyote seven times, the first time was when he invited Coyote to drink from the maguey. Retell in your group and write down the deceptions in order.

(2)   Then, Coyote repeatedly confused one thing for another, starting in Episode 3 when he perceived the boulder falling because of the movement of the clouds. This occurred four more times in Episodes 4, 5, 6, and 7. Retell the Coyote's confusions in sequential order.

(3)   Opossum, when confronted by Coyote for his deceit in Episode 3 alleges that it was not he (the "Boulder Opossum") but rather the "Pulque Opossum." This occurs four more times, etc.

For example, comparing this type of narrative (the temporal/arbitrary schema) with *Coyote and the Shadow People* (logical/causal) develops students' awareness of how texts across the different genres are organized.

• Why are the series of deceptions and confusions that Opossum provokes so difficult to remember in the original order?
• What other stories that you have heard are more like *Coyote and Opossum*, and which are more like *Coyote and the Shadow People*?

Advanced students will be able to go beyond recognition and differentiation to actually producing prototypes of each narrative subcategory.

Taking dictation

Collectively, students and their families can provide a significant portion of the reading material that schools do not have at their disposal in the form of published books. Dictating narratives to the teacher, or to another competent scribe, however, goes beyond the important functions of preserving and sharing, and creating resources for literacy teaching. In the process of mentally formulating and then narrating a story, for the purpose of writing it down, children intuitively begin to make modifications that take into account not only the needs of the scribe, but also begin to reflect more deliberately on the form and structure of their discourse. Children start to think of their verbal expression in terms of *composing*, creating a text. The outcome will be a product that can be read, contemplated, discussed, and even analyzed for its adequacy as a story. This process of reflection is closely related to the idea of communicative awareness, where the speaker or writer must think about the audience's ability to recreate the narrative they are reading or listening to.

In fact, the "first draft" of a student dictation will pass through an editing phase where the considerations of coherence, completeness, and clarity will guide the revision process. Patterns of written composition are different from the patterns of conversational speech. Each is complex in different ways, something that for all students should become an important language learning objective. And in case there may exist any doubt in their minds, both the language of wider communication and the ancestral language share both of these kinds of discourse pattern. Students will also come to appreciate that the patterns of oral narrative begin to approach those of formal writing, the more elaborate and practiced the oral narrative, the more it resembles the written story.

Taking student dictation, also known as the Language Experience Approach (LEA), has been part of the basic instructional repertoire of generations of elementary school reading teachers (Hall, 1978). Again, its objective is not only to supplement the lack of published children's literature. LEA stories, by their very nature, are highly predictable and make the necessary connection between oral and written language in a context-embedded and concrete way. What students begin to do intuitively in regard to making their dictations approach higher levels of formality, teachers will extend and systematize. Dictated traditional stories share the same quality of predictability; and even in their original, unedited, form they reflect higher levels of structure, even when recited by the youngest beginning readers in the class.

Dictation can be taken either individually or as a whole class activity. In the latter case the act of transcription will often be combined with the editing phase as students offer revisions, or suggest corrections of their classmates' versions. The teacher must decide here to what extent, and under which circumstances, the students' dictations (their actual utterances) are recorded verbatim, or are "edited" during the act of transcription. Short of changing the actual sense of the discourse, there is no hard-and-fast rule. Clearly, incomplete sound patterns or mispronunciations (or what are perceived as such) are not represented in writing. If the teacher/scribe feels it is important to substitute grammatically correct forms for non-native-speaker errors that students produce, when the correction is apparent or obvious, it may be necessary to briefly and very succinctly explain the substitution. On the other hand, various kinds of minor surface-level error may not warrant commentary, unless of course students call attention to them. An important note of caution here concerns the dialectical variation that may exist in the IL speech community that will be reflected in students' choices of words and expressions. The classroom teacher must at all times hold up the highest standard of tolerance and flexibility, even in the face of students' objections to the "non-standard" usage of their peers (also see Chapter 4 on how teachers should respond to codeswitching). Being able to differentiate between legitimate variants of the language and clearly non-native learner errors is often difficult and requires a high level of *grammatical** competence on the part of the teacher. When in doubt, accept the grammatical structure or lexical item that students offer.

Since few indigenous languages have definitively resolved the issue of orthographic standardization, the broadest latitude is called for in this area, especially from student written productions. In the same way bilingual IL-speaking teachers must not hesitate to perform their responsibilities of scribe alleging less-than-perfect command of its written conventions. Establishing a community-wide consensus on spelling standards is an important and worthwhile objective. Meanwhile, teachers of the language must continue to experiment with the forms they have learned, working through their own hypotheses and conceptions of the writing system for authentic expressive and communicative purposes.

Lastly, we do not recommend that teachers discourage students from copying the dictated versions. Beginning readers and writers often look forward to this activity for sound pedagogical reasons: (1) students appropriate their own copies to read again, in private, to keep and have, and to share with friends and family; (2) practicing the skills of letter formation, word segmentation, spelling, and punctuation represents an aspect of literacy development that children themselves often perceive as significant and essential (not without reason, certainly). Placed in proper perspective, these represent important literacy sub-skills that correspond to what are sometimes termed "surface features" or "bottom-up" skills. On the one hand, they are separate and independent from the higher-order comprehension abilities and global composition strategies. But control over the literacy sub-skills also interacts with the macro-level "top-down" strategies. The relationship is one of *interdependence*. For example, the editing process depends necessarily on being able to inspect and reread one's own manuscript. As maturity in the composing process develops, writers reflect and edit as they proceed from paragraph to paragraph. Language awareness develops with the opportunity to manipulate language, the *wording itself.* The clearest, most legible, and artfully composed versions will eventually become part of the classroom library of traditional narrative.

Applications of cloze to IL literacy

The technique of systematically deleting words from a text, for the purpose of presenting readers with the task of making the passage meaningful and interpretable again, has been usually associated with assessment. In this chapter we will discuss the cloze procedure as an instructional approach. As such it offers teachers of indigenous languages particular opportunities, especially for the non-native speaker, and even the monolingual teacher. Keeping in mind the necessity of constantly generating teacher-made learning materials, creatively applying cloze to the IL reading curriculum will enrich and diversify classroom literacy lessons. Primary among the advantages are:

(1) Students must focus on text comprehension and aspects of sentence structure in the passage to complete the task. Research indicates that the greater part of the reader's attention during a cloze reading task is directed at grammatical and meaning relationships at the sentence level (Cohen, 1994; Chávez-Oller *et al.*, 1994); however, depending on the design of the cloze task, and teacher scaffolding, the student will also take into account text-level meaning relationships.

(2) Various possible modifications can increase context support and decrease the information processing load (if this is necessary) for beginning readers, and L2 learners.

(3) As a teaching tool, and by its very nature, cloze lends itself well to cooperative learning group work in which students reflect upon and compare criteria for constructing coherent texts, word choice, grammatical compatibility, etc. For young readers attempting solutions to cloze, our experience suggests that the operations involved in reintegrating, making a passage whole again, are intrinsically motivating on some level, as long as the degree of difficulty is controlled. Indeed, students generally show an avid interest in the activity, and remain on task for extended periods, especially if peer collaboration is encouraged.

(4) Cloze reading tasks can be easily constructed and produced for students in any language, even by teachers with minimal levels of proficiency in the indigenous language. The ten steps outlined in Table 3 have proven to be highly successful in situations where no literacy materials were available in the language of the community (Francis, 1999b; Francis & Navarrete Gómez, 1999). When there is nothing to

read for children in the IL, as is the case for all but a few isolated cases, producing materials locally is one temporary alternative to the NL monopoly over reading primers and language arts workbooks. Teachers should keep a file of all the literacy-related activities they generate for future editing and publication.

Choosing the appropriate text for cloze is the first important decision the teacher must make. For students who are unfamiliar with the procedure, who are beginning readers, or who are reading in their second language, highly predictable, narrative texts are a good place to begin. Working on a cloze passage of a story that was read aloud to the class, for example, increases to an even greater degree the predictability of the text. The same applies to stories that are already familiar to students (narrative material from the oral tradition, even texts taken from students' reading anthologies and basal readers). Keep in mind that, when working with whole texts, longer than one or two sentences, the task of reconstructing a complete and integral copy is never a mechanical or memoristic-type activity, even if the students have just heard the entire story. To be able to "remember" anything from an oral reading of a narrative, the listener had to have focused his or her attention on the meaning relationships at some level. Beyond remembering phone numbers and birthdays, memory depends on complex integrative processes involving the assimilation and reorganization of information so that it can be stored in some useable (i.e. retrievable) form.

As readers become more experienced, the teacher can select texts that are predictable in different ways, especially, not predictable in the more obvious and transparent way that the standard narrative tends to be. In this case solution of the cloze task will depend less on the support that previous knowledge provides, and more on the ability of the reader to concentrate his or her attention on the meaning relationships and grammatical patterns in the cloze passage itself.

In steps 2, 3, and 4 the teacher is presented with further opportunities to adjust the difficulty level of the cloze passage. As in all language teaching, the two dimensions that are constantly shifting (fine-tuned according to the next round of language learning challenges that the student is presented with) are: the degree of extralinguistic context support available, and the amount of new information that must be processed at one time – "processed simultaneously or in close succession" (Cummins & Swain, 1987: 151–156).

The decision to display word choices depends on other factors related to context, familiarity, and information load – all, in turn, related to the level of L2 proficiency of the reader. Especially for students reading in their second

Table 3 Teaching reading comprehension in a language you may not know: Being creative with cloze

The following procedure can be followed either by retyping the text, or with scissors, paste, and correction fluid.

Step 1 Choose a story

Select a reading passage, for beginners preferably a story or other highly predictable text. Try to pick a story that is no more than two grade levels above the instructional reading level of the students.

Step 2 Segment the passage

Divide the text into sections of two or three paragraphs each, depending on the reading and/or language proficiency of the students. Maintain paragraphs intact.

Step 3 Word deletion

Leave the first sentence of the text intact. Tentatively select what appear to be content words in predictable locations (i.e. towards the end of sentences or phrases). As a rule, try to avoid deletion of the first word of a sentence. Make sure not to delete too many words; a ratio of one deletion for every 10th running word is reasonable. One for every 5th word is generally too difficult. Replace each deleted word with a space. Maintain the length of each space constant. For focused lessons on grammatical patterns, for example, deletions can target function words.

Step 4 Display choices along with one distracter

Below each section arrange the deleted words in random order, and add one distracter.

Step 5 Make copies

Retain a copy for yourself with the deleted words written in.

Step 6 Training session

Show the students how to solve the problem with a sample teaching passage, either in your L1 or the students' L1. Discuss each choice that students offer in terms of how well it "fits". "Does the sentence make sense now?" Remember there may be more than one answer for any particular omission, and note that student responses may be compatible, grammatically and semantically, at the sentence level, but may not be compatible with the story as a whole. But again this too may be permissible, depending on the circumstances.

Step 7 Pre-reading access to previous knowledge

If you know what the story is about, before students get to work, introduce the story, in your L1 if necessary (characters, setting, problem, etc.), and elicit predictions.

Step 8 Grouping

Preferably, students work in committees, discuss among themselves, and try to reach agreement for each response.

Step 9 Overview

Before trying to fill in the answers, students should read straight through, silently or as a group, the entire passage, then return to the beginning.

Step 10 Solution

Students discuss and arrive at possible solutions in each committee. Discuss as a class the alternatives. Again, often more than one answer is possible, and students may choose to use their own words to complete the text instead of the alternatives provided. Students may also decide to change some aspects of the original meaning of the story.

See Appendix C for sample cloze passages with choices and distracters.

language, for whom searching their limited L2 mental dictionaries presents an additional challenge, providing alternative responses from which to choose is often necessary to avoid random responses. And as they gain confidence and proficiency, the same cloze passage, now without alternatives (moving from a closed-ended to a more open-ended format), will require them to rely on their own word choices, to search their own second language vocabulary store.

As a rule, if the passage is long, it is advisable to segment the text (as shown in the examples given in Appendix C), always paying close attention to its structural components. For example, in the case of a narrative, maintain intact episodes or scenes that form integral segments within the story. Here it is useful to recall our own experience with cloze as students and why our recollection of the task is probably somewhat less than fond and enthusiastic. Most likely presented in a testing situation (often timed), the format insured a high rate of error (and frustration): (1) long passages, (2) frequent deletions, (3) no alternative responses, and (4) no context support outside of the text itself – made difficult or impossible to interpret by (2).

Deleting content words (nouns, verbs, adjectives, and adverbs, as opposed to grammatical function words) in highly predictable locations facilitates the task for beginners. Depending on sentence level context, other grammatical categories can be predictable as well; and with increased proficiency, the deletions can focus on specific language skills: prepositions, definite versus indefinite articles, and referents within the text involving pronouns, for example. At first, the reader's attention will be focused on sentence-level context, subsequently, and depending on the kind of deletions chosen, compatibility of the reader's word choice will involve text-level context as well. In all cases, deleting too many words defeats the purpose of cloze as an instructional tool, that of teaching students new reading comprehension strategies that depend less on context outside of the text and more on the information provided in the text itself.

To maximize the language learning potential of cloze, teaching students specific strategies for how to utilize "within text information" is essential (steps 6 and 7 in Table 3). Since these text-processing strategies are universal, the instruction and even the practice passages can be provided in the teacher's dominant language if this is not the same as the language of the cloze activity itself. On the one hand, perhaps first, the focus is on grammatical compatibility. At the sentence level, does the inserted word result in a sentence that conforms to the grammatical patterns of the language? Does it "sound" like the IL (or the NL as the case may be), "even though you may not know what it means, could someone say this in the language?" Then, does the choice make sense: is the sentence meaningful, and "does the sentence now fit with the rest of the story?" or does it contradict something in a previous sentence or paragraph? The most advanced readers will begin to detect anomalies and contradictions in regard to *subsequent* sections of the passage. While the objective is to develop the use of context "within the text," always maximize access to previous knowledge before reading. Facilitating access to pertinent background knowledge in no way contradicts or works at cross-purposes to the "text-dependent" strategies.

Probably the greatest benefit of this kind of classroom assignment is realized when students are given the opportunity to compare and contrast different options, turning the activity into a true problem-solving task. When different linguistic options become the object of discussion and conscious reflection (and ideally dispute and the confrontation of different points of view) for the purpose of reestablishing meaning and coherence, students are engaging in a particular variety of higher-order thinking about language that is the bedrock of academic literacy. Preferably, for steps 8, 9 and 10, the groups are on their own, struggling to come to consensus without the teacher's intervention.

From beginning to end, the monolingual teacher can play an active role in organizing the cloze activity, introducing students to new comprehension strategies, explaining procedures, etc. However, on all *linguistic* questions he or she cedes authority to the more capable bilinguals in the class. It goes without saying that this kind of teaching opportunity is invaluable for the affirmation of the indigenous language when the bilinguals with high levels of competence in the indigenous language become models of correct usage. The bilingual teacher, of course, has at his or her disposal the full range of instructional and linguistic resources to enrich this and all other IL literacy teaching opportunities that go far beyond what has been outlined here.

In summary, the primary focus of students' problem-solving activity is on meaning relationships (indeed it would be impossible, cheating aside, to reintegrate a deleted text in any other way). At the same time, readers must become more sensitive to the textual constraints themselves; that is, not any word that comes to mind (e.g. based on previous knowledge alone or on an accompanying illustration) will be the best choice.

A concluding note about teaching skills

In this chapter on literacy we have not included a section on the teaching of decoding strategies (building children's sight vocabulary, teaching the letter–sound correspondences for the writing system, phonemic and morphological awareness, etc.) This is not because we deem this component of literacy to be unimportant; rather, it is because we have very little to add on this point to the additional readings listed below. In fact, it would be a mistake to conclude that an exclusively literature-based, text comprehension-oriented approach is sufficient for beginning literacy teaching. We have chosen to emphasize the importance of reflection on narrative genres as one example that happens to make a good connection with the existing IL oral and literacy traditions. However, reflection on language structures at the "lower levels," or on the "bottom-up processes" as they are sometimes called, is also a necessary part of learning how to read and write. The methods and lesson plans described are easily adaptable to literacy teaching in any language as long as the teacher keeps in mind that languages choose, so to speak, from a universal inventory of linguistic features. That is, the *specific* phonological, morphological, and syntactic patterns used as examples in textbooks on reading instruction may not be applicable, but the general approaches that are outlined do apply.

Additional reading

Reading, Writing, and Learning in ESL: A Resource Book for K-12 Teachers by Peregoy and Boyle (2001) is a true classroom handbook for teachers, as the subtitle suggests. Virtually all the numerous activities described are applicable to, or can de modified for, literacy teaching in the indigenous language. Chapter 4 emphasizes the fundamental continuity between school-related oral language development and literacy, with many practical suggestions on how to bridge these two aspects of academic discourse.

Learning in Two Worlds by Pérez and Torres-Guzmán (1992) focuses on the bilingual class (as opposed to ESL, making it a useful companion to the above book). Examples are taken from English and Spanish, but again are applicable to Native American languages, keeping in mind our limitation in the area of published materials. Chapters that are strong on methods and materials are 4: Early years of reading and writing, 5: Developing proficiency: and 6: Literacy in the content areas. This book is a good follow-up to Ovando and Collier (1998) on integrating mathematics, science and social studies with language learning in general.

Writing in a Second Language: Insights from First and Second Language Teaching and Research by Leeds (1996) is a collection of studies focused on teaching strategies for Composing, Revising, Teacher Feed back and Assessment of student compositions (including peer evaluation).

Teaching Reading Skills in a Foreign Language by Nuttall (1996) completes the circle by providing the teacher with classroom strategies from a different perspective, that of the foreign language student. The numerous practical guidelines apply to all L2 reading situations, for example under Word Attack Skills: Freeing students from the dictionary, Learning when to ignore difficult words, What makes words difficult, and Inference from context.

Chapter 7

Language Assessment

Evaluation as a Component of the Indigenous Language Teaching Program

Language assessment is a broad field with an extensive research base; and in recent years some of the most important advances have been made as a result of the expansion of educational programs serving bilingual students. All second language teachers know how important well-designed assessments are for effective teaching. Together with the growth of interest in assessment of bilingual learners as a whole, indigenous communities and the educators that serve them have begun to develop assessment procedures for measuring or estimating different aspects of proficiency that a speaker may possess in the indigenous language. This, among the many important issues related to the testing and evaluation of Indian children, is the focus of this chapter.

Before we can begin to observe, take samples of language, or estimate ability, the first step must always be to determine what is the purpose of assessment: what precisely will the results be used for? This seemingly obvious consideration merits serious and well-informed reflection; in fact, the omission of this essential prerequisite often results in unnecessary errors of judgment, and precipitous and inappropriate classification of learners. Among the appropriate and educationally relevant assessment objectives, from our point of view (indigenous language development and additive bilingualism), we can identify perhaps some of the more important.

(1) *Estimating language dominance*: minimally, teachers need informal screening procedures for determining bilingual children's primary language or languages. Among other possible schemas, we could propose five broad categories of basic language competence that are important to take into account in planning language instruction, in particular beginning literacy:
(a) monolingual indigenous language (IL);
(b) monolingual national language (NL);
(c) primary language IL, child NL learner (beginner or intermediate);
(d) primary language NL, child IL learner (beginner or intermediate);
(e) balanced bilingual (equivalent competence in IL and NL).

(2) *Ongoing classroom assessment of academic language proficiency:* how well can students perform on grade-level tasks related to the content areas, involving academic discourse, higher-order comprehension, writing, etc.; and to what extent can these academic language proficiencies be applied to tasks in the NL and in the IL?

(3) *Progress in second language learning:* which grammatical structures, and new L2 vocabulary, for example, have been mastered, and which still require some kind of direct instruction?

These three purposes of classroom-based language evaluation can be grouped under the broad category of assessments that are most effectively carried out using *criterion-referenced* measures. The pertinent comparison in each case is a predetermined criterion or standard, a specific language skill or set of abilities, as in objectives (2) and (3), or an overall language competence profile, as in (1). The focus of comparison in these cases is not the performance of other individuals as in norm-referenced tests, but rather a set of learning objectives or a broad category of interrelated knowledge structures.

The IL community may decide to take on a more ambitious assessment project that attempts to estimate, for example, actual levels of proficiency in each language that children or adults (e.g. candidates for bilingual teacher) speak. In this case, a systematic study, the objective of which is to establish a *community language database*, is necessary. A norm sample, based on actual language use in the IL community (to which performance on the test will be compared) must be gathered following a carefully designed plan. We refer readers to a concise, non-technical, introduction to the requirements of *norm-referenced* test construction published by the Arizona Department of Education, *American Indian Language Proficiency Assessment: Considerations and Resources* (1983). Briefly, the following steps are recommended:

(1) A committee of local teachers and community members works in collaboration with a linguist and a test construction specialist to first identify the purpose of the evaluation instrument, and then proceed to gather information. First and foremost, the committee must decide whether the assessment instrument will sample aspects of fluency associated with everyday conversational language, or school-related discourse proficiencies involving context-reduced uses of language, tied to literacy, or both. In the last case (assessing both conversational fluency *and* higher-order academic language use), we recommend keeping these two distinct aspects of language proficiency conceptually separate from the beginning. Native speaker competence in the language is necessary for all phases of planning and test construction.

For further reading on this subject we refer readers to the discussion in McGroarty *et al.* (1995) on the central tasks and challenges in designing a standardized language assessment for an indigenous language.

(2)   Since one of the objectives of the project is to arrive at a proficiency scale, a broadly based, representative sample of language use must reflect language use both by speakers who command complete, adult-level, proficiency, and by those who fall short of the native speaker norm (child learners, NL-dominant bilinguals with partial knowledge of the IL, including those who have lost proficiency in the language).

(3)   Video or audio recordings must be analyzed and rated by recognized competent speakers in collaboration with a linguist.

(4)   Construction of items, including the determination of what kinds of interview procedure and stimulus material are culturally appropriate for the age group selected. In the assessment of academic language proficiency, one could argue that not all items must reflect IL speakers' shared, local community-based, cultural knowledge. However, if interpersonal communicative fluency (or basic grammatical competence and vocabulary knowledge) is the objective, the introduction of culturally-foreign items may confound the results (i.e. at the point of interpreting the data, there will be uncertainty regarding the source of incorrect or null responses – in this case, lack of basic linguistic knowledge or lack of general world knowledge).

(5)   Submission of items for community review to elicit the observations of native speakers of the language, including teachers, who are also familiar with the local culture.

(6)   Selection of a representative sample of speakers for trial testing, reflecting a cross section of language abilities in the indigenous language.

(7)   Analysis of trial test results, deletion/rewriting of inappropriate or otherwise defective items, leading to final revision.

(8)   Final field testing that includes evaluation of the instrument for desirable technical features, and for the establishing of community norms. Steps (7) and (8) are repeated at regular intervals to confirm the original findings and to make necessary revisions.

In summary, both criterion-referenced and norm-referenced assessments are appropriate and useful in evaluating different aspects of language proficiency. How useful and appropriate one or another turns out to be will depend on: (1) the specific purpose of the evaluation; (2) the component or components of language knowledge that are being targeted; (3) practical considerations related to the availability of community-based resources for researching the indigenous language itself; and (4) patterns of use among both bilingual and monolingual speakers. The reader may also have noticed that *standardization* can be a desirable feature of language assessment. In our example of the steps involved in designing a norm-referenced test, the uniformity of various aspects of the assessment is in fact necessary to allow for meaningful interpretation of the results. The individual speaker's performance is compared to the same norm sample; otherwise comparisons would not be possible. For the same reason, each interviewee responds to the same items, a standard procedure is used in presenting the test items, and a uniform set of scoring criteria is applied. In principle, standardized tests are not incompatible with either the structure of indigenous languages, or culturally related language use patterns associated with the IL speech community. Errors are often committed in the way standardized test results are interpreted and used; however, it would be a mistake to ascribe special circumstances to the language and culture of Indian communities that exclude, as a general rule, one or another assessment approach. This point, precisely, leads us to the consideration of the fundamental principles of language assessment.

Any discussion of the assessment of indigenous language speakers' proficiency should review the two basic guiding concepts in the field of testing and evaluation: validity and reliability. The general principles of language assessment apply with equal force to all situations of bilingualism, and to the entire range of assessment approaches: standardized testing, teacher-designed formal testing, informal classroom-based assessment of language abilities, structured interviews, checklists and open-ended questionnaires, portfolios, and ethnographic observation. As a field, the assessment of IL speakers' language proficiency is very new and , to date, has been primarily the domain of researchers. Nevertheless, under all the above categories, including standardized measures, the first steps have already been taken by educators in this important aspect of *teaching*. The concepts of validity and reliability will serve as our twin guideposts in examining the various methods and how educators can put them to good use.

Validity

(1) In regard to a given language assessment validity does not refer to the method or procedure itself, and not even, strictly speaking, to the information that the student's responses provide. It refers to how the information is *interpreted*; that is, what meaning is attributed to the results that were gathered.

(2)   In relation to the interpretation of the results (i.e. to what extent it actually sheds light on the aspect of language proficiency that the teacher needs to know about), validity is a matter of *degree*; thus, it is not accurate to say that the results of an assessment are simply valid or invalid.

(3)   And, related to (2), validity is *specific* to a particular objective. An interpretation may be appropriate, or valid, in regard to one kind of language learning outcome and perhaps less so for another. For example, a test of IL vocabulary knowledge, in which the child responds by selecting the correct pictorial representation of words that the examiner reads aloud, will reflect his or her level of listening comprehension to a certain degree. The test will not provide an exact measure of this aspect of language proficiency, but will most likely approximate the exact measure sufficiently to be able to provide useful information to the teacher. The test results will also be related to his or her ability to use this vocabulary knowledge, for example, in telling a story or explaining a procedure. But it will be related to this expressive ability to a lesser extent, or in a much more indirect way, because other linguistic and cognitive skills each play an important role in higher-order uses of language. Here again, it would be a mistake to say that the *test* is invalid because an erroneous conclusion would be the result of *misinterpreting* the results. It would also not be correct to simply declare that our hypothetical test of vocabulary knowledge is completely invalid as a measure of the more complex ability since vocabulary knowledge does play a role. In other words, the results of the vocabulary test would reflect the more complex ability to a degree; we could argue that it does so to a limited degree, but this judgment is different from one that discards the results out of hand as "invalid."

Thus, in order to avoid misinterpreting assessment results, two questions should be foremost in the bilingual teacher's mind:

(1)   what aspect of language proficiency will the method that was selected hopefully reveal?

(2)   to what degree will the results reflect this aspect of language proficiency?

All of this assumes, of course, that the aspect of language proficiency that was selected is an important learning objective in the first place. For a more complete discussion of the concept of validity, see Linn and Gronlund (1995: 47–80), Genesee and Upshur (1996: 62–67), and Kubiszyn and Borich (2000: 297–310).

Reliability

(1) Similarly to considerations of validity, reliability does not refer to the assessment instrument itself. However, in contrast to validity, when we consider questions of reliability we are not concerned with the interpretation of the results, but rather with examining the results themselves. In this sense reliability is solely a *statistical* consideration; by itself it cannot answer the question of what the assessment data mean.

(2) By definition, reliability refers to an estimate of how *consistent* the results of an assessment are. In other words, are test scores, or other information gathered, free from unsystematic variation? Information that an assessment provides is reliable if we can be relatively confident that whatever is being measured or observed is done so in a uniform and systematic way. Reliability is also a matter of degree, and always refers to a specific kind of consistency (e.g. when considering reliability among different examiners' observations, are the samples of language performance themselves consistent, and are there factors unrelated to the assessment's objective that may cause the student to respond in an inconsistent way).

(3) As one might expect from point (2), a set of scores, for example, that appears to measure a language skill in a consistent way offers no guarantee that it will be interpreted appropriately. In other words, reliability does not by itself ensure validity. A reliable set of results only provides the consistency from which valid interpretations can be made. Looking at this relationship from the point of view of validity, to be able to even begin to interpret in a meaningful way the information that was gathered, that same sample of information must have been gathered consistently and systematically. Thus, a minimal level of reliability is *necessary for validity,* but reliable results do not automatically lead to valid interpretations (Linn & Gronlund, 1995: 87–111, Genesee & Upshur, 1996: 57–62).

Taking as an example our hypothetical test of IL vocabulary knowledge (the child selects a graphic representation among a set of choices in response to the interviewer's verbal prompt), an advantage of this kind of assessment measure is that it tends to be free of one kind of unreliability: problems associated with examiner judgment (i.e. accurately and consistently marking the child's responses as correct or incorrect) are reduced to a minimum. Therefore, in this case, this kind of reliability would be high, by itself a positive feature of the test. However, the results (which again in this respect will tend to be highly consistent) may not provide the information that the teacher needs. If the objective of the evaluation is to measure the child's ability to perform complex, higher-level, comprehension tasks, or to be able to use the IL in culturally appropriate ways in different social settings, then the fact that the results are reliable in this case provides us with information that is of only limited usefulness (although as we suggested in point (2) in the discussion of validity above, the information is of limited usefulness to a degree). A moment's reflection will suggest that it is even possible to measure the wrong thing (e.g. a skill that is irrelevant to the purpose of the assessment) in a very consistent way. This, in fact, is what often occurs in the assessment of indigenous students' language proficiency.

On the other hand, an example of unreliability would be the following. An interview-type evaluation of grammatical competence is administered to a child speaker of an indigenous language where responses are marked as either grammatically correct or unacceptable. In this case the examiner speaks one of the various regional dialects of the language, is unfamiliar with the others that the students in school speak, and the test instructions provide vague guidelines that happen to correspond only to his dialect.

In an attempt to judge the acceptability of the children's responses a certain number that sound "foreign" to the examiner (but are actually grammatical) may be marked "unacceptable," and others that belong to the same category are marked "correct." Further complicating the situation, among the children's responses that are actually ungrammatical, the examiner will mark some as "correct" because he understands, more or less, the child's intention. Others that are equally ungrammatical, but that sound unfamiliar, are marked "unacceptable." Thus, the lack of consistency in marking makes any subsequent analysis of the results extremely difficult, and valid interpretations would not be possible.

A similar problem with reliability, related to dialectal variation, could arise in an assessment of vocabulary knowledge. The child listens to the stimulus word and points to one of four illustrations. Significant variations in pronunciation and actual differences in what things are called in the respective dialects will introduce an element of inconsistency in children's scores, making the results less reliable. Remember, this kind of unforeseen factor that affects the degree to which responses are marked in a systematic way does not affect reliability in an all-or-nothing way, but rather it affects reliability to a certain degree.

Perhaps the examiner is conscious of this dilemma and proceeds to design a more "open-ended" measure of vocabulary: scenes from everyday life in the community are displayed to the child and all responses are recorded, even those that are unfamiliar to the examiner. This procedure will eliminate the source of the dialect-related inconsistency, but may introduce another that the more "closed-ended" method had successfully controlled for. The more loquacious students (or those that are more talkative than others on this particular occasion) will produce a larger number of responses than the more reserved or more reflective students. As any experienced teacher can attest, this kind of variation in children's responses is unrelated to vocabulary knowledge *per se*.

As the reader may have already suspected, in regard to language assessment at least, it would be misleading to suggest that there is one set of methods that is appropriate for indigenous students, and another that is inappropriate. As is often the case, the teacher/evaluator must carefully weigh the relative merits and shortcomings of different approaches, and in a conscious way reflect upon the *trade-offs* between two or more alternatives. The most thorough and comprehensive approach (if in fact a more complete and representative sample is required) will involve combining contrasting methods that tend to *compensate* for each other's limitations.[31] This more responsible and professional perspective on language assessment is possible because we no longer reject, out of hand, one or another approach as "invalid" or "biased." Indeed this kind of more reflective approach allows us to pinpoint more successfully which aspects of an assessment tool are less useful, inappropriate, or completely irrelevant for the *purpose* at hand. In all cases, the primary overall purpose of assessment is to improve teaching and maximize learning, specifically in regard to day-to-day planning of instruction. Other objectives, often associated with standardized tests of academic achievement, are also of interest to classroom teachers and IL communities whose objective is to promote additive bilingualism. However, the results of these tests should be interpreted in an appropriate way, a point to which we will return later in this chapter.

Discrete Point and Integrative Assessment

At this point it will be helpful to introduce the distinction between discrete point and integrative approaches to language assessment. By definition, a discrete point test seeks to isolate one aspect of language proficiency for examination. For example, the examiner might be interested in the speaker's knowledge or control over some aspect of one subsystem of language in particular (pronunciation, grammar, vocabulary), or two or more, or even all of them. However the discrete point approach will consider each aspect of language proficiency (or linguistic subsystem) separately. For example, after reading a story, the teacher takes the opportunity to provide direct instruction on the formation of two common past tense forms utilized in the narrator's voice (simple past and past continuous). To assess whether students can use the forms correctly in their own writing, the teacher may choose to design a series of tasks that require one or another form:

Yesterday the boy was _____ the horse. (riding, rode, ride)
Last week we _____ working in town. (are, were)
The goats _____ the road when the girl stopped the traffic. (crossed, cross, crossing)

On the other hand integrative approaches attempt to assess language proficiency in a more holistic manner, presenting the student with a given task that will require the application, so to speak, of all of the discrete aspects of language, in an integrative way. As the term implies, performance will require a concurrent and integrated use of all of the categories of language ability. A mistaken, one-sided, view of this distinction often leads to the idea that only integrative measures of language can yield results from which valid interpretations are possible. However, we must keep in mind that claims about validity cannot be judged in the abstract, but rather in relation to a purpose, in this case we should ask: what aspect of language proficiency is the object of examination? For example, if the objective of the assessment is reading comprehension, generally, a kind of integrative measure might be more appropriate, because the ability to construct meaning beyond the sentence level and form a coherent mental representation of a text requires the simultaneous and integrative application of grammar and vocabulary knowledge, general world knowledge, and discourse competence. Discrete point tests would provide a more focused, or narrower, perspective on one or another aspect of reading comprehension.

As with other aspects of language assessment, the distinction between discrete point and integrative approaches is not a matter of clear-cut, mutually exclusive, categories. Any kind of language task that involves meaning, as in our example of the discrete point test of past tense, will be integrative to some degree; and assessment approaches that are considered to be holistic vary in the degree to which they call upon the entire array of linguistic and cognitive skills that are applied in typical naturally occurring language use. For example, a cloze task (see Chapter 6) is integrative to a degree; i.e. it calls upon grammatical and vocabulary knowledge in a holistic way at the sentence level primarily and to a certain degree at the level of the text as a whole. But at the level of the text as a whole a cloze test would be integrative to a lesser extent.

In the evaluation of IL proficiency, sometimes measures of the more integrative type may be preferred for a number of reasons: (1) widespread dialectical variation makes reliable scoring of discrete point grammatical or

---

Voices 7 (Quechua)

Manas imatapas yachaniñachu atrasus kayky; huk umawansi umaykuta kutichinqaku.
(They say that we can't know anything, that we are backwardness itself, that they will exchange our heads for better ones.)

Pichqa pachak hukman papakunam waytachkan chay ñawikipa mana aypanan qori tuta, qollqi punchao allpapa. Chaymi ñutquy, chaymi sonqoy.
(Five hundred kinds of potatoes grow where your eyes don't reach, in the golden night, the silver day, of the land. That's where my brains are, that's where my heart is.)

José María Arguedas (1938) quoted in Harrison (1989: 189)

---

vocabulary items difficult; (2) the lack of normalization and standardization; (3) a representative language database, including the study of the developmental stages of child language acquisition, may not be available. Integrative measures that focus on broader criteria (e.g. on higher-level language proficiencies such as coherence in story retelling) can side step, to a certain degree, issues such as grammatical acceptability. They also have the added advantage of being closely linked to classroom teaching objectives related to the development of academic language skills. However, in principle, discrete point assessment of specific language structures is as compatible with the indigenous language as it is with the national language. In this regard, one guideline to keep in mind when designing assessment tasks is the following: the higher-level, global, language proficiencies that depend more on conceptual knowledge and the ability to comprehend and manipulate different text patterns can be effectively evaluated by measures that are more integrative in nature. The more specific the information about the knowledge of particular language structures (correct use of pronouns, verb tense, vocabulary knowledge, etc.) that is needed, the more the test approaches the discrete point end of the continuum.

A Hypothetical Case Study: Misinterpreting Test Results

Let us take a closer look at a particular assessment instrument used for evaluating language dominance, *The Window Rock Oral Language Test: Navajo/English Bilingual Proficiency* (WROLT). This is one of the few tests that have actually been developed for indigenous language speakers. Before reviewing the WROLT, we want to re-emphasize what in this discussion is the basic idea that underlies validity. A test is not valid or invalid by itself; neither are the scores valid or invalid by themselves, but rather validity refers to the particular purpose that the results will hopefully serve. That is, the results (the information provided by the child's responses) must be interpreted correctly. For example, a bilingual assessment instrument such as the WROLT, which appears to provide consistent and generally reliable information (i.e. an adequate sample of children's language that can be scored and analyzed), is as good as the evaluator's interpretation of that same information.

Classroom teachers also observe their bilingual students' language performance on a daily basis, reflecting upon and recording information similar to the actual items on tests. Again, problems of validity arise when observations, informal assessments, and even direct student responses to interview items are *misinterpreted*. A hypothetical case of a normally developing six-year-old bilingual child (for example, dominant in English with partial grammatical competence in Navajo) will illustrate some of the errors that may arise when proficiency levels are assigned and students are categorized. The teacher must also always remember that children's scores represent a *sample* of what we assume is their true language proficiency; and that sample must be a fair representation of their true language proficiency (actual performance that would be observed outside the testing situation, and knowledge that exists but may not be observable in typical everyday language use).

In English, our bilingual child (we will call him Peter) easily manages conversations in concrete, face-to-face situations, with people he knows, and when topics are familiar. With immediate family and friends, when talking about something that is physically present, or about a topic for which all the conversants have complete background knowledge, Peter's verbal expression is fluent. Grammatical errors are those typical for the average six-year-old, and his vocabulary knowledge is adequate for his communicative needs. In other words, there is no evidence to suggest that he is different in any qualitative way from other native speakers of English in his knowledge of the basic grammatical patterns and access to the everyday vocabulary that characterize the native speaker. In the case of our hypothetical young bilingual, we will assume that he has not received any significant exposure to more abstract language use, such as stories from the oral tradition, or from regular visits to the library. As a first approximation, we could present a profile of Peter's language proficiency as follows:

(1) age-appropriate command of the basic linguistic structures of his primary language;
(2) typical for a child his age, normal development of *Basic Interpersonal Communication Skills** (BICS – which consists of (1) plus the social-interactive rules of conversational language use that all normal children learn in their speech community by a certain age); and
(3) he has yet to learn about and master the rudiments of CALP (topics are more abstract, comprehension requires mentally constructing coherent passages linking one sentence to another, higher degrees of metacognitive processing, more than one abstract category or concept manipulated at the same time, etc.).

Peter's parents and his kindergarten teacher may be concerned about his ability to do well in school, especially in beginning reading and writing, but we would still describe his language development as normal (even typical) for a child who has not been exposed to classroom-type discourse and literacy instruction. As such, ascribing to him a "deficit" of some kind would also be incorrect.

In fact, the problem of misinterpreting test results, as we will see in our hypothetical case, begins by failing to distinguish between BICS and CALP, or more precisely, the difference between knowledge of the language itself (age-appropriate grammar and vocabulary that is usually most clearly evidenced in a child's performance in BICS-type situations) and degrees of higher-order, academic-type, discourse abilities. The question that should be asked at the very beginning is: precisely upon which aspect of language proficiency will the evaluation shed some light? Often in language dominance assessment in schools, elements of both aspects (conversational ability and literacy-related academic discourse ability) are included in the items. Unless these two kinds of language ability are clearly distinguished, results can be difficult to interpret. The decision regarding which categories of language proficiency and which language skills schools should evaluate is one that belongs to educators and communities. However, in the area of language dominance testing we propose that, in the interpretation of results, aspects of BICS and CALP be separated so as to avoid the unnecessary and misleading label of "semilingual" that is often applied to large numbers of Indian students. Indeed, this characterization seems to be applied more often to speakers of indigenous languages than to other bilingual populations. For example, the label of semilingual is rarely used today to describe Spanish/English bilinguals in the United States, or French/English bilinguals in Canada.

Let us see how this might occur in the case of our six-year-old bilingual.

As in most language-dominance tests, the WROLT presents a series of illustrations for the child to interpret. In Part 1 (Auditory comprehension), most items involve concrete referents where the listener responds to the tester's description or question simply by pointing to the correct illustration: "Which one of these trucks can carry more things?" "Which lady has finished cooking her meal?" On the other hand, one item that may cause difficulties for Peter is the last question, which requires him to complete a short narrative: "Raymond and his father got up early one morning and went fishing. They caught some fish. Then they went home. What happened next?' Out of ten items, Peter will receive credit for nine if he misses this one. The next section, conversation, requires the evaluator to judge vocabulary, grammar, fluency, pronunciation, and comprehension, globally, on a five-point scale. In Peter's case, some of the criteria for *limited proficiency* (level 3 out of 5) might apply to his performance on the series of four illustrations that form part of a short narrative: "the respondent can name some of the common objects and recount the essentials of the story," "is able to construct sentences of simple subjects and predicates," and "gives responses consisting of single words or isolated phrases." "Fluency" (above level 3), on the other hand, is defined as the ability to "put words and sentences together into connected discourse" (Window Rock School District, 1981: 20). Peter will be able to attain "level 3," as would be expected of any normal six or seven year old. Level 4 and above, constructing "connected discourse," depends on experience with this kind of discourse; and he may not score high enough to receive credit for this level.

In assessing productive language abilities in young children, a common response to a series of story scenes is that the subject describes each scene in isolation from the others. This produces a discourse that actually turns out to be descriptively adequate with reference to each scene taken by itself, but lacks any apparent connection between one and another. Each utterance is grammatical, typically consisting of simple sentences or phrases, or even single-word responses. Here it is important to emphasize that single-word responses and "incomplete sentences" are often appropriate if the interaction between examiner and child begins to approximate natural conversation. More complex grammatical structures and discourse features that are normally in evidence in complete stories and connected discourse usually require the child to narrate the story independently. In this case, again, the six-year-old with no prior experience with extended, independently produced, discourse (as in stories) may respond by describing details he or she *sees* in one scene after another. However, the series of descriptions may not form a coherent "connected discourse." The use of "discourse markers" that link phrases and sentences to one another, and the more complex relationships between independent and dependent clauses (as called for in "level 3"), may not be in evidence.

The final section (part III – Association) requires the child to complete a series of analogies. Items are presented verbally without visual context support: "We're not going to look at any more pictures now. We're just going to talk. I'm going to tell you a very short story. But I will not tell you the end of the story." (Window Rock School District, 1981: 29).

Here the requirements of the task clearly cross over into the academic language domain: a grammatically correct response alone does not suffice. What is required is one that also makes explicit what semantic relationship exists among a set of words. In the items: "Birds fly, dogs _____" and "Mothers weave, children_____" the child is asked to apply context-reduced language abilities closely tied to school-related discourse, and it would not be surprising if our subject fails most of the items. Calculating the total score for parts I, II, and III, Peter might not surpass the cut-off for "limited proficiency" in English. The total score in Navajo (his weaker language) would be lower, suggesting the misleading interpretation of "semilingual." This conclusion is misleading because a significant number of items on the test for each language correspond to CALP-type discourse abilities.

However, if the child's responses are grammatical, even if they consist largely of incomplete sentences (especially in conversational-type interviews) there is no reason to suspect that linguistic development is not normal, or is "limited." In at least one of his languages, our hypothetical bilingual subject has acquired age-appropriate conversational proficiency (grammatical knowledge of the language, basic vocabulary, and the social/ interactive language-use rules associated with BICS).

If it can be demonstrated that in neither language the bilingual child has acquired BICS-type abilities, *and* he or she reveals notably immature grammatical competence in both, we might be able to make the case for gathering more information to explore the possibility of "double limited proficiency" or semilingualism. In this instance there would be cause to suspect a disability of some kind; and an exhaustive assessment battery to determine possible special educational needs would be called for. In all cases we proceed cautiously, avoiding premature categorization. As we pointed out in Chapter 4, in any interview involving cross-cultural communication (even when, for example, both the interviewer and interviewee are native speakers of the indigenous language), we can never underestimate the intervening effects of cultural expectations on the part of the child. Lack of response in situations of adult/child verbal interaction does not necessarily indicate lack of knowledge. In situations where culturally determined conversational norms do not coincide, we must be even more uncertain about interpretations of "uncooperative" behavior, non-reciprocal responses, or no response at all. To be consistent, it is preferable to reserve the term "deficit" for true impairments and disabilities, the kind that are inherent or intrinsic in some way. To reiterate, late-developing CALP-type abilities (as in the case of our hypothetical six-year-old WROLT interviewee) do not by themselves indicate a deficit, because the only factor responsible for this difference may be relevant experience, a factor that is easily remedied.

When categorizing a child as semilingual, teachers may be referring to academic language skills; that is, in a particular case, there is no suspicion that the child's basic conversational skills are deficient. Rather, the student (e.g. after two or three years in school) has not learned about academic language proficiency; the student cannot read in either language, and has difficulty comprehending academic discourse in classroom settings (the teacher's lecture or lengthy explanation of an abstract concept, oral stories that are not familiar, complex procedures presented verbally, etc.). Since in general we consider these skills as part of "language proficiency," especially in school, and as long as the distinction between BICS and CALP is kept in mind, one could perhaps, in this sense, apply the concept of less-than-adequate "proficiency" in both languages. This hypothetical student is at risk academically, and may indeed not catch up to grade level expectations in the area of literacy-related language skills, just as is the case with large numbers of monolingual English speaking students, for example. Thus, this kind of achievement gap is not peculiar to bilingual students, and perhaps the characterization of "semilingual" is not really very useful in this case either. For example, what would we call monolingual students who lack the same set of school-related language proficiencies? Sometimes labels and categories are helpful (e.g. in the case where a child's legal right to receive certain kinds of special educational service is specified). Often, however, it is better to *describe the circumstances* that a learner encounters in school and identify areas in which literacy-related academic discourse ability has not developed adequately, and avoid labels and categories.

A final possibility would be the case of the child IL speaker who under the pressure of the forces of the national language begins to lose his or her primary language at a very rapid rate, while the NL is replacing it, again under the unfavorable circumstances of subtractive bilingualism (see the discussion of the additive/subtractive distinction in Chapter 5). Perhaps during this transitional period, as IL grammatical structures are being lost, the child is still struggling to learn the new NL grammar, which in turn continues for a period of time to be incomplete. However, the most likely outcome here is that the second language continues to develop, sooner or later achieving completeness (i.e. in regard to basic grammatical knowledge, conversational vocabulary, and the social rules of face-to-face verbal interaction). Here, a kind of "semilingualism" would be a strictly transitory phenomenon (McLaughlin *et al.*, 1995); although the attentive reader will take note here of another possible negative consequence of subtractive bilingualism. Such a period of rapid loss of competence in L1, during which time L2 development may be slow to take over the important comprehension functions in school, is hardly the most favorable condition for learning CALP and learning how to read and write.

Measuring Language Dominance

The following procedure we would recommend as an informal teacher-made screening for language dominance. It is important to emphasize here that educators need not wait for test developers to provide them with formal, standardized, language assessments. For most situations of indigenous language bilingualism, the design and elaboration of such instruments is not something that we can expect to be completed in the near future. Meanwhile, teachers must plan language instruction based on the most accurate needs-assessment that they can design themselves.

In the case of language dominance, in fact, a reasonably reliable estimate can be made in the absence of a previous study of community-wide language use patterns and levels of IL linguistic development among child native speakers. The reason for this is that, instead of attempting to devise a scale of proficiency for each language, as in our example above of a norm-referenced test, a comparison can be made simply between the two languages for each individual child. The relevant comparison would not be with levels of proficiency of other IL speakers (as in norm-referenced testing) but rather "internally": an approximate measure is taken to determine which language, the NL or the IL, is the primary or dominant language. Depending on the degree of IL loss in the community, a number of children will receive scores that indicate a balanced proficiency, or equivalent competence in IL and NL. Again, for a teacher-made informal screening measure, there would be no need to determine levels of proficiency in each language, only a balance score as in the example given at the beginning of this chapter.

Bilingual interview

A "bilingual interview" similar to one that has been piloted in Mexico in three separate bilingual indigenous communities (Francis, 1992a) could include three sections and an optional fourth:

(1) greetings and conversation;
(2) vocabulary knowledge;
(3) description of story scenes or episodes in interview format, and
(4) independent oral narrative based on the illustrations in (3).

For each section, a parallel set of illustrations is available to elicit language from the child: one set for a hypothetically monolingual NL evaluator, and another for a hypothetically monolingual IL evaluator. That is, two persons interview the child: the first playing the NL speaker role (at no point during the interview resorting to the IL or providing translation) and vice versa. Each examiner simply prefaces the interview by requesting that the child answer in either IL or NL, as the case may be.

(1) Greetings and conversation

So that the interview conforms as closely as possible to the cultural expectations of a normal verbal interchange, the conversation should open with a customary greeting, an appropriate "how are you" question, and a brief series of questions that an adult normally would ask a child. That is, in this section the examiner's queries should represent *genuine questions*, as opposed to "known information" questions. For example: (1) The child is asked his or her name only if, from the perspective of the child, *the examiner does not know it*: (2) Do you have any brothers? Any sisters? (3) How many? (4) Who is the oldest (or biggest)? (5) Who is the youngest? In this section, as the nature of the questions indicates, one word replies are appropriate and acceptable, as are non-verbal responses that show comprehension, or responses given in the other language than that spoken by the examiner. Notations to this effect can be useful for subsequent analysis.

(2) Vocabulary knowledge

To avoid the dilemma of dialectical variation, a set of open-ended items can be prepared consisting of everyday scenes that would normally elicit a broad sample of words that are part of the child's everyday productive vocabulary. Here, the examiner accepts all words the child offers, regardless of whether they appear to correspond to the scene. In fact the child should be encouraged, as part of the standard instructions, to name objects that do not appear in the illustrations, but that one would have the occasion to observe (or others that are "hidden" from view, etc.). Refer to Appendix E for sample plates of: Market, Front Yard/Exterior of House, Interior of House, and Corn Field. A simple pilot test of the plates can be applied to ensure that the two scenes that will correspond to the IL indeed are equivalent to the NL pair in the number of lexical items they in fact elicit.

Again, all verbal responses are simply recorded regardless of the language to which they belong. If reminding the child to answer in the indigenous language is considered important (for example in situations where conversing with a teacher, at school, in the IL is viewed as unusual or contrary to language-use norms) this should be done a *standard* number of times, for example only once.

(3) Description of story scenes

After explaining to the child that the next series of illustrations represents a story (refer to Appendix E for sample narrative strips) request that he or she examine the series and think about the events that are represented (remember to indicate to the child that the series of pictures actually does "tell a story"). For each scene, formulate two questions that are sufficiently open-ended to elicit a complete grammatical phrase or sentence. (e.g. What is the lady doing here? In this picture, why is everyone getting dressed? The food has been prepared, what will happen next? Why is the man walking with a cane? Tell me; what happened here? What will the girl do now?). As in all sections, the examiner speaks only the assigned language, and accepts and records all responses regardless of the language chosen by the child for his or her response.

Marking the responses can be based on global criteria of comprehensibility. For example, if the child's response is comprehensible, and indicates that he or she in fact understands the question, the item can be marked acceptable. Complex grammatical analyses of responses would be unnecessary: if the utterance contains age-appropriate local *errors** that do not affect meaning, the response is marked as acceptable. For major, *global errors*, that make the response impossible to interpret by a native speaker of the language, it is marked as unacceptable.

Since all responses are recorded on the answer sheet, the examiner can also indicate in which language the child produced the answer: IL or NL – the same language of that part of the interview, or did the child switch? If the basic grammatical pattern of the response corresponds to the IL, for example, codeswitching or borrowed vocabulary would not affect scoring or be counted as an error.

(4) Independent oral narrative

As an optional assessment, the examiner may request the narration of the same story without the interactive support of the dialogue. The child narrates independently from beginning to end his or her version of the events. This application provides interesting data regarding children's ability to produce a comprehensible and complete rendition of the story that they had the opportunity to think about in the previous section. However, the examiner must keep in mind that what is being evaluated in the independent narration section may begin to cross over the line into the domain of academic, literacy-related, language proficiency (depending again on which aspects of the child's narration will be selected for evaluation). Performance among native-speaking kindergartners and first graders with a complete command of age-appropriate grammatical structures will vary considerably. The actual variation in scores assigned will vary depending upon the criteria that the examiner sets for degrees of story completeness and coherence, for example, if this aspect of the child's storytelling ability is selected.

Scoring

The next step would consist of simply counting the total number of responses produced in the IL and the NL, separately, in sections 1 and 2, and then proceeding to compare the results. Separately again, count the total number of acceptable responses to Section 3 that were given in each language and compare – do not combine the scores of the four sections into a single total score. Similarly for the optional section 4, one possible scoring scheme would count the number of comprehensible sentences (up to a maximum of 5 points), and then proceed to assign a global score (0–5) for coherence. Again, since students' responses are not being compared either to an arbitrary cut-off score, or to the performance of other students, the interpretation is greatly facilitated. The total number of IL responses is simply compared to the total number of NL responses, *separately, for each section*. If an index, or balance score, is necessary or desirable, the following calculation (based on the child's responses to Section 1 and Section 3) can provide a rating for summary purposes:

$$\frac{\text{Total number of responses in IL - Total number of responses in NL}}{\text{Total number of responses in IL + Total number of responses in NL}} \times 100 = \text{Percentage}$$

For sections (1) and (3) only, the resulting index or percentage can be applied to a scale (Table 4) that reflects relative dominance or balance between the two languages (Francis, 1992a, following Baetens-Beardsmore, 1986)

For purposes of estimating the relative balance between IL and NL, section 2 (Vocabulary) is not comparable to section 1 and 3 because codeswitching and borrowing vary widely. Also, children's conscious awareness of whether a given vocabulary item "belongs" to the IL or the NL involves complex judgments related to factors largely independent of vocabulary knowledge *per se*. And remember, since section 4 may involve aspects of CALP, it is conceivable that a normally developing six- or seven-

Table 4 Language dominance scale

Language dominance scale	*Range of scores*
Monolingual IL, or NL beginner (level 1)	+75 to +100
Primary language IL, NL learner (level 2 or 3)	+10 to +74
Balanced bilingual (equivalent competence in IL and NL)	+9 to -9
Primary language NL, IL learner (level 2 or 3)	-10 to -74
Monolingual NL, or IL beginner (level 1)	75 to -100

year-old may score low in both languages. This last finding would not by itself indicate language deficit or language impairment.

For classroom assessment purposes, however, the above calculations would normally be unnecessary; in most cases, simply by visually inspecting the balance between the scores for each section, an approximate estimate of language dominance can be made.[32] And in this regard it is important to re-emphasize that all estimates of language proficiency are subject to the effect of uncontrolled factors that result in greater or lesser degrees of error. Since some amount of *error of measurement* is inevitable, teachers must interpret all scores, ratings, judgments, and even anecdotal notations as tentative to one degree or another, and subject, in all cases, to confirmation by other measures. First and foremost among these are the daily verbal interaction with students, and the ongoing informal language assessment that should always be an integral part of instruction.

Evaluating Literacy-Related Language Skills

In Chapter 6 we discussed cloze and retelling from the point of view of literacy instruction, tasks that lend themselves ideally to small group cooperative learning activities in the second language. Modified to be suitable for individual problem solving, both can serve the purposes of assessment of academic language proficiency. Both cloze and retelling offer a number of advantages:

(1) Since they are teacher-made instruments, content can be controlled to closely correspond to the actual language-learning objective of the day.

(2) In the case of cloze and *written* retelling, design and administration

does not require high levels of proficiency in the IL (in a pinch, even a non-speaker can construct the assessment with minimal consultation from an intermediate or advanced-level speaker). For example, the construction of a multiple-choice or sentence fill-in test of reading comprehension calls for at least near-native proficiency. Of course, scoring and interpretation of student responses does require IL proficiency;

(3)   Generally corresponding to the integrative category, the focus of evaluation is on higher-order literacy skills; Valdez Pierce and O'Malley (1992) classify them under the broad category of "performance assessment." In all cases, cloze and retelling involve working with complete texts (or substantial, integrated, passages) that oblige the student to apply *text-level* comprehension strategies.

Cloze as an assessment tool

Follow the procedure outlined in Chapter 6 (Table 3 – Being creative with cloze) for test construction; instead of solution in small groups, students solve the cloze individually. Here, bilingual teachers, with IL proficiency, can modify the task to:

(1)   target certain grammatical categories when deleting words (e.g. discourse connectors, content words, prepositions, different verb forms);

(2)   adjust the level of scaffolding; i.e. control the amount of information to be processed (e.g. segmenting the text into shorter passages, offering a list of correct options plus distracters)

Scoring and interpretation always require high levels of grammatical and vocabulary knowledge, whether or not students were supplied with a list of choices that included the exact words deleted. Each response can be evaluated for compatibility with the text as a whole, leaving open the possibility for acceptable synonyms, acceptable student responses not displayed on the list of options, and partially correct responses of various degrees (e.g. compatible within the sentence, not compatible with previous text information) (MacLean & d'Anglejan, 1986).

Another scoring option that simply marks the responses for exact word replacement can provide useful assessment data in regard to the overall class profile: level of general text difficulty of reading material for the group as a whole, or to determine how heterogeneous the class is in regard to IL reading skills. However, the exact-word scoring method is not recommended for interpreting individual results, and *never for purposes of providing corrective feedback* to students (responses that are grammatically acceptable and meaningful can be, and often are, scored "incorrect").

These two methods of scoring correspond to an important distinction regarding the aspect of language assessment that is related to processing and analysis of results: qualitative and quantitative. As in our first scoring option for cloze, students' responses are *interpreted* (each one individually) according to a given set of criteria that the evaluator determines as important, for example, knowledge of grammar patterns and meaning. Most importantly, *qualitative* scoring allows the evaluator to discern degrees of acceptability, identify error patterns, and even examine the learners' working hypotheses of how the second language functions based on their present stage of partial knowledge. This approach offers obvious advantages for the assessment of IL proficiency where standardized forms have never been established, or where it may be difficult to distinguish between a dialectical variation and a clearly non-native, learner-language, form that no native speaker of the language would produce.

From the above, the reader may already have anticipated one of the advantages of *quantitative* scoring: marking responses is free of the dilemmas of judgment, and does not demand vast amounts of time and concentrated effort or special training. A well designed multiple choice test, for example, can be scored quickly and accurately. However, what is gained in time and a certain type of reliability is lost in nuance, and usefulness in regard to some of the purposes of assessment. First and foremost among these is the opportunity for teachers and learners to examine and reflect upon their current performance and develop a consciousness about their own learning strategies: where they were last month, and to take note of the discrepancy between current knowledge and the next stage of learning. But again, as with most of the other considerations we have discussed in this chapter, the scoring method will be dictated by the kind of information that is required and the purpose of the assessment. Practical considerations of time, expertise, material resources, will determine if the objectives are attainable, and will counsel educators and researchers regarding how important certain kinds of information really are. Davies (1990: 24–26) discusses "Practical constraints," as do Genesee and Upshur (1996: 56–57).

As with any language assessment that requires a special kind of task or procedure (potentially unfamiliar to students in all situations, or unfamiliar to them in the context of using the indigenous language for this purpose), special care should always be taken to pre-teach the procedure itself. For example, cloze involves supplying, in writing, missing words to make a text meaningful, re-integrating it, so to speak. This specific task is not what readers do when they process text in typical silent reading situations; and one could imagine perhaps that children presented with a test of this kind in the IL (already the "marked" language for literacy) may find the procedure even more anomalous. Thus, providing for previous experience and practice in the rules of the new game is essential for reliable results and valid interpretations. Our own studies of the applicability of cloze to IL literacy contexts have confirmed that there is no impediment to its use when the above conditions are met (Francis, 1997, 1999a, 2000c). To re-emphasize an idea that we have been arguing for in previous chapters: nothing about indigenous languages as such or about any particular speech community precludes the application of instructional methods or assessment approaches that have demonstrated their efficacy in non-indigenous contexts.

Retelling

Retelling, or re-narration in the case of stories, can take two forms: oral or written; both forms are considered a highly integrative measure of language proficiency. The task also combines receptive (comprehension) and expressive skills, although it is the latter that is directly evaluated. Contrary to appearances, as we pointed out in Chapter 6, a re-narration test involves much more than rote memory. In fact, rating or scoring a re-narration will have to take into account the wide range of student reconstructions that may be generated from the same model. The model, however, plays an important role in providing students with a schema from which to mentally assemble their own version. Depending on the circumstances (language proficiency in the IL, age, grade level, availability of written material), the combination of what kind of model to present and the requested response format will reflect the objectives of the assessment: (1) oral presentation – oral re-narration, (2) oral – written, (3) written – oral, (4) written – written. In addition, any of the models can be presented accompanied by a series of graphics that provides visual context support.

In the case of oral retelling, if the analysis requires anything beyond the most global and holistic-type rating, an audiotape version will be necessary for reference. For most teachers, who will rely on the one-time, un-taped, oral retellings, a concise, structured, rating scale that clearly indicates the distinctions among the different categories will help minimize problems of unreliable scoring. Each category should reflect a specific set of skills or clearly identifiable characteristics of different levels of proficiency. For example, the following (Table 5) could serve as an eight-point rating scale for evaluating the re-narration of a traditional story that contains the standard components of a setting, a problem or

Table 5 Evaluating the re-narration of a story

Level 0	No response or unconnected comments unrelated to the story
Level 1	Attempt at describing one or another episode or character trait – but no structure
Level 2	A purely descriptive sequence, not connected temporally
Level 3	An action sequence - descriptive sequence is temporally connected, but not causally linked
Level 4	An action sequence with temporal and causal links
Level 5	An action sequence with temporal and causal links that also mentions a problem or goal-oriented behavior
Level 6	Level 5 plus the complicating factor of an obstacle that obstructs the solution to the problem
Level 7	Level 6 with an ending

Adapted from Stein & Albro (1997)

need, a journey or a struggle by the protagonist, attempt at solution, complication, and resolution.

Another option (among others, depending on the actual structure of the story model) would be: score for levels 0–6, and assign one point to any level above level 1 if the retelling includes an ending. For alternative evaluation schemas, most of which require a written version or transcription, consider "Retelling stories as a diagnostic tool" (Mandel-Morrow, 1988). Whatever kind of rating scale is chosen, however, the levels or components to which credit is assigned must both reflect the broad structural patterns of the model story, and allow for enough flexibility to accommodate acceptable and coherent variations that students will produce.

Especially with written re-narrations, the evaluator can combine an integrative approach to eliciting the actual language sample with a discrete point method of scoring specific language structures. Apart from global, text-level, coherence, the student's re-narration can be examined for anything from sound pattern transfers from L1 to L2 (evidenced in spelling), to error patterns that reflect partial grammatical knowledge.

If the objective of the evaluation is strictly the ability to recite or compose a coherent discourse in general (as opposed to knowledge of, and proficiency in, the various expository text patterns) then re-narration of traditional stories offers two distinct advantages:

(1) The cultural content can be controlled to ensure that unfamiliar concepts and problems, characters' motivations that seem unusual or inexplicable, or contexts that are completely alien, do not confound the results. For example, with young children, we would not be sure if a score of 1 or 2 on our story structure rating scale is the result of an inability to construct a coherent story, or an inability to interpret a model *coherently* because the cultural context is uncommon or peculiar.

(2) Along the same lines, the choice of the narrative genre minimizes the uncertainty regarding access to a recognizable *text* pattern. Again, in the case of a non-narrative pattern, would a score of 1 or 2 result from the inability to produce a discourse for which the corresponding schema exists? Or would it result simply from the fact that the child has not had contact with the discourse pattern in question, and indeed does not possess a mental representation of it?

Narrative happens to be the most universally available of all text patterns. However this, in turn, implies an important limitation from the point of view of the assessment of higher-order language proficiencies: being also the first to emerge, developmentally, proficiency in the re-narration of stories does not automatically extend to the more abstract and complex expository patterns. However, discourse ability in the area of narrative certainly bodes well for subsequent development along these lines.[33]

Other methods of eliciting writing samples (or an oral, monologue-type, discourse) involve one or another degree of spontaneity, or where the weight of planning the composition is shifted, to a greater degree, onto the student's shoulders. Without a completely formed model to work from, the narrator must attend to the task of constructing the story with fewer cues regarding structure, setting, theme, etc. That is, the starting point, framework or "scaffold," assigned by the evaluator has fewer cues or readily available patterns to immediately begin the construction of a coherent discourse. For example, the model may consist of a series of graphics, representing the episodes of the story, as in our example of the oral interview for language dominance. Again, since the task of mentally constructing an appropriate model is now added to the evaluation, we could say that the aspect of academic language proficiency that is being measured is now more complex, more cognitively demanding. This of course is an option that is always open to the evaluator. However, the more we reduce the scaffolding that structures the language task in question, the more we run the risk of coming up empty handed, and not being sure why. All extended language expression (written composition, oral narrative, etc.) begins with a purpose, is driven by a goal, and is organized around a framework of some kind. Often we ask students to execute such tasks without ensuring that they have had the opportunity to plan, and to search their long-term memory for the appropriate schemas. These schemas fall into two categories: (1) content – *what* the text or story will be about, and (2) organizational structure (what we have called genre) – which pattern corresponds to this content, or in other words, *how* it will go together? In assessment terms, we might not be sure what exactly the failure to produce a coherent story, for example, can be attributed to. Among the different possibilities a few come to mind:

(1) a temporary absence of ideas;
(2) an appropriate schema exists, but the ability to "call it up" is blocked in some way;
(3) the student has stored a wealth of experiences, and there is no shortage of ideas, but they are not organized, because he or she has yet to learn how. For very predictable stories, his or her everyday experiential knowledge suffices, for more complex, less predictable, stories, the lack of an organizing schema may result in an inability to assemble the parts into an integrated whole;
(4) the story schema exists at a rudimentary level that allows for comprehension, but it is not sufficiently advanced for purposes of producing a narrative independently.

Performance and portfolio approaches

We have described a few examples of performance-type measures: retelling for evaluating comprehension, and the oral language interview. Under this category of individually administered assessments would fall oral reading miscue analysis (Goodman, 1995); if scored with open-ended criteria, it would also lend itself well to situations where the IL has yet to establish standardized forms. The portfolio, as a self-referenced approach (in contrast to norm-referenced and criterion-referenced), offers language learners the opportunity to actively reflect on their own language development. This metacognitive aspect of active self-assessment that portfolios are particularly suited for (Genesee & Upshur, 1996) compliments our emphasis on developing in children a reflective and analytical stance toward reading comprehension, writing, learning the L2 grammar system, and oral expression in the academic discourse mode. As such it becomes a more integral part of learning and teaching, through which students can intervene more directly in the process of actually setting objectives for their own and their community's language development. Since IL revitalization can only proceed on the basis of an autonomous self-management of language planning on the community level, the IL bilingual teacher will want to promote this same consciousness within his or her classroom. As is common to other evaluations of a non-test type, gathering representative exemplars of student performance is not restricted by language (IL or NL), is not complicated by problems of translation of items or tasks to the IL for example, and does not depend on learners understanding or being pre-taught procedures that are peculiar to a test format or are "contrived" to a high degree. Valdéz-Pierce and O'Malley (1992), and Valencia *et al.* (1994) describe special applications of portfolios to literacy learning.

At the same time, our recommendation in this area parallels that to which we alluded in discussing other assessment techniques. The decisive advantages that make any method particularly effective for one kind of measurement or reflective activity also suggest one or another limitation when the object of scrutiny presents a different array of features. As with other kinds of tool, the more useful for broader or varied purposes it may be, the less effective it will be for a particular specialized task, and vice versa. On the other hand, the better an implement becomes for cutting through one kind of material, the more its aptness for a different kind of material is diminished. Language teachers need access to a broad range of instruments to accommodate the multiplicity of learning objectives and learning contexts that present themselves in so many different ways.

A note on interpreting standardized tests

A critical assessment of standardized, norm-referenced, testing goes far beyond the scope of this book; and within the domain of evaluating proficiency in the IL, few standardized measures are available. However, in closing the discussion on the topic of this chapter we believe it is important to emphasize two important practical considerations:

(1)   Standardized, norm-referenced, tests of academic achievement have a specific purpose and usefulness. Since scores that the test provides reflect comparisons with other students selected from the national population as a whole, results are generally not appropriate guideposts for day-to-day planning of instruction.

(2)   On the other hand, in the case of indigenous students who are learning the NL as a second language, norm-referenced measures can offer valuable information. In comparison to a national sample of native speakers of English, for example, beginning English language learners will on average score lower on language-related measures, indicating

to the teacher the gap that still remains to be closed. As such, a norm-referenced comparison can provide evidence for L2 learners' progress, with a clear ultimate objective in sight and periodic indicators of the *rate* of progress toward the goal. However, as very broad and "superficial" measures (as they must be by design), the usefulness of norm-referenced evaluations for other purposes is limited. This "trade-off" applies as well to the norm-referenced type tests of IL proficiency described at the beginning of the chapter. Collier and Thomas (1998) offer a more complete discussion of the appropriate use and correct interpretation of different kinds of standardized tests.

The teaching of indigenous languages necessarily implies evaluating the different aspects of learners' language proficiency: for planning purposes prior to instruction, integrated into daily teaching activities during instruction for the purpose of setting interim objectives, and as a means of measuring the ultimate effectiveness of instruction. In fact, recent attempts at developing language assessment instruments for indigenous languages reflect the seriousness with which communities view the questions of children's literacy learning, of their advances in L2 proficiency, and the development of their ancestral language. Different kinds of assessment will be useful and appropriate for the wide range of purposes tied to these three closely related objectives.

Additional reading

A basic text is Linn and Gronlund's *Measurement and Assessment in Testing* (1995), now in its seventh edition. The authors do not address the special circumstances of second language assessment; however, the chapters on Validity and Reliability are among the most complete and comprehensive (and non-technical) in the literature.

Classroom-based evaluation in Second Language Education, by Genesee and Upshur (1996) narrows the discussion of assessment to consider the second language learner, maintaining a good balance between Evaluating without tests (section II) and Evaluating with tests (section III).

A more comprehensive teacher's guide to evaluating second language students is *Instructional Assessment: An Integrative Approach to Evaluating Student Performance* by Fradd Homlar and McGee (1994). With the classroom teacher in mind, Chapters 3, 5 ,6 are replete with workable and practical procedures. A good follow-up to our discussion of semilingualism is one of the central concerns of indigenous teachers: Differentiating Language Disorders from the Effects of Limited Opportunities for Language Learning (Chapter 4).

For a short course on language assessment, try *Classroom Testing* by Heaton (1991). Chapters 3–6 are categorized by skill area testing: Listening Skills, Speaking, Reading, Writing, with examples and sample items for each.

Chapter 8

Conclusion: A Teaching Model for Realizing the Potential of Additive Bilingualism

As is evident from our brief review in Chapters 2 and 3 of the first experiments in bilingual education and biliteracy (beginning in the 16th Century), the present situation of extreme inequality between indigenous languages and national languages is simply a matter of social and political circumstance. Certainly it is an accident of history that the indigenous languages of the Americas came to be excluded so completely from the domains of schooling and literacy. As is widely recognized today, it is a bilingual approach that is capable of realizing the full potential of language and literacy development for child second language learners. Drawing on this resource of bilingualism would reap the same kind of benefit for indigenous children learning an L2; no scientific evidence or supposition leads us to doubt this conclusion. The most effective language program will be one that finds support among all the points of the "continuum of biliteracy" (Hornberger, 1998).

Our own recent series of experiments on the degree and extent of access to higher-order discourse abilities when bilingual indigenous children attempt solutions to literacy tasks in their IL has confirmed that any transient or circumstantial limitation to this access is either unessential, or readily surmountable. For a review of the findings: see Francis (2000c) and Francis and Nieto Andrade (2000). This leads us to our concluding discussion, recapitulating for one last time the proposals we have been arguing for in the last seven chapters – the applicability to indigenous language bilingualism of two central aspects of Cummins' Common Underlying Proficiency model, recently summarized in its most complete presentation (Cummins, 2000):

(1) A core of higher-order discourse proficiencies, plus general analytical abilities related to *metalinguistic awareness**, forms part of the fundamental underpinning of literacy and other categories of language-related academic achievement. This Cognitive Academic Language Proficiency (CALP) begins to develop in early childhood through contact and experi-

ence with uses of language that make use of these proficiencies and abilities. CALP develops in a different way and independently in many respects from both universal grammatical competence in children's primary language, and their ability to use their primary language for interpersonal communication of the everyday, situation-embedded, conversational kind (another kind of *discourse** proficiency).

(2) These academic-type discourse proficiencies and analytical abilities, since they are not strictly "language bound," are at the disposal of the bilingual child (ready for use) in any language in which he or she attains a certain minimum level of mastery of grammar and vocabulary.

Both of these concepts have a particular relevance to indigenous language bilingualism. While we still do not understand completely and precisely how they apply, there is no reason to suppose that indigenous languages or their speech communities are somehow exempt from the general principles; future research and classroom practice will suggest new and interesting refinements to the theory. Adapting slightly Cummins' double-iceberg schema (Figure 4), we can see how both indigenous language (IL) and national language (NL), benefiting from an additive-type bilingual development, draw from the Common Underlying Proficiency, which they both "share." The language proficiencies of the cognitive/academic kind, not "bound" to either NL or IL, are "available" from this common store for application to problem-solving tasks, "shared" again between NL and IL. CALP develops by means of a diverse set of contributions and through different mediums and modalities, to mention just a few that come to mind that are related to literacy:

- problem-solving activity that children engage in of progressively more advanced levels of abstraction and complexity,
- solving problems posed in L2 learning to which conscious learning strategies have to be applied (unlike L1 acquisition in early childhood),
- similarly, solving problems posed in the higher-order domains of language proficiency such as literacy (in both L1 and L2),
- learning specific comprehension strategies that are called upon for specific kinds of discourse and text,
- applying orthographic principles to a second language, or an IL that has not previously been used for literacy,
- extending comprehension strategies to oral tradition performances, poetry, oratory, and ceremonial discourse,
- listening to instructions and learning procedures of increasing levels of sophistication.

As should be evident, the double-iceberg model shows itself to be particularly illustrative of another general principle of IL bilingualism and bilingual teaching: it depicts clearly how the contributions of both IL and NL form part of students' developing CUP, how the "origin" of one or another particular proficiency is secondary in the sense that it is now available for tasks performed in either language. In any case, because mental representations undergo internal restructuring and recombination, "inputs" from one or another "source" do not remain stored in their original form. Contributions to a common store of cognitive and academic-type proficiencies through the medium of IL or NL, through written or oral modality, etc., build a shared network of proficiencies that can be tapped for oral or written language tasks, in NL or IL. Again, it is the notion of a CUP (a model of language use that maintains a distinction between language itself, the sectors labeled IL and NL in Figure 4, on the one hand, and the discourse knowledge system and analytical abilities on the other) that most clearly leads us to recognize the role that indigenous languages can play in children's development. The way that the related distinction between CALP and conversational discourse is framed further clarifies the rationale for a bilingual approach, even when only one of the languages of instruction can draw on resources of an extensive literary tradition. CALP is not synonymous with written discourse or literacy (narrowly defined), and does not emerge from experience with writing alone, as we confirmed in Chapter 4.

Figure 4 suggests a cross-cultural pedagogy based on what we have repeatedly referred to in the previous chapters as general principles of language learning. These are subject to limitations, constraints, circumstances, and opportunities that social conditions impose (or facilitate),

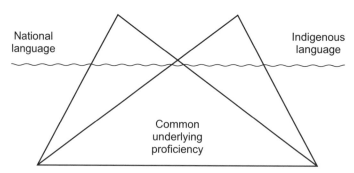

Figure 4 The common underlying proficiency model

Source: Cummins, 1991

none of which however alters in any substantive way the general principles. In reference to indigenous languages we could begin (a fitting conclusion for the final chapter) with a short list:

(1) The unfolding of first language acquisition in early childhood follows universal milestones, based on internal developmental mechanisms independent of culture, an inheritance that cannot be altered by the most unequal relations of power and opportunity between IL and NL. Good news for teachers: proceed with absolute confidence that each new generation of first graders consists of competent speakers of at least one language, whose knowledge of the basic grammatical systems in either IL or NL, or both, is commensurate with that of any other child from any other culture, and has not been diminished by possible unfavorable external factors.

(2) All existing IL cultures and speech communities have at their disposal a body of higher-order genres and discourses that not only are compatible with school-based academic language proficiency, but stand as an ample reservoir from which to draw resources for language and literacy development. This universal principle holds both for communities with an available collection of written works, and for those whose oral tradition has not been transcribed.

(3) No indigenous language is inapt for literacy, and no set of sociolinguistic restrictions or imbalances definitively blocks bilingual children's access (for example through the medium of the IL) to CALP-type discourse strategies.

(4) Learning a second language (NL or IL) proceeds under more favorable conditions if children's bilingual development is additive. Readers will recognize this concept as another version of the well-known maxim: L2 learning is favored by high levels of proficiency in the child's L1. Young children benefit in many ways from early exposure to a L2, obviating any across-the-board restriction on or delay in the teaching of second languages in school. The child's knowledge of an IL presents no more of an "obstacle" to learning the NL and developing advanced literacy skills than would knowledge of another European language.

The CUP model's focus on school-related language abilities helps us understand what should be ideally the proper balance between IL and NL in relation to the academic content of the curriculum. As we pointed out in Chapter 5, it would be a mistake to create a division of labor between the languages such that only the NL is reserved for the higher-level academic objectives. Such a compartmentalization would in effect simply reproduce the *subtractive diglossia* of society (refer to Chapter 3) – the NL being the displacer, the IL the subtracted. Outside of school, when the languages are separated according to function (or according to the perception of what their function should be), this kind of diglossia usually reinforces the imposed limitations on the IL. Within the school, since planning decisions can be more easily implemented, allocation of the languages for instructional purposes can actually have, in the long run, the opposite effect.

Thus, it is of central importance that the indigenous language be integrated into the curriculum in a way that promotes the development of literacy and academic language proficiency. The greater part of our suggestions in Chapters 4, 5, and 6 follow from this starting point: putting the IL at the service of fostering higher-order academic skills; and as we were able to see, this necessary goal is entirely realizable. If, for example, IL-medium teaching comes to be viewed (e.g. by parents) as taking instructional resources and time away from the core academic objectives tied to literacy, support for a bilingual approach will be seriously undermined. If this perception in fact corresponds to an actual shift away from these objectives, then the rationale itself for an indigenous language component to the curriculum is called into question, rightfully so. Specifically, this could occur in both kinds of program model: (1) IL revitalization/enrichment for NL-dominant children, and (2) bilingual instruction for IL-dominant second language learners of the NL. In the first kind of program model, IL-medium instruction might come to be restricted to frequent daily activities focused on learning elementary grammar and vocabulary in isolation from content instruction; or IL teaching might be integrated into highly context-embedded and cognitively undemanding content unrelated to literacy development for a significant percentage of the weekly teaching schedule. In the second type of program ((2) – IL speakers who are second language learners of the NL), since published literacy materials in the IL are scarce or non-existent, the indigenous language might be (by default and lack of teacher initiative) relegated to activities that do not promote literacy learning. Both of these scenarios represent a serious degrading of children's opportunities for academic language development and an implicit downgrading of expectations for achievement. To re-emphasize, if a way cannot be found to integrate the IL into literacy-oriented language teaching, the very justification for its inclusion into the school program is weakened. At most, the IL would be reserved for non-academic or highly context-embedded classroom activities outside the sphere of cognitively challenging CALP-type learning.

All this leads us to another argument in favor of a bilingual policy in school. Additive bilingual development is the most favorable platform from which to achieve the goal of high levels of proficiency in the national language and full command of literacy in the national language, an objective that cannot be neglected today in any indigenous community school. This argument has perhaps fallen into disfavor in some circles because of its unfortunate association with narrowly conceived early-exit transitional bilingual models. But, especially for the second language learner of the NL, this objective must remain among those of highest priority. Use of the IL in literacy teaching, more critically at the initial stages, can make an important contribution. From a common-sense perspective, classroom verbal interaction that is engaging because it includes a language the child understands, will be more conducive to integrating children into all aspects of school life and school work, and *keeping children in school* – by all accounts the most effective means of promoting the learning of the national language. A similarly favorable atmosphere is created for the NL-speaking indigenous child when the language of his or her community is no longer excluded from the classroom. This common-sense approach (which also happens to be correct) applies as well to the different components of school life and schoolwork, beginning with learning how to read and write. In other words, putting the IL at the service of fostering higher-order academic language proficiencies entails building a stronger base of CALP-related abilities, which in turn prepares the way for a more effective and complete learning of the national language. Fortunately, this objective is entirely compatible with that of indigenous language revitalization, if this, in fact, is or comes to be a consciously assumed goal of the IL-speaking community itself.

In the coming years, the integration of indigenous communities into the broader economy and social fabric of each nation state, region, and beyond into the international networks of trade, labor markets, and cultural and technological interchange will only accelerate. IL-bilingual education and indigenous education generally will need to rise to the challenge and be up to the formidable tasks that these historically-necessary integrative tendencies will place at the doorstep of every school. Our view flows from the idea that the most effective and democratic integration, in regard to literacy and schooling, would proceed on the basis of a pluralistic language policy. A curriculum plan that keeps its sights fixed on the development of academic language proficiencies, based on the CUP model or one like it, at this point at least, offers teachers one means to maintain high standards and expectations for bilingual children and second language learners, a hedge against the paternalism that continues to plague much of the field of Indian education.

Our anonymous informant in Voices 8 makes a pointed reference to his linguistic inheritance, asking rhetorically, "… left to me as a gift, how can you take it away from me?" One aspect of this inheritance is truly inalien-

Voices 8 (Náhuatl)

Upon being queried on his stance ("are you sad or are you happy") toward the eventual disappearance of Náhuatl in his town:

Neh, solamente nimoyolcocoa para ce, para ce demanda, para ce reclamaroz ce cosa ihuaxca, quihtoz, "Pos xiquitta onechcuilihqueh in noaxnoh." "Pos ¿quen omitzcuilihqueh?" Pos ihquin huan ihquin, moyolcocoa nialmahtzin por tleca onechquixtilih. Tla non notexihca tlahtol onechmotlaocolilihtehuac … Noherencia, ¿quen tinechquix-tiliz?

(As for me, I am sad only for such a, such a petition, such a demand, for one who would claim something of his own, who will say, "Well look, they took away my donkey." "Well, how did they take it away from you?" Well like this and like this, one is sad in his soul because they took it from me. Surely it is the language of my inheritance which was left to me as a gift … As for my inheritance, how will you take it away from me?)

Anonymous informant from Tlaxcala, interviewed by Hill & Hill (1986: 86–87)[34]

able in the most absolute sense, and corresponds to the endowment that each generation of children receives from its ancestors, that equips them to acquire a mother tongue. This uniquely human capacity cannot be taken away, being so robust that only the most extreme sort of depravation or trauma can diminish it or obstruct its course of development. The capacity for second language learning is also universally available, perhaps in a different way. Indigenous languages have a legitimate and vindicatable claim on these endowments, and, in the context of a democratic educational language policy, can make an important contribution to child development in many ways.

Chapter 9
Resources for Schools and Communities

Books

Cantoni, Gina (ed.) (1996) *Stabilizing Indigenous Languages*. Flagstaff, AZ: Northern Arizona University. On WWW at http://www.ncbe.gwu.edu/miscpubs/stabilize/index.htm.
   The proceedings of the 1994 and 1995 Stabilizing Indigenous Languages Symposiums with sections on needs and rationale, language policy, families and communities, and education.
Fishman, Joshua (1991) *Reversing Language Shift: Empirical and Theoretical Foundations of Assistance to Threatened Languages*. Clevedon, UK: Multilingual Matters.
   A classic study of endangered language revitalization efforts worldwide, along with Fishman's graded intergenerational disruption scale for threatened languages.
Fishman, Joshua (ed.) (2000) *Can Threatened Languages be Saved? Reversing Language Shift, Revisited: A 21st Century Perspective*. Clevedon, UK: Multilingual Matters.
   Provides practical case studies and a theoretical discussion drawing on research from five continents. Advances the idea of a collective pursuit of "reversing language shift" as part of the broader goal of cultural democracy.
Hinton, Leanne (1994) *Flutes of Fire: Essays on California Indian Languages*. Berkeley, CA: Heyday Books.
   Includes information on California Indian languages and the Master Apprentice Model for passing on endangered indigenous languages in an advanced stage of erosion from elders to young adults.
Hornberger, Nancy (ed.) (1997) *Indigenous Literacies in the Americas: Language Planning From the Bottom Up*. Berlin: Mouton de Gruyter.
   Chapters from both North America and Latin America on language planning issues related to the role of writing.
McLaughlin, Daniel (1992) *When Literacy Empowers: Navajo Language in Print*. Albuquerque: University of New Mexico Press.
   A study of the Rock Point community in the Navajo Nation, with a report on how the community's bilingual school teaches reading and writing in the Navajo language, and insights into the community's attitude towards Navajo/English bilingual education.
Reyhner, Jon (ed.) (1997) *Teaching Indigenous Languages*. Flagstaff, AZ: Northern Arizona University. At http://jan.ucc.nau.edu/~jar/TIL_Contents.html.
   Twenty-five papers from the 1997 Stabilizing Indigenous Languages Symposium on the role of tribal organizations and schools, teacher education, curriculum and materials development, language attitudes and promotion, and general overviews related to bilingual indigenous education.

Reyhner, Jon (ed.) (1992) *Teaching American Indian Students*. Norman: University of Oklahoma Press.
Information on the historical suppression of American Indian languages in schools and recent efforts at using American Indian languages in bilingual education programs. Foreword by US Senator Ben Nighthorse Campbell.
Reyhner, Jon (ed.) (1990) *Effective Language Education Practices and Native Language Survival* (Proceedings of the 9th annual NALI Institute). Choctaw, OK: Native American Language Issues. (ERIC Document Reproduction Service No. ED 342 512). On WWW at http://jan.ucc.nau.edu/~jar/NALI_Contents.html.
Eleven papers from the 1989 Native American Language Issues conference, including papers on Rock Point Community School and Maori adult language revitalization efforts.
Reyhner, Jon, Cantoni, Gina, St. Clair, Robert and Yazzie, Evangeline Parsons (eds) (1999) *Revitalizing Indigenous Languages*. Flagstaff, AZ: Northern Arizona University. On WWW at http://jan.ucc.nau.edu/~jar/RIL_Contents.html.
Eleven papers describing language revitalization efforts and the use of writing and technology. The introduction provides an overview of current thinking on American Indian language revitalization efforts.
Rosier, Paul and Wayne Holm (1980) *The Rock Point Experience: A Longitudinal Study of a Navajo School Program (Saad Naaki Bee Na'nitin)*. Papers in Applied Linguistics, Bilingual Series: 8. Washington, DC: Center for Applied Linguistics.
Classic study of a Navajo community school with a successful K-2 Navajo/English bilingual program.
Silver, Shirley and Wick, R. Miller (1997) American Indian languages: Cultural and Social contexts. Tucson: University of Arizona Press.
A general introduction to American Indian languages and linguistics, as well as the cultural and social domains in which these languages are spoken.
St Clair, Robert N. and Leap, William (eds) (1982) *Language Renewal among American Indian Tribes: Issues, Problems, and Prospects*. Rosslyn, VA: National Clearing house for Bilingual Education.
Twelve essays focusing on sociopolitical factors, language renewal projects, and linguistics.

Programs and Organizations

American Indian Languages Development Institute (AILDI)
An annual summer training institute for indigenous language teachers and activists. A 20-year history of AILDI can be found on WWW at http://jan.ucc.nau.edu/~jar/TIL_9.html. For more information contact: AILDI Coordinator, University of Arizona, Department of Language, Reading and Culture, PO Box 210069, Tucson, AZ 85721-0069. Phone +1 (520) 621-1068. Website: http://w3.arizona.edu/~aisp/AILDI2002.html
Centro de Investigaciones y Estudios Superiores en Antropología Social (CIESAS)
Publications, research, and advanced study in Mexico, including a *Maestría en lingüística indoamericana*. CIESAS, Juárez 87, Tlalpan 14000, México DF.E-mail: ciejuare@juarez.ciesas.edu.mx. Website: http://www.ciesas.edu.mx.
Endangered Language Fund (ELF)
ELF supports with small grants efforts by Native communities or scholars to do work related to endangered language, including preserving the texts of a Native

culture, developing videotaped language instruction, and "generation skipping" language learning. For more information contact: ELF, Department of linguistics, Yale University, PO Box 208236, New Haven, CT 06520-8236. E-mail: elf@haskins.yale.edu . Website: http://sapir.ling.yale.edu/~elf/index.html.

Foundation for Endangered Languages (FEL)
FEL publishes a newsletter, holds annual meetings, and supports efforts to preserve indigenous languages with small grants. For more information contact: FEL, Batheaston Villa, 172 Bailbrook Lane, Bath BA1 7AA, England. E-mail: nostler@chibcha.demon.co.uk. Website at: http://www.bris.ac.uk/Depts/Philosophy/CTLL/FEL/.

Indigenous Language Institute (ILI)
Collaborates with indigenous communities to revitalize the languages of the original inhabitants of the Americas. For more information contact: ILI, 560 Montezuma Ave. 201-A, Santa Fe, NM 87501. Phone +1 (505) 820-0316. E-mail: ipola@ipola.org. Website: http://www.ipola.org/.

The Society for the Study of the Indigenous Languages of the Americas (SSILA)
An international organization founded in 1981 with a focus on American Indian linguistics. Membership is open to anyone interested in the scientific study of the languages of the Native peoples of Americas. Publishes a quarterly newsletter and a monthly e-mail bulletin. For more information contact: SSILA, P.O. Box 555, Arcata, CA 95518. Phone +1 (707) 826-4324. E-mail: gollav@axe.humboldt.edu. Website: http://www.ssila.org.

Special Issues of Journals

The Winter 1988 (Vol. 47, #4) issue of *Human Organization* was largely devoted to indigenous languages. Individual articles of interest include William L. Leap's "Indian Language Renewal" (pp. 283–291) and Elizabeth A. Brandt's "Applied Linguistics, Anthropology and American Indian Language Renewal" (pp. 322–329).

Freeland, Jane (1999) Maintaining and Revitalizing Indigenous Languages in Latin America: State Planning vs. Grassroots Initiatives. *International Journal of Bilingual Education and Bilingualism* 2 (3).

Hamel, Rainer Enrique (ed.) (1993) Políticas del Lenguaje en América Latina. *Iztapalapa: Revista de Ciencias Sociales y Humanidades* N. 29.
Articles and discussion on language planning from: Mexico, Brazil, Peru, Uruguay and Quebec.

Henze, Rosemary and Davis, Kathryn (eds) (March 1999) Authenticity and Identity: Lessons from Indigenous Language Education. *Anthropology and Education* 30 (1).
Five articles discuss lessons from Alaska, California, and Hawaii.

Kirkness, Verna J. (ed.) (1989) Language is a gift from the Creator. *Canadian Journal of Native Education* 16 (2).
Includes five papers on "language renewal in the broad sense, ranging from the issue-oriented to the practical, and from placing the focus on the historical context and the national situation, to the case study of one community's approach to language renewal."

Lipka, Jerry and Stairs, Arlene (eds) (Winter 1994) Negotiating the Culture of Indigenous Schools. *Peabody Journal of Education* 69 (2).
Includes twelve articles on indigenous education, including a report by Lucille J. Watahomigie and Teresa L. McCarty on "Bilingual/bicultural Education at Peach Springs [Arizona]: A Hualapai Way of Schooling."
McCarty, Teresa L. and Zepeda, Ofelia (Winter 1995) Indigenous Language Education and Literacy. *Bilingual Research Journal* 19 (1). On WWW at http://www.ncbe.gwu.edu/miscpubs/nabe/brj/v19n1/index.htm.
Contains articles in four sections. Part 1: Conceptualizing indigenous literacies, Part 2: The status of indigenous languages in the US and Canada, Part 3: Models of indigenous language education, and Part 4: Synthesis and discussion: The Role of indigenous communities in language and culture renewal.
McCarty, Teresa L. and Zepeda, Ofelia (eds) (1998) Indigenous Language Use and Change in the Americas. *International Journal of the Sociology of Language* 132.
Eighteen articles assessing the status and role of indigenous languages in the Americas, with a special focus on the ideological and social forces that influence their use and vitality; a number of the contributors are speakers of the languages in question.
McCarty, Teresa L.; Watahomigie, Lucille J. and Yamamoto, Akira Y. (eds) (1999) Reversing Language Shift in Indigenous America: Collaborations and Views from the Field. *Practicing Anthropology* 21 (2).
Nine articles focusing on how applied linguists can work with indigenous communities to reverse language shift.
Fuentes, Nancy (1999) *Profiles of Native Language Education Programs: A Source Book for Arkansas, Louisiana, New Mexico, Oklahoma, and Texas.* Austin, TX: Southwest Educational Development Laboratory. On WWW at http://www.sedl.org/pubs/lc05/.
Describes 24 programs and gives teachers and other educators who serve American Indian students in the Southwest access to organizations and resources that can help them meet the educational needs Native students.

Internet Indexes, Sites, and Discussion Groups

Centro Cultural Abya-yala
Publishes *Pueblos indígenas y educación*, and a wide selection of books on bilingual education, indigenous languages and cultures, Networks and information from Mexico, Central America, and South America. At http://www.abyayala.org/.

Endangered-Languages-L Forum
An e-mail list with associated web pages providing a worldwide communications vehicle and a central electronic archive for anyone working on or interested in the study and documentation of endangered languages. At http:/ /carmen.murdoch.edu.au/lists/endangered-languages-l/.

Index of Native American Language Resources on the Internet
Comprehensive index of Native American language web sites. At http://www.hanksville.org/NAresources/indices/NAlanguage.html.

Language Policy
Extensive information on language policy issues in the United States, including those related to endangered Native American Languages, maintained by author

Jim Crawford. Website at http://ourworld.compuserve.com/homepages/ JWCRAWFORD/.

Native American Languages Links
Linguist Wayne Lehman maintains this site with more than 80 useful links to web sites on specific American Indian languages. At http://www.mcn.net/~wleman/langlinks.htm.

Native American Language Resources
The University of Southern California's Center for Multilingual, Multicultural Research site with links to sites and full text publications concerning Native American languages. At http://www-rcf.usc.edu/~cmmr/Native_American.html#language resources.

Teaching Indigenous Languages
Extensive collection of full text materials on revitalizing and teaching American Indian languages and links to other related resources and organizations. At http://jan.ucc.nau.edu/~jar/TIL.html.

Ethnologue:Languages of the World
Country index, maps, language families, listing of 6,800 "main languages," site search for 41,000 alternate names and dialects. At http://www.ethnologue.com/web.asp.

Videotapes

E Ola Ka 'Olelo Hawai'i. (1997). 'Aha Punana Leo (PO Box 1265 Kea'au, HI 96749). Tells the story of more than a century of decline of the Hawaiian language. and the revival of its use in the past two decades; features interviews, archival footage, and visits to Hawaiian language immersion classrooms. Describes how Hawaiian language activists learned about Maori "language nest" immersion preschools, implemented them in Hawaii, and then expanded Hawaiian language immersion instruction into the public schools of Hawaii. In Hawaiian with English subtitles, 28 minutes. $12.95 [2002 USA prices]. E-mail: hauoli@leoki.uhh.hawaii.edu. At: http://www.ahapunanaleo.org/index.html.

Online Articles, Chapters and Papers

Bennett, Ruth, Mattz, Pam, Jackson, Silish and Cambell, Harold. (1999) *Coyote Steals Daylight*, with "Writing activities at six levels with sample Hupa language activities built around the story." Website at http://jan.ucc.nau.edu/~jar/RIL_Contents.html.

Crawford, James (1998) Endangered Native American Languages: What is to be Done, and Why? In Thomas Ricento and Barbara Burnaby (eds.), *Language and Politics in the U.S. and Canada: Myths and Realities.* Mahwah, NJ: Lawrence Erlbaum. http://ourworld.compuserve.com/homepages/JWCRAWFORD/brj.htm.

Guidelines for Strengthening Indigenous Languages. Adopted by the Assembly of Alaska Native Educators, Anchorage, Alaska, February 6, 2001. Includes guidelines for Native elders, parents, language learners, Native communities and organizations, educators, schools, education agencies, linguists, and media producers.) On WWW at http://www.ankn.uaf.edu/standards/Language.html.

McCarty, Teresa L. (1994) Bilingual education policy and the Empowerment of American Indian Communities. *The Journal of Educational Issues of Language Minority Students* 14, 23-42. E-mail: akindler@ncbe.gwu.edu. At http:// www.ncbe.gwu.edu/miscpubs/jeilms/vol14/mccarty.htm.

McCarty, Teresa L. and Dick, Galena Sells (1996) Mother Tongue Literacy and Language Renewal: The Case of Navajo. Literacy online: Proceedings of the 1996 World Conference on Literacy. At http://www.literacyonline.org/products/ili/webdocs/ilproc/ilprocMc.htm.

Organización de Estados Iberoamericanos (OEI) (1997). Educación Bilingüe Intercultural, *Revista Iberoamericana de Educación*, N. 13.At http:// www.oei.org.co/oeivirt/rie13.htm#Intro.

Reyhner, Jon (1993) American Indian Language Policy and School Success. *The Journal of Educational Issues of Language Minority Students* 12, Special Issue III, 35–59. At http://jan.ucc.nau.edu/~jar/BOISE.html.

Reyhner, Jon and Tennant, Edward (1995) Maintaining and Renewing Native Languages. *Bilingual Research Journal* 19 (2), 279–304. On WWW at http:// jan.ucc.nau.edu/~jar/Main.html.

Other Materials

Kipp, Darell (2000) *Encouragement, Guidance, Insights and Lessons Learned from Native Language Activists Developing Their Own Tribal Language Programs*.
     Pamphlet presenting "a conversation with twelve visiting Native American Language Activists providing guidance and an analysis of some of the essentials for developing immersion language programs." Available for $10.00 [2002 USA price] from the Piegan Institute, PO Box 909, 308 Popimi Street, Browning, MT 59417. E-mail: piegan@3rivers.net.

Notes

Study Guide to the Notes

We invite the reader to peruse the following notes to the chapters, both incorporating them into the discussion from which they sprang forth, and separately, depending on specific interests and inclinations toward further study (to this end they are grouped by chapter). To facilitate this selective reading we recommend the following groupings, which in some cases might even serve as a short (very short) invitation to the allied discipline in question. For the reader so inclined, looking back to the respective Chapters and forward to the Glossary will suggest other points of reflection and leads for more in-depth research. For this purpose, the citations, found in all three sections, will be especially helpful for further reading.

Language policy, language planning, and sociolinguistics

Notes: 1, 2, 4, 5, 6, 8, 9, 10, 17, 23, 25 and 34

Glossary terms: autochthonous, boundaries, diglossia, ethnolinguistic vitality, integration, language shift, lingua franca, prestige, vernacular.

Language learning and basic linguistic concepts

Notes: 3, 13, 14, 18, 19, 20, 21, 22, 24, 26, 27, 28, 33, and Glossary terms: alphabetic, borrowing, codeswitching, coherence, cohesion, competence, dialect, discourse, dominant language, dramatic irony, error, expository text, extralinguistic information, formulaic structures, foreshadowing, genre, grammatical, input, lexical, literary, metalinguistic awareness, metaphor, parallelism, phonology, pragmatic system, prosody, redundancy, register, reported speech, representational speech, schema, situational factors, syntax, text.

Bilingual program models and literacy

Notes: 11, 12, 15, 16, 33 and Glossary terms: concurrent translation, context embedded, immersion, scaffolding.

Language assessment:

Notes: 31, 32

Chapter 1

1. The accuracy of official estimates of the number of Indian language speakers varies from country to country. Usually drawn from the periodic national census statistics, the process itself of locating and interviewing respondents during door-to-door canvassing is plagued with numerous obstacles. Unlike information regarding access to electricity and housing characteristics that can be directly observed, estimates of language proficiency depend on the ability or willingness of the respondent to supply the relevant data and the interviewer's ability to interpret responses. For example, false negative responses to the questions "Do you speak an indigenous language? What indigenous language do you speak?" (item 6, second section, on the Mexican census questionnaire) are possible for a number of reasons: the respondent is non-Spanish speaking, purposeful denial in the presence of a representative of the federal government, prestige value of Spanish mono-lingualism in many communities, uncertainty regarding how to report partial or incomplete competence, infrequent or domain specific use of the indigenous language. Local and national underestimates of language proficiency are probably common. For example, in Mexico, while the 1990 Census counts 5,282,347 IL Speakers (7.5% of the total population above 5 years of age), a national survey by the General Directorate of Indigenous Education (DGEI), drawn from its own commu-nity surveys the previous year, had estimated over 9,400,000 (DGEI, 1990a).

The Pame language was brought to the attention of the census bureau in 1910 with 1673 speakers, apparently declining to 71 in 1921. From 1930 to 1970 the Pame "disappeared" from the national count, only to "reappear" in 1980 with 5,649 (Citarella, 1990).

Census results in the United States have been repeatedly criticized by language minority groups for undercounting non-English speakers, especially among immi-grant groups. The inability or unwillingness on the part of census takers to gain access to remote or economically depressed areas is cited as a contributing factor.

2. Our proposals for early L2 teaching stems in part from the widespread rejection, on the part of parents, of bilingual educational programs that postpone instruction in the national language for an extended period during the early primary grades. In fact, parent's objections have turned out to be consistent (at least in part) with recent developments in dual language curriculum design (Krashen, 1991, 1996). Early introduction of the second language in bilingual education, especially in context-embedded subject areas that involve lower-level cognitive demands, is beneficial for language development in general, and for learning the NL, in the long term, the principal language of schooling.

Attempting to exclude the national language from certain domains in the hope of "substituting" the IL and artificially "normalizing" its use in this way is as uto-pian as it is impractical, given the high levels of bilingualism and national language monolingualism. Similarly utopian is the notion that preserving, in some way, sec-tors of indigenous language monolingualism will serve the ends of language preservation. While the participation in family and community networks of non-English and non-Spanish speakers represents a source of both integrative and in-strumental motivation for a majority of the community to maintain their bilingual proficiency, indigenous language monolingualism cannot be a policy and planning objective (even implicitly, as in the acceptance or justification of levels of incom-plete learning of English or Spanish in school) for any age group, least of all school-age children. In this regard, the formulation "imposition of the national language," while perhaps valid in historical terms (although even here it lacks precision in many cases), today, is flatly anachronistic.

3. Researchers of language development have been especially interested in the relationship between first language (L1) acquisition and second language (L2) learning. In regard to the acquisition of native speaker competence, a key feature is that of *completeness*. First language acquisition follows remarkably regular developmental patterns and stages for all languages. They are *universal*; that is, independent of cultural and social factors. By a certain age all normally developing children evidence a command of the grammatical system of their first language that sets them apart, even to the casual observer, from most speakers of the same language who have learned it later in life as an L2. The child's first language competence evidences completeness in the sense that nothing in his or her performance would lead another native speaker of the same language to surmise that he or she is not also a native speaker. This is possible as early as five or six years of age. While L1 acquisition is universally successful and complete (in the sense described above), L2 learners typically evidence a wide range of achievement, even after many years of intense study and extensive use in natural communicative contexts. Many learners attain levels that are native or near-native (e.g. in the case of elementary school-age immigrants to the United States, or American Indian children learning English as a second language). By adolescence many of these bilingual young people are barely distinguishable from native speakers of English. Most L2 learners, however, fall short to some degree or another of complete mastery (in particular in regard to the subsystems of syntax, morphology, and phonology). Again, the wide variation in ultimate attainment of language competence in L2 learning is not evident in L1 acquisition. In part, in an effort to explain this phenomenon, linguists have posited the existence of a Language Acquisition Device (LAD), product of the human genetic endowment. In other terms, in their L1 children have access to a Universal Grammar (UG), a set of innately given principles that places necessary constraints on the acquisition process such that the complex structures of the language can develop. Precisely, these constraints (i.e. limiting the options among all the possible rules that logically could be constructed by the child) make it possible for the cognitively immature child to quickly build up the different interacting systems in the absence of any kind of systematic instruction.

In some cultures, researchers have identified and described a certain style of parental verbal interaction termed "motherese" that purportedly helps children learn the grammatical system of their mother tongue. Interestingly, some of the features of "motherese" are similar to what L2 learners find useful in the modifications that their teachers make during instruction in the target language; see Chapter 4: Language Learner Sensitive Discourse. However, cross-cultural research, particularly in "non-Western" societies has strongly suggested that the motherese style is not universal; for example, Crago *et al.* (1997) provide an extensive report on Inuit family interaction patterns that depart in some important respects from the motherese schema. Nevertheless, children from all cultures attain complete grammatical competence in their mother tongue roughly on the same developmental schedule.

Children are capable of this achievement even without access to complete information about the full complexity of the linguistic system they end up knowing. For example, the grammatical knowledge that children attain apparently does not require what is called "negative evidence." That is, exposure to positive examples alone is sufficient to set the appropriate parameters for the first language. But interestingly, for older L2 learner's exposure to positive examples may not be sufficient. In fact L2 learners may require, or greatly benefit from, focusing on incorrect patterns and comparing them to the target language patterns, something again that the young child does not need in order to acquire his or her L1 (Gregg, 1996). For an introduction to the research, read Scovel (1998) and Ellis (1997). A very readable survey, especially regarding the debate on *critical periods* in L1 and L2, can also be found in Bialystok and Hakuta (1994); and for a more advanced treatment of the theoretical foundations of second language learning, read Sharwood-Smith (1994), and on the concept of completeness, Schachter (1988). For an introduction to the study of the science of language and language development, a good place to begin is Akmajian *et al.* (1995), Chomsky (1999), Pinker (1999) and Fromkin (2000).

Some evidence suggests that access to the LAD, or UG, may begin to diminish with age, or perhaps begin to diminish during the period in which the development of the L1 is approaching completeness. For example, students who learn an L2 in immersion programs, even after as many as eight years of extensive contact with the target language, typically fall far short of native-speaker levels in grammatical competence (involving various structures that native speakers of the target language acquire in early childhood) when they use the L2 in communicative settings in the classroom. Refer to the findings of the many investigations of French immersion in Canada which is to date, by far the most comprehensive body of research in the area of L2 learning (Harley *et al.*, 1990; LeBlanc, 1992; Pawley, 1985; Genesee, 1987; Lapkin *et al.*, 1990; Danesi 1991 and Hammerly, 1987, to mention only a few), and for immersion teaching internationally, refer to Johnson and Swain (1997).

Thus, early exposure to the indigenous language in family networks, as well as in more formal, community-level settings, such as preschool programs, probably represents an indispensable ingredient in IL development. See the reports on Maori "language nests" in New Zealand (Shafer, 1988; J King, 2001), and Hawaiian preschool immersion (Slaughter, 1997). While children still can count on full access to the LAD and the principles of UG, special measures would be appropriate to provide input in the indigenous language, even under circumstances where the national language appears to be dominant and the child seems to prefer English or Spanish. For example, anecdotal reports from Mexico (Francis, 1997, 2000b) suggest the possibility that many children entering primary school, seemingly monolingual in Spanish, also have acquired much of the indigenous language during the preschool years, which in turn begins to evidence a surprisingly rapid development, in school, thanks to contact with children whose productive ability in the IL is complete. The existence of a critical period in L1 acquisition and the possibility of a continued access to UG in L2 learning is still the subject of lively debate among language development researchers (Singleton & Lengyel, 1995; Birdsong, 1999; Gass, 2000; DeKeyser 2000). In any case, even if the theories of a LAD or a UG turn out not to apply, the bilingual child with significant contact with the IL before the age of six stands a better chance to develop an additive form of bilingualism in later childhood than does the indigenous preschooler (already dominant in the NL) with only minimal contact with the IL. This is also K. King's (2001) conclusion based on research on prospects for language revitalization of Quechua in Ecuador.

Chapter 2

4. In part owing to the difficulty of defining indigenous identity in a country that is over 90% mestizo (Mexico), official estimates of the Indian population now resort to a single criterion: ability to speak a language of American origin (along with, of course, self-identification as Indian). Previous to the 1960 census, attempts were made to broaden the criteria for "indigenous" taking into account descriptors related to "racial" features, ethnic identity, dietary customs, traditional dress, and even categories of footwear, or their absence. None of these solutions to the problem of under-counting the indigenous population turned out to be workable (i.e. capable of providing demographers with a reliable method). For a discussion, see Valdés and Menéndez (1987).

5. Demographic factors often override all other considerations regarding the vitality of a minority language. Where conditions arise (or are created) such that a speech community is prevented from reproducing, the language can enter into rapid decline even without being displaced by another language. An example from recent European history would be that of Yiddish where the physical extermination of a significant percentage of its speakers shifted, within the space of a few years, the language to a stage of advanced decline. Indigenous languages in the United States whose only speakers are beyond childbearing age face the same virtually inevitable outcome.

The contact with diseases of European origin, beginning in the 15th century, did indeed produce such a precipitous demographic/linguistic collapse for a number of language groups. In Mesoamerica, the impact of the epidemics was nothing short of catastrophic. Gruzinski (1991) estimated that in central Mexico alone, of a pre-Columbian population of more than 25 million, less than 17 million remained ten years after the conquest of the Aztecs. By 1548 the population had fallen to 6.3 million, by 1568 to 2.6, and by 1585 to 1.9 million. For a fuller discussion of the various investigations of the population decline in Latin America, see Whitmore (1992), whose own demographic study of the Central Basin of Mexico roughly coincides with the above estimate, but projects a somewhat less abrupt decline for Mesoamerica as a whole.

However today, demographic factors appear to actually be working in favor of the reproduction of many IL-speaking populations. For example, a recent front-page article published in the *Arizona Daily Sun* (March 2, 1999) reported a dramatic 75% reduction in infant mortality among Navajos since 1974 (from 27.1 deaths per 1000 births to 7.9 in 1996). In Mexico, two contrary, or contrasting, tendencies may contribute to a reversal in the relative decline of indigenous language speakers. In the general population during the last 30 years, the growth rate has declined to less than 2% – down from 3.5%, from an average of 6 or 7 children per family to 2 or 3 (Aguilar Camín, 1998). Large families, however, are still the norm in most indigenous communities. In previous generations, high infant mortality rates canceled out any potential demographic advantage vis-à-vis the national language. The major expansion of the national health care system to rural areas during this same period has resulted in equally significant changes in survival rates among potential indigenous language speakers.

6. Succeeding Peruvian governments turned out to be less enthusiastic about the status of Quechua as an official language of the nation, and the ambitious proposals for bilingual education were implemented only on a very limited scale. The current constitutional provision represents a retreat from the 1975 decrees. However, the influence of the new ethnolinguistic consciousness on official policy is still evident in the formal recognition of indigenous language rights; "recognition" extended to Aymara, at the same time as the scope of the "official use" of Quechua was reduced. Articles 83 and 35 read:

> Spanish is the official language of the Republic. Quechua and Aymara are also in official use in the zones and the form which the law establishes. The other aboriginal languages as well make up the cultural patrimony of the nation.

The State promotes the study and knowledge of the aboriginal languages. It guarantees the right of Quechua, Aymara and other communities to receive primary education in their own tongue. (*Constitución política del Perú* 1982, quoted in Hornberger 1989)

Chapter 3

7. It should be noted in passing that in Latin America the term *America* refers, collectively, to all the countries of the Western Hemisphere. Also, *Indian*, is equally Pan-American both historically and in current usage. In this regard, the international scope of our discussion is highlighted in very concrete terms by the situation of a number of language communities that straddle the US–Mexican border, in the Arizona/Sonora region alone, adding a geopolitical dimension to the cultural and linguistic *nepantla* ("in-between-ness") of the Tohono O'odham, Cocopah, and Yaqui.

8. Here, the use of the term *national language* refers to the language of wider communication, or "common" language of the nation-state. For the purposes of this discussion the special, and unique, circumstances of Paraguay and Guaraní (the country's "national language") should be considered separately; see Corvalán (1988) for a historical and current sociolinguistic survey. In any case, our use of the term "national" implies no juridical category, although in various Latin American countries the language of wider communication enjoys "official" status. In the United States, some states have attempted to impose English as the only "official language." However, the federal Constitution has never recognized, and probably never will, any language as official. A case in point for the futility of legally restricting language use is the state with the highest number of IL speakers, Arizona (Navajo approximately 120,000, Hopi 5,264, Tohono O'odham 11,819, Apache 12,693, Havasupai-Hualapai-Yavapai 1007, Yaqui 406, Cocopah 321, Mohave 234, Maricopa 181) (Grimes, 1999). In 1988, a narrow majority approved an English-only referendum, only to be overturned ten years later as unconstitutional by the Arizona Supreme Court (*The Arizona Republic,* April 29, 1998).

9. Diglossia was defined by Ferguson (1959) as a situation of *language contact* where there exists within a given speech community a kind of coexistence between two language varieties, each "specialized" for, or "assigned" to, certain functions and/ or social contexts: literature, school, administration of public affairs, religious ceremony, informal speech, intimate conversation, the family, etc. Fishman (1967) extended the concept to all situations of functional distribution or sociolinguistic asymmetry to include different languages as well as dialects of the same language. More recently, an alternate interpretation of diglossia has been proposed by various authors to emphasize the tension that characterizes diglossia and the unstable aspects of asymmetrical language contact; preferring the formulation: *language conflict* (Hamel & Sierra, 1983; Roth Seneff *et al.*, 1986; Coronado, 1989).

10. In its initial formulation, diglossia (Ferguson, 1959) was conceived of as a stable system (involving, originally, variants of the same language), *barring the impact of certain destabilizing factors*: (1) the spread of literacy to socially marginalized sectors; (2) a breakdown in the linguistic and cultural isolation of these same sectors, along with the amplification of communication networks; and (3) the development of sentiments for autonomy and sovereignty tied to movements towards a greater degree of linguistic standardization on some level. Thus, we could say that Ferguson anticipated the present day discussion of those aspects of diglossia that are character-ized by asymmetrical *and* unstable relations of language contact (see Note 9).

Far from involving a purely theoretical discussion on the relationship between oral and written language, for example, the issue of language choice in literacy in-struction and academic discourse is often one of the most critical points of contention, or cooperation, as the case may be, between parents and bilingual teachers. In bilingual communities, strongly-held views and deeply-felt attitudes (although both often re-flect contradictory perceptions and postures) on language use in the classroom are always among the central themes in school–community relations.

11. Here it is important to note the distinction made by Shearwood (1987) between "pragmatic vernacular literacy" and "high vernacular literacy." The former has as its typical example the personal letter, where participants are known to each other: "an addresser–addressee relationship similar to face-to-face conversation" (Shearwood, 1987: 636). The latter corresponds to the formal oral genres sometimes referred to as "oral literature," that, in turn, would directly sustain the development of the indigenous language, in oral and written form, for academic purposes. In high vernacular literacy "the nature of the addresser-addressee relationship [becomes] abstracted from face-to-face interaction" (Shearwood, 1987: 637). Remember that while formal, context-reduced, discourses are typically associated with writing (and that writing is especially well suited for certain academic and formal uses of language), written messages can also be highly context-embedded, interpersonal, conversation-like, and informal. The same holds true for the different language functions in oral form; some oral genres are highly structured and formal, and require deliberate attention to forms and patterns on the part of the speaker and the listener (although to a lesser extent for the listener). And of course oral forms are best suited for interpersonal communication of the conversational kind.

12. Two recent studies of biliteracy development examined school-age children's response to literacy tasks in Náhuatl and Chichimeca (Francis & Nieto Andrade, 1996), and Hñähñú (Francis & Hamel, 1992; Hamel, 1995). Under adequate peda-gogical conditions, the access to proficiencies related to text comprehension and text construction when bilingual children are faced with literacy tasks in the IL is less restricted than one would expect, given the adverse social circumstances of language contact. Subjects were directed to perform reading and writing tasks in the indigenous language, which for the vast majority corresponds to the language of oral communication only: outside of school in most domains, and in school for informal, interpersonal communication among peers, but not in the classroom with teachers. Students applied decoding skills and comprehension strategies to reading passages in Náhuatl and Hñähñú with little difficulty. This was in part due to the generally close correspondence between the respective writing systems and Spanish orthography, but perhaps more importantly because the skills associated with Cognitive Academic Language Proficiency (CALP) are readily available when performing literacy tasks in any language in which a certain minimum threshold of competence has been attained. This condition was satisfied, since subjects were fluent speakers of Náhuatl or Hñähñú in addition to Spanish. Access to the common underlying proficiencies of text-processing and comprehension were facilitated by ensuring sufficient prior knowledge contextualization for each reading task, what research in L2 reading has described as "top-down support" (Devine, 1988; Carrell, 1989, and in the area of studying indigenous language literacy, Francis, 1992b, 1998a, 1998b, and Hausler & Masayesva Jeanne, 1987). Similar results (for which the same factors are responsible) were obtained in composition tasks in the language that previous to the study was, for most students, never used for writing.

Chapter 4

13. Some researchers have suggested a possible alternative version of Cummins' (1989) hypothesis that cognitive development is favored by high levels of bilingualism. Reporting on results from a study of kindergarten and first grade learners, Yelland *et al.* (1993) propose that enhanced *metalinguistic** skills, for example, are not dependent on an equivalence of competence in the two languages, per se. Subjects who were exposed to limited instruction in the second language (one hour per week for six weeks) performed significantly better in a "word awareness" assessment than did their monolingual peers. This finding would concur with Bialystok's proposal that it is perhaps a kind of "imbalance" between proficiency in L1 and L2 that promotes enhanced awareness of language structures. Increased cognitive demands are placed on the bilingual child who, on a regular basis, must find "solutions to the problem of communicating in the absence of adequate linguistic resources" (Bialystok, 1991: 138). This kind of struggle (in the mental domain), on the part of the bilingual child, under normal conditions, should represent a positive influence for the development of discourse competence, analytical and reflective thinking, and general cognitive development. Thus, for the majority of young bilinguals, who probably do not enjoy equivalent proficiency in both languages, using their second language implies testing alternatives and making choices regarding linguistic forms earlier and more often (also see Díaz, 1985). For many indigenous child bilinguals, the "tension," which is a product of the conflict on the sociolinguistic level, might be related to a more sophisticated awareness of language in regard to different social functions, and especially the conflictive relationship between the indigenous and the national language (Francis, 1998a; Francis & Ryan, 1998). The critical factor here would include not only the imbalance itself, but also a "positive bilingual development," not subtractive, where the indigenous language is valued and continues to develop, as a linguistic system and as a tool for abstract thought.

Research on the role that metalinguistic awareness plays in language development promises to help unlock some of the persistent conceptual puzzles in understanding the nature of literacy-related academic language proficiency. In children, the ability to consciously reflect upon and perform higher-level cognitive operations on language develops in a parallel and independent manner from the acquisition of basic grammatical competence. As such, this ability forms part of the central core of CALP. While literacy contributes an important, probably indispensable, ingredient to the development of the higher, more advanced, levels of the different kinds of metalinguistic ability, language use in the oral medium must play a role as well. Reflection on discourse patterns in narratives and other structural genres (on the part of listener and performer) fosters the ability to step back and contemplate the different forms in which discourses and texts present themselves. Also, reflection on the "lower levels" (sentence grammar, word structure, and sound patterns) contributes to literacy learning in many ways, not only in the more obvious area of writing (e.g. self-correction, editing, revision), but to the development of reading comprehension skills, especially when the reader must shift toward more "bottom-up" type strategies. Bilingual children may benefit from their exposure to two different linguistic systems as they engage in learning tasks that require reflection and analysis. Indigenous language bilingual children can profit from the same opportunities if teachers learn how to take advantage of the already existing resources at hand: the formal oral genres discussed in Chapter 4 and their extension to the written domain. For further reading on the development of metalinguistic awareness, see Gombert (1992), Bialystok (1991, 2001), Birdsong (1989), Cumming (1990), Garner (1994), Francis (1998a), Edwards and Kirkpatrick (1999).

14. Note the two usages of the term "native." One refers to peoples, communities, or tribes that are considered indigenous to the Americas – *Native* here being synonymous with Indian. In reference to language ability, linguists refer to *native* competence to describe the knowledge that a person possesses of their primary language, synonymous in this book with mother tongue or dominant language. For example, an individual may exhibit near-native competence in his or her second language (Spanish, English, Navajo, Zapoteco, etc.). To avoid confusion, and to be consistent with orthographic convention, the former is capitalized, the second, written in lower case.

15. The reader may be familiar with one of the variants of the Canadian Immersion model where kindergarten and first graders are taught exclusively in the second language, including all beginning literacy instruction (known as Total Early Immersion). We do not recommend this particular application that would, in effect, put many of our students at risk in the area of literacy learning. Excluding the primary language from initial literacy instruction can make it more difficult for many children to get the necessary strong early start on decoding, for example, and research evidence has not demonstrated conclusively that more rapid rates of L2 acquisition result under such conditions. Total L2 early immersion programs may "work" in some contexts for children who enter elementary school with the development of their basic literacy skills, through L1, already well under way (a not uncommon situation in many immersion schools). Hernández-Chávez (1984) and Valdés (1997) present a critical examination of Immersion, in particular in regard to the learning needs of language minority students.

16. The level of L2 proficiency of a child learning to read and write in his or her second language is not the only factor to keep in mind. In a very schematic way we can frame the problem in terms of an interaction between two factors: level of L2 learning and level of proficiency in academic-type discourse skills. To simplify the argument, let us consider the prototypical cases of four children entering first grade who are still not "literate," do not read and write, per se; four different "preliterate scenarios":

(1) the child understands and speaks the language of literacy instruction and comes to elementary school with a strong foundation of oral CALP-type language skills (i.e. a high level of literacy-related discourse competence);
(2) the child understands and speaks the language of literacy instruction, but only possesses minimal CALP-type discourse competence;
(3) the child is monolingual and speaks a different language than his or her teacher, but has developed a high level of literacy-related discourse competence;

(4)   the child does not understand the language of instruction and comes to school with only basic conversational skills, i.e. minimal CALP-type discourse competence.

All other variables aside (for now), case (1) will probably encounter no insurmountable obstacles to literacy learning and higher-order written language proficiencies. Along similar lines, readers may recognize the characteristics of case (3) which opponents of bilingual education often point to. This is the immigrant child who in his or her country of origin acquired a solid foundation of CALP-type literacy-related proficiencies but upon arrival does not receive bilingual education, and excels in both English and the content area subjects. This student might have profited from bilingual education in the host country (e.g. L1 development), but is integrated successfully and completely into the L2 mainstream.

Case (2), corresponding to the second argument against bilingual education, represents the broad category of children for whom linguistic competence, per se, is not at issue in their unsuccessful experiences with initial literacy learning. Here, we are referring to the large number of children, who are native speakers of the language of literacy instruction, and who fail to attain adequate levels of proficiency in reading and writing.

On the other hand, initial literacy instruction with a significant L1 component (not necessarily exclusive, as some early bilingual education models proposed) would appear to be the optimal approach for case 4. This is the preliterate, monolingual, first-grade student with little or no previous contact with the higher-order discourses, the fundamental antecedents of literacy. Exclusive L2 literacy for this child would represent, in general, the most unfavorable set of circumstances, exceptions aside and all things being equal. For another point of view, see Wagner *et al.* (1989) for an interpretation of research findings that calls into question the disadvantages of exclusive L2 literacy teaching.

In bilingual programs of the very early-exit transitional type, the indigenous language plays a limited role of introducing sound/symbol correspondences in the IL and practicing patterns that children will apply to word analysis and word identification skills in the second language. Simple sentences and short texts in the IL may even form part of this kind of literacy program. However, the objective here is to shift, as soon as possible, to exclusive L2 reading instruction: i.e. to introduce the concept of phoneme/letter matching at the minimum level, concentrate on the pairings that students will perceive as similar in the national language, and work for a rapid "transfer" of these decoding strategies when all literacy instruction is in English or Spanish. While we cannot reject, out of hand, the possibility that students may profit in some way from such abbreviated transitional methods, the approach that one-year-early-exit models adhere to results in a great missed opportunity.

In practice, the general approach exemplified in the series of IL primers produced in Mexico, for example, still promotes this very limited transitional perspective. While it is clearly not the official policy of the Dirección General de Educación Indígena (DGEI), the failure to develop curriculum and materials that go beyond the initial stage of introducing the basic alphabetical principles represents a kind of implicit recognition that additive, developmental, bilingual programs for indigenous languages are still not feasible. For examples of student primers and teacher guides, see DGEI (1988a) and DGEI (1986).

We should clarify here that our less-than-enthusiastic assessment of transitional bilingual education is primarily reserved for the early-exit variety. Depending on teachers' attitudes and perspectives toward additive bilingualism, late transitional program types, in actual practice, approach the characteristics of full-scale developmental dual language instruction. The limitation often involves purely practical considerations (e.g. shortage of qualified personnel) as in the case described by Dick and McCarty (1997), the Navajo bilingual program at Rough Rock, that at the time of publication extended only through grade three. Our view is that such would-be developmental bilingual programs mark a step forward, a conquest upon which more complete and comprehensive programs can be built. In the case of IL-dominant NL learners, it should also be evident that even early-exit transitional approaches can (if implemented correctly) offer children significant L1 support for early literacy development precisely when they might need it most, even if in the long run the L2 comes to replace the indigenous language as the person's primary language. In other words, even in situations of language loss, the transitional use of the IL is justified if it intervenes at a critical stage of initial literacy learning and contributes to the academic and cognitive development of the child.

17. We are indebted to Pedro Atzatzi (1991) for his transcription of the oral poem *Los vaqueros vasarios*, recently recorded in the indigenous community of San Isidro Buensuceso, Tlaxcala. Notably, as the only remaining example of this verbal art form in a town where over 90% of the population speaks Náhuatl, *Los vaqueros vasarios* is recited entirely in Spanish. This is perhaps another example of how the national language continues to encroach upon traditional domains normally associated with use of the indigenous language, in the present case the traditional Saint's Day from which the town takes its Christian name. Judging from some of the archaic expressions and terms, this particular introduction of Spanish into the poetic tradition of the region probably dates from an earlier period when few San Isidrans spoke or understood Spanish at all (regarding the concept of the social distribution of language functions, refer back to the discussion of diglossia in Chapter 3 and in Notes 9 and 10). Again, in situations of a sharp imbalance between the vernacular and the national language, a clear allocation of languages is not possible, with the boundaries constantly shifting. From the point of view of IL revitalization, domains to which poems like *Los vaqueros vasarios* belong would have to be reclaimed (redeemed, without at the same time implying the exclusion of the national language). In the same way, domains traditionally "reserved" (or so perceived) for the national language can be expanded to create "shared spaces," perhaps always conflictive and unstable, but in a way such that the direction of the constantly shifting language boundaries is not permanently one-sided.

18. For further reading on the subject of American Indian verbal art see Chapters 5 and 6 of Silver and Miller's (1997) study of the indigenous languages of the Americas. Although the extent and formality of instruction in storytelling and myth telling varies, in all cases special learning contexts are required. For example, among the Northern California tribes, elders organized intensive highly structured training periods devoted to the teaching of mythology. Instruction would even take on institutional forms, as well as being long and arduous. In contrast, among the Mohave and Yuma, training was more informal; however, procedures for standardization of both the presentation and the narratives themselves set these formal genres apart from conversational discourse. For example, recitations were given in the presence of elders who were charged with giving a critique of the narration

(Silver & Miller, 1997: 124). Esthetic oral genres are built around sets of rules that do not apply to ordinary speech, the practice of explicit and organized reflection upon the performance of novices being a practice that would not be observed in typical language socialization practices of the everyday kind. In fact, rules of conversational interaction normally preclude commentaries about a speaker's style or correct usage. The special expectations that apply to the contexts of performance are reflected in the rules that govern the grammatical and discourse patterns of the genres themselves, rigidly prescribed in the case of ceremonial discourses, less so in storytelling and myth-telling.

Genre-specific patterns mark verbal art at all levels of language, including specialized vocabulary, grammar and *prosody**. Their primary function is tied to esthetic effects, making the words themselves and the wording itself prominent in different ways, rather than their meaning (in the narrow sense) (Silver & Miller, 1997: 130–145). This in fact is one of the defining features of verbal art in general, both oral and written, tradition and modern. On this subject, also consult Velie (1991), Hinton (1994), Bauman (1977), Tannen (1987, 1989), and Messineo (2000) especially on the analysis of oral genres for pedagogical purposes.

19. Errors refer to structures that do not conform to the grammatical rules of a given language (or rather the patterns of mental grammar shared by a given speech community). That is, a native speaker of the language would tend to judge errors as patterns that are unacceptable, immature, or foreign, even if he or she might be able to make a good guess as to the intended meaning. When linguists point out that all languages are rule-governed, they are referring to the fact that the way words and phrases are combined to produce sentences is not arbitrary or haphazard; and that phrases are not simply strung together in a linear way. Grammatical patterns should not be viewed either in terms of how "logical" the rules seem to be, or the degree to which they always must represent meaning in a straightforward way. For example in the domain of morphology, in regard to marking plural in English, it is common to hear a teacher (a competent native speaker of English) say: "now children, everyone, put your heads down," a sentence that may sound strange to speakers of other languages that would tend to mark "head" (at least of the human kind) as singular. English speakers, when addressing a group of persons often extend this seemingly curious plural marking to other body parts that usually do not come in pairs of two. In the area of syntax, in English, we take the verb "to sleep" to be intransitive (i.e. it can only be inserted into a verb phrase that has no direct object): "The mother sleeps" but not "The mother sleeps the child." However, in other languages (e.g. Spanish) verbs like "sleep" may be both intransitive and transitive, in the latter case (transitive) corresponding to the English expression "put to sleep." Both of the following are grammatically correct: "*La mamá* (the mother) *duerme* (sleeps);" and "*La mamá* (the mother) *duerme* (puts to sleep) *al niño* (the child)." Regarding the Mohave speaker's tendency to delete pronouns in English, here again, to speakers of other languages that also allow pronoun dropping (e.g. Spanish again), English may sound too redundant in this case. The rules of language that are represented in the mind are complex, but they are not "illogical" either. Researchers who study error patterns produced by L2 learners have found that even when structures do not conform to the grammatical rules of the target language, they are far from arbitrary or random (an interesting parallel with L1 acquisition).

20. Our view of Cummins model of CALP is that it provides teachers who work in IL communities with a coherent theoretical framework for developing a dual-language curriculum that has the best chances of promoting additive bilingualism. It appears to be particularly compatible with Krashen's "variable threshold model" for teaching a second language in the elementary grades. And the way that the distinction between higher-order discourses (associated with the academic domain) and conversational discourse is posed, such that it cuts across the oral-written "divide," is especially relevant to the indigenous language bilingual situation. However it is only fair to point out that since the first exposition of Cummins' analysis of CALP and BICS, the model has been at the center of an ongoing polemic. For an in-depth study of this important debate we recommend the following early critiques: Edelsky *et al.* (1983), Troike (1984), and Martin-Jones and Romaine (1986), and Cummins and Swain's (1983) initial reply. More recently the debate continues with Edelsky (1996), Wiley (1996) and MacSwan (2000), and Cummins' (2000) second round defense. The reader will have to chart his or her own course through this interesting discussion. From our perspective the differences appear to be not only persistent and deep going, but at this point probably represent two irreconcilable approaches to how bilingual proficiency should be conceived – after 20 years, too much water under the bridge. The opposition seems to turn around the question of to what extent are different aspects of language proficiency independent/interdependent and autonomous from each other, and to what extent is language ability global, undifferentiated, and integrated. This same theoretical debate finds its expression in different perspectives in regard to language assessment, broadly speaking: analytical approaches compared to holistic methods.

21. In her now-classic paper, Poplack (1980) discusses the codeswitching patterns among Spanish speaking bilinguals in New York City:

> The phenomenon of codeswitching has been a point of contention in assessing community identity. While intellectuals have seen language mixture to constitute evidence of the disintegration of the Puerto Rican Spanish language and culture, community members themselves appear to consider various bilingual behaviors to be defining features of their identity. The opinion that codeswitching represents a deviation from some bilingual "norm" is also widespread in educational circles. It is our contention here that codeswitching is itself a norm in specific speech situations which exist in *stable bilingual communities*. Satisfaction of this norm requires considerably more linguistic competence in the two languages than has heretofore been noted. (Poplack, 1980: 588) [emphasis added]

In the same article the author introduced the principle of the *equivalence constraint*: "switches will tend to occur at points in discourse where juxtaposition of L1 and L2 elements does not violate a syntactic rule of either language" (Poplack, 1980: 586). If the equivalence constraint in fact imposes this kind of pattern, the fluent bilingual will tend to be inhibited from switching within a grammatical structure where a rule from one language does not coincide with the rule of the other. For example in the sentence:

I got a lotta *blanquito* [white] friends.

the principle would be violated because Spanish, in this case, does not allow the adjective *"blanquito"* (white) to precede "friends" (Poplack, 1980: 600). Rather, the sentence follows English word order, one that is not shared, in this case, with Spanish. The fluent bilinguals studied by Poplack typically switch between Spanish and English as in the following example:

> *Si tú eres puertorriqueño* (If you are a Puerto Rican), your father's a Puerto Rican, you should at least *de vez en cuando* (sometimes), you know, *hablar español* (speak Spanish). (Poplack, 1980: 594)

Exactly how bilinguals maintain the compatibility between their two language systems in mixed language sentences is still not well understood. For example, it is probably related to couplings between L1 and L2 at a more abstract underlying level rather than just fitting the respective surface structure patterns into place. In any case we can be pretty sure (for fluent bilinguals at least) that the combinations are systematic and rule governed. For a comprehensive review of the research on codeswitching, see Milroy and Muysken (1995), and Myers-Scotton (1993), and for codeswitching involving an indigenous language, Hill and Hill (1986) and MacSwan (1999).

Another type of codeswitching that teachers might observe would involve the alternation between two dialects that a child has knowledge of, or between the standard monolingual variety of a language and a variety heavily influenced by the other language spoken in the community. In this case, as Romaine (1994: 63) points out, "switch sites" would be more difficult to identify since the two linguistic systems share a good number of the same patterns.

Chapter 5

22. Claims, often made by educators, and at times by students themselves, regarding the tendency of Indian children to be "visual learners" are ironic indeed. If this were true, yet another pretext would have to be offered for lower average levels of achievement in literacy (a good candidate for "visual" processing of language). For societies that have developed *verbal* art forms to a high degree, and have relied on the *oral* tradition for centuries for purposes for which non-indigenous cultures rely on writing, we would conceivably suppose just the opposite: that indigenous students prefer "oral learning styles." As it turns out, neither learning style hypothesis rests on particularly solid theoretical ground, actual evidence being even harder to come by. However, the danger in ascribing to any culture a particular dependence on visual context support is very real. All language learners, especially in their L2, require additional context support for oral language input when their control over the language structures in question is less than complete (visual support being among the principal varieties). This is true, as well, for other domains of learning; e.g. at first, abstract concepts require concrete examples, illustrations, and "hands-on" experiences. As learners develop proficiency over structures, concepts, and other objectives, they become less and less dependent on context. For example, after mastery is achieved, a student may be able to follow and comprehend a class lecture about a topic for which he or she required significant amounts of visual support before. To suggest that some children (by nature, or because of "culture") are inherently or permanently "visual learners" implies something about their general ability to progress toward more decontextualized processing of information and more cognitively demanding language use. While it is entirely conceivable that such a condition can apply to individuals, it is quite a different matter to describe entire communities or cultures in this way. Again, educators should be wary of sweeping claims about the basic cognitive and linguistic hardware of any ethnic group, social class, or language community. See Pinker (1994), and Jackendoff (1994) on how language, thought, and culture interact.

23. The application of the concept of diglossia to the school curriculum (Ruiz, 1988; Baker, 2001) could be viewed as a response, of sorts, to a variety of diglossia at the speech community level that Hamel (1997) describes in terms of *asymmetric language conflict*. In the latter case the national language serves:

> the classical "high" and the ILs the "low" functions. Different from diglossia in both Ferguson's and Fishman's sense, forms and functions are not neatly separated; on the contrary, domain invasion and language mixing occur as part of a process of socially motivated language change. (Hamel, 1997: 109)

Asymmetric diglossia compartmentalizes language functions in situations where the playing field is uneven to begin with. On the one hand, it reinforces the *exclusion* of the IL from the domains it has lost or historically never occupied. On the other hand, compartmentalization is simply not applied to the NL; in reality, it cannot. Within the boundaries of community institutions that come under some measure of local control, where a stable or "balanced" diglossia can be maintained, a kind of allocation of language functions that in fact *favors IL development* is possible, in principle.

24. An interesting distinction in regard to L2 teaching is that between inductive and deductive learning. For second language students, attempting to "acquire" the basic grammatical structures of a language solely through exposure to comprehensible input appears to be problematic. Research has shown that, even after thousands of hours of contact with the L2, high school immersion students continue to reveal clearly partial knowledge of basic grammatical patterns (Harley *et al.*, 1990). On the other hand, it also appears that these same learners benefit from direct instruction, in particular, inductive learning activities based on the "concept attainment" approach. Key to inductive learning is the generation of hypotheses that lead to successive approximations of the concept (or grammar rule, in our case). Especially for complex rules positive evidence appears to be insufficient. Complete mastery apparently depends on conscious attention and reflection upon *negative evidence* as well – negative evidence here referring to examples that are incorrect (Woolfolk, 1996: 346–362). Some types of error correction that call attention to the gap between the learner's incomplete grammatical knowledge and the target language structure in question appear to advance the process along. Learners begin to consciously "notice the gap" (Ellis, 1993). Older, more cognitively mature, L2 learners can profit from these inductive approaches because they have at their disposal more sophisticated information-processing strategies.

Curiously, young children acquiring their L1 do not seem to profit (or at least not very much) from such inductive methods in the development of the basic grammatical knowledge. On the one hand, they are cognitively too immature to take advantage of anything but the most rudimentary direct instruction-type "teaching." But more to the point, it is clear that they do not need to. A good part of first language acquisition appears to be more of the deductive kind. The basic principles and constraints of language are already available so to speak; and apparently with exposure to *positive evidence alone*, grammatical knowledge develops (see Sharwood-Smith, 1994, on the inductive/deductive distinction in L2 learning). If older L2 learners begin to lose access to the Language Acquisition Device, they also begin to lose (in the same degree) the ability to apply this peculiar kind of deductive process to language learning. For an introduction to the concept of the LAD and the role it plays in the development of L1 grammar, see Chapter 11, "Language acquisition in children," in Akmajian *et al.* (1995), on vocabulary development in children: Bloom (2000).

25. Incorporating traditional IL discourses into the school language learning program, for example in the person of recognized narrators from the community, is actually more complex than it appears at first glance. Indeed our reference to "pretexts" for excluding these discourses from the classroom is primarily directed toward postures that view them as unworthy or inherently inappropriate for the higher-order language functions of the academic domain. However, we could draw a distinction between, on the one hand, attitudes toward traditional narrative that fail to appreciate or understand their value, and on the other, perspectives whose purpose is to preserve and venerate them, maintaining their ties to the original or customary context in which they are transmitted. For example, it is often pointed out that some traditional narrative genres (e.g. Coyote stories in the Navajo tradition) are situation- and occasion-specific; and that their presentation outside of this context would result in a violation of community norms. In other words, the story itself cannot be removed from the situation in which it is normally performed without compromising its integrity.

Between these two perspectives, which can be portrayed as completely counterposed (explicit devaluation and its opposite: reverence and veneration), we could speculate about a range of intermediate viewpoints: conceptions of the traditional genres, and their corresponding domains, that are more ambivalent rather than clearly defined. Conflicting and countervailing influences from both of the opposite perspectives result in doubts and second thoughts about appropriateness, for different reasons. Clearly, in the case of explicitly prescribed cultural practices, teachers can only proceed on the basis of extensive consultation and broad agreement. In the case of attitudes that manifestly reflect devaluation, the school's responsibility is that of patient explanation and education. Along the intermediate ranges that reflect contradictory attitudes and ambiguous postures, full consensus is rarely possible, but a broad and good faith consultation is necessary.

For a discussion of context and traditional oral genres, refer to Taylor (1988), Lord (1991), Bowra (1963), Leavitt (1991), Ong (1982), Johansson (1993), Zepeda (1995), and Montemayor (1992).

26. Studying the problems of misunderstanding highlights an important distinction that is often missed in discussions of language and culture – that the two are not inextricably intertwined, forming a kind of single, undifferentiated, one-ness. Scollon and Scollon (1981) make the cut, so to speak, between "grammar" and "discourse":

> The grammatical system gives the message while the discourse system tells how to interpret the message. The greatest cause of interethnic problems lies in the area of understanding not *what* someone says but *why* he is saying it. This information about why people are speaking is not signaled in the same way in

all ethnic groups, and so some misunderstandings can result even where the grammatical systems are nearly identical. By the same token, even where grammatical systems are quite different, communication can succeed if there is agreement about the discourse system...This system is learned through a long and highly involved process of socialization and communication with caregivers. It is unconscious and affects all communication...This discourse system is closely tied to an individual's concept of identity. Any change in the discourse system is likely to be felt as a change in personality and culture. (Scollon & Scollon, 1981: 12)

This relationship between two aspects of the knowledge of language can be observed in the case of languages that cross ethnic and cultural boundaries. For example, speakers of English, Spanish, and French, around the world, share the same basic grammatical system, allowing them to understand what words refer to and what utterances and texts are about. However, many of the stereotypes and prejudices that persist within these global speech communities are the direct result of patterns of misunderstanding that, in turn, stem from differences in the rules of how the discourse system contributes to meaning. The knowledge that one possesses of these rules is closely tied to cultural knowledge. Variation in how the rules of the discourse system are set for turn taking, proximity, *prosody*,* greeting and leave taking, showing deference and respect, etc., lead to errors of interpretation that are difficult to monitor and reflect upon. An example from the American Southwest is the linguistic (i.e. grammatical) closeness between Navajo and Apache that is not reflected to the same degree in cultural practices and cultural expectations. Thus, culture is intimately related to one aspect of language use, what linguists refer to as the pragmatic* system. Theories that propose a close relationship with other subsystems, such as syntax and morphology, are more controversial.

Chapter 6

27. There are a number of useful surveys of the research on biliteracy focused on classroom applications. Good introductory texts are Williams and Snipper (1990), Pérez and Torres-Guzmàn (1992), Nuttall (1996), Peregoy and Boyle (2001), and Nurss and Hough (1992). A collection of papers that gives a more in-depth treatment of the central issues in teaching reading in bilingual contexts with a focus on the particular problems encountered by the student reading in his or her second language is Carrell *et al.* (1988); a recent review of the research is in Geva and Wang (2001).

The most important advances in the field of biliteracy continue to emanate not from bilingual education but rather from ESL and Foreign Language teaching, probably due to their preoccupation with the issue of second language reading and writing. This focus is actually more pertinent to the teacher of Indian students than might appear at first glance. Three L2 literacy scenarios present themselves:

(1) In a large percentage of cases today the ancestral language of the community is not the primary language ("linguistically" speaking) of students. Here, reading and writing in the IL is a kind of enrichment biliteracy instruction, and the general theory and practice of L2 literacy is directly applicable.

In the case of children who are proficient speakers of the IL, we can consider two additional variants:

(2) For IL-dominant or monolingual children, literacy instruction is almost always in their second language, more often than not exclusively so.

(3) For bilinguals, again since beginning reading and writing were usually taught in English or Spanish, extending literacy to the other language involves *a kind of L2 literacy*. However, since the balanced bilingual enjoys full command of the basic linguistic systems of the IL, the extension or "transition" in this case is truly of a different kind, different from both (1) and (2) (also see Note 12).

28. Driven, perhaps, by the principle that each dialect group of a language should be represented by its own unique orthography (and to each phoneme a corresponding grapheme), early attempts at designing alphabets by modern-day missionaries have resulted in writing systems that are quite complex. The following text (a story about three *campesinos* on a trip to the city, and the troubles that they encounter on the way because they do not speak Spanish) is an example of attempting to represent the shifts in tone in Chinanteco:

$Gaang^2 dsea^2$ 'i ja^2 $t\ddot{t}ig^2$ $Juni coo^2 n\acute{e}e'^{24}$ $caliseng^2 gaang^2 dsea\~nu^{12}$ 'i ja^2 $tiing^2 j\acute{u}'^{24} cami'^4$ $ju\~n\acute{t}$ $f\iota^{23} coo^2 f\ddot{t}$ '$ep\acute{t}'^4$. $Jo coo^2 jmii^{24} cas\acute{u}i\~n^3 roo^2$ '$e cangol\acute{u}i\~n^4$ '$e cangojm\ddot{t}t\ddot{t}i\~n^2 ju\~n\acute{t} f\iota^{23}$ ciudad. (Summer Institute of Linguistics, 1984)

The matter of an optimal "method" for representing speech in written form is actually very complex; among the great variety of orthographies that have evolved to their modern versions there does not exist any one system that is ideal or "complete." All writing systems involve one kind of compromise or another. However the purpose of an orthography is not to represent *all* the sounds of a language. For example, only a very narrow portion of the full range of the prosodic features of speech is marked graphically in punctuation, and often punctuation follows grammatical patterns rather than intonation or tone groups (for examples, Halliday, 1989). In general, alphabetical writing tends towards representing patterns at a higher level than the speech sounds themselves (see the Glossary for the distinction between allophones and phonemes). In English, maintaining constant the orthographic marking for plural in "dogs" and "cats" facilitates both decoding, for the reader, *and* spelling (even though one of the words, is "not spelled the way it sounds." Other principles even override phonology: for example, in "sign" and "signal", and "machine" and "mechanical," spelling patterns are maintained constant despite their phonemic structure being different.

Practical writing systems of the alphabetic type, designed for use by speakers of the language can dispense with many of the phonetic and phonological details, so to speak, since the other linguistic systems, plus context, provide enough redundancy to resolve ambiguities of meaning. Exact *transcriptions* of speech are more useful for non-native speakers of a language for purposes of study and analysis, for anthropologists, linguists, and missionaries whose low level of grammatical competence may not allow them to take advantage of the natural redundancy in language that native speakers can, and in fact must, avail themselves of to process written language efficiently.

On a related note, tendencies toward standardization of the orthographic system, and away from dialect-specific spelling patterns, stem from some of the communicative and expressive functions of writing itself. Among others, the less an orthography is tied to any one particular dialect, and the more it can incorporate or bridge different dialects of an IL, the greater is the usefulness of writing for communication among the various local speech communities that share the same language. For a discussion, refer to Cerrón-Palomino (1993), Cerrón-Palomino and López (1990), Díaz-Couder (1990), Pardo (1993), Hornberger (1996), and Rudes (2000). For an introduction to writing and its relationship to spoken language, see Chapters 2 and 3 in Halliday (1989), and for a more in-depth discussion: DeFrancis (1989), Olson (1994), Bennett and Berry (1991), Burnaby and Anthony (1985), Coronado (1988), Hasler (1987), Pellicer (1993), and Prem and Riess (1983).

29. The myth of Orpheus and Euridice is surely one of the most prominent examples of the universality of traditional narrative themes. The recording, transcription, and translation of *Coyote and the Shadow People* forms part of the extensive ethnographic and literary work of A. Phinney, of Columbia University, himself a member of the Nez-Perce tribe to which this coyote story belongs. Cultural differences provide for interesting variations; Swadesh (1966) reports on a Nutca version where "Orpheus" travels by canoe and is counseled and guided by an elderly woman from his tribe whom he finds on a beach far from his house.

30. Reiss (1967), in his discussion of the nature of connotation in literature, addresses the issue of the relationship between text meaning and reader/listener meaning, what Rosenblatt (1994) refers to, perhaps from a different point of view, as *transaction:*

> Those who do not really understand literature often remark that, since creative writing is frequently not clear, it may mean something different to each reader. The implication is that every reader brings his own set of preferences and prejudices against which he places the work - which of necessity, becomes a mirror image of his views. (Reiss, 1967: 21)

> One of the easiest and least rewarding pastimes is to read meanings into works. It is possible, as many have said, to make something mean just about anything we want; but what is much more difficult - and rewarding - is to understand what something means *in and of itself.* (Reiss, 1967: 22) [emphasis added]

Chapter 7

31. Davies (1990) emphasizes how in language testing the requirements of reliability and validity must be balanced one against the other. Just as in teaching, the analytical and the integrative appear to be in conflict. However, this "tension" actually reflects different aspects of language learning, especially in the case of L2 learning. Just as it would be an error to contend that all aspects of L2 learning follow integrative and holistic principles, excluding all analytical and structural approaches from language assessment unnecessarily restricts us to only one set of evaluation tools. At first glance, an analytical, discrete-point, approach to assessment would favor reliability (reliable results), and integrative methods would favor validity (valid interpretations). "Adding to the stock of discrete items, the smaller the bits and the more of these there are, the higher the potential reliability. Validity, however, is increased by making the test truer to life, more like language use" (Davies, 1990: 34). Thus, depending on the purpose of the evaluation, a certain measure of "uncertainty" may have to be tolerated, since the price we pay for ever-higher degrees of precision is a kind of downgrading of authenticity. At the same time we must be mindful of this trade-off in the opposite direction: the more global and holistic the evaluator's judgments are, the more difficult it becomes to control inconsistency and subjectivity.

32. When estimating different aspects of language proficiency, as in the case of our proposed "Bilingual interview," it is important to remember that raw score totals for each sub-test are not comparable, and cannot be added together to calculate a global, overall, score. For example, the number of responses produced on an open-ended vocabulary task, as in section 2, will vary widely, while the number of responses to section 1 (greetings and personal questions) and section 3 (questions based on story illustrations) is fixed. In addition, one point awarded for a vocabulary word produced in section 2 is not equivalent to one point for an acceptable response consisting of a complete grammatical sentence in section 3. Another interesting problem arises in situations of intense language contact where bilinguals freely resort to lexical borrowing (mainly when speaking in the IL). The balance score for vocabulary knowledge will reflect this tendency depending on the particular sociolinguistic context (e.g. degree of NL influence and stage of IL erosion). Even among children who possess a complete command of the IL grammatical system, quantitatively, the balance in vocabulary may tend to tip toward the NL. Thus, if a "dominance index" were calculated based solely on responses to the vocabulary section, the mistaken impression may be given that an actual balanced bilingual is NL-dominant because of an "imbalance" in the total number of lexical items produced in each language (refer to the discussion in Chapter 6 on validity). A vocabulary test reflects language competence only to a certain degree; in comparison to a test that elicits complete sentences or connected discourse, we would say that a vocabulary test does so to a much lesser degree. Choice of vocabulary is constrained by social and contextual factors in a way that demonstrating grammatical knowledge is not.

Also, consider the criteria for marking a given response as IL or NL. In many cases, large numbers of lexical items have entered the indigenous language from the many years of intense contact with the European languages (review the discussion on codeswitching and borrowing in Chapter 4 and Note 21). In the case of loan words that the IL borrowed during a previous historical period, and that native speakers have fully incorporated into the IL lexicon, such items should probably be counted on a test as IL vocabulary. For example, in Náhuatl, the words *axno* ("donkey" from Spanish) and *koton* ("shirt" from English) have been phonologically integrated into the language. The archaic term for "name" in Spanish, *gracia*, is still used in greetings: *"Tlen mo gracia"* [What is your name].

33. A very promising line of research on the development of higher-order language proficiencies has focused on the emergence of narrative in young children, and the differences between this "mode of thought" and what Olson (1994) and Bruner (1986) term "paradigmatic modes" (associated with expository texts, the essay, the logical/mathematical proof). According to Olson:

> Narrative is more fundamental in that we invent stories and continuously revise them in the attempt to make events, including our lives, comprehensible to ourselves and others. (Olson, 1994: 134)

Following Olson, Gombert (1992) summarizes some of the research findings, distinguishing between "a *prospective* approach to narrative which contrasts with a *retrospective* approach to expository text," the explanation for the distinction being related to the involvement of schema. Expository discourse requires a more "bottom-up" (i.e. retrospective) type of processing, one that cannot rely upon the more predictable patterns of narrative for constructing coherence.

When subjects are confronted by a narrative, the schema provokes expectations which permit the structuring of new information *as and when it appears*. This method of processing, effective in 6-year-olds, is of the top-down type in which cognitive representation directs the structuring of the perceived linguistic information. (Gombert, 1992: 147)

Expository texts are approached in a retrospective way, each piece of new information being related to the information *given earlier in the text*. This hypothesis might well help explain the fact that it appears to be easier to detect violations of prior knowledge in narrative than in expository texts. (Gombert, 1992. 145)

Related to this distinction is the shift from "early narrative" (5 and 6-year-olds), which is situation- dependent, toward "late narrative" which becomes more and more independent of the immediate, situation-dependent, context. Here "late narrative" serves as a kind of bridge toward the more abstract school-related genres. For more discussion, refer to Mandler (1984) and Gee (1989).

Chapter 8

34. Hill and Hill (1986), who recorded this interview on the topic of community perceptions of language loss, center their analysis on how informants reconstruct the line of questioning that researchers prepare, consciously or unconsciously going beyond the interviewer's presuppositions (in this case that the indigenous language is indeed in danger of being lost). Such interchanges often provide the occasion for informants to effect a "shift of the discourse into a whole new set of terms" (Hill & Hill, 1986: 87), allowing for the introduction of unanticipated subtleties and pointed commentaries reflecting the contradictions and ambivalences of the language conflict between NL and IL.

To a similar query we made in Tlaxcala, to Don Heriberto Conde, we can take note of a similar attempt on his part to portray the complexities of the *mixed feeling* of many IL speakers toward the question of language loss, a fitting final entry to our *Voices from the communities* series, on this occasion given in Spanish (and translated to English).

Voices 9

I speak just like before not having forgotten Náhuatl, it suckles you, can't forget it, it can't be bought, it would be like forgetting the milk from your mother's breast, like a lamb it lulls you to sleep, it embraces you, it can't be bought, can't be rented. It's a thing of pride for Imelda [his granddaughter] that she speaks both.

(Before she learned Spanish)

It was very hard for her, in first grade she cried, she suffered, she wasn't civilized yet ... at times I make my daughters-in-law speak Spanish so that they don't suffer, so that they don't speak all mixed up, half-speech ... they hear both, they start understanding.

(At a subsequent point during the interview making a point about the historical and cultural value of the indigenous language)

You can't forget because it's our mother dialect, the more a man knows the more he is worth. It would be good to set up a school where Náhuatl could be taught; maybe in Mexico City they already have them, start them from when they are little so that they don't forget. I have a great satisfaction that I haven't forgotten, it is an ignorance to be ashamed to speak your dialect. If I don't express myself well, then yes, if I talk in half-speech, [but] in Náhuatl, no. Here, you're talking with your fellow countrymen, your people, to the contrary.

(Then upon reflecting upon the possibility of Náhuatl being forgotten in his town, the situation is portrayed in different terms.)

... for the necessity of leaving to go to work, if they civilize us enough, yes we will lose it; it would be more competent, more civilized, no one would come around and humiliate us, it would open the way up for the development of our town. It would be good...very satisfied!

(Returning to the original theme of the conversation, and without calling attention to any possible contradiction in regard to his earlier remarks.)

It's a good thing, If it were lost it would be lost to history, like a memory, it's an inheritance of our people.

(And in summary)

With a true, legitimate, Indian you can't talk to him; he hides. The poor Indian, you look at this poor man that just puts up with it, he doesn't know how to defend himself. A civilized person wouldn't permit it. A noble girl, who doesn't know, people take advantage of her, [but] if she has schooling...

Original text in Spanish recorded in Francis (1997)

Appendix D

35. As a historical document, the UNESCO declaration on the use of vernacular languages in education marks an important turning point, coming as it does during the great wave of post-World War II independence struggles in Asia and Africa. Also, in Latin America, findings from the *Proyecto Tarasco* (Chapter 3) played an important role in undermining the notion that only European languages were suitable for literacy learning (even in situations where children are monolingual speakers of a non-European language). The common-sense proposal that young children learn reading and writing most effectively when they understand the language of instruction met resistance largely because of political motives. A similar politically motivated opposition to bilingual approaches to literacy instruction persists today; in addition, some educational researchers have suggested that the UNESCO principles are of limited applicability. Strong opponents of bilingual education reject the "vernacular advantage concept" across the board (Porter, 1990); and more recently, in the United States, the debate has sharpened considerably with the passage of Proposition 227 in California and Proposition 203 in Arizona that seek to dismantle bilingual education outright (Crawford, 1997; Krashen, 1999).

Keeping in mind that the UNESCO report dates from before the emergence of the field of modern linguistics and its applied subdisciplines, its conclusions remain remarkably current. With few exceptions, research on language development, second language learning, literacy learning, and language teaching is still grappling with the central issues raised in the passages we have taken excerpts from the document. One notable exception is the original (and now largely discredited) concept of bilingual literacy teaching that envisioned two separate and consecutive stages: an exclusively L1 stage for the purpose of "consolidating" mother tongue literacy, free from the potentially "confusing" interference of L2 learning, followed by a subsequent transition to the second language. As we pointed out in Chapter 5, there is nothing in the concept of the "first language advantage" that necessarily implies that initial reading and writing must be taught exclusively in the L1 for an extended period of time. Children can benefit in many ways from literacy instruction in *both* the language that they understand best (as native speakers) and the language that they are learning as a L2 (Francis, 1999a, 2000a). Optimally, for a beginning reader who at the same time is at the very initial stages of L2 learning, the greater part of literacy learning should (if this is possible) be carried out through the language he or she understands, especially the learning of decoding skills that rely on knowledge of the linguistic subsystems. Second language literacy perhaps could be introduced initially through highly context-embedded reading activities of the holistic kind (these correspond, in the case of the NL, to the ubiquitous environmental print that the child is in contact with on television, on the way to school, at the market, etc.) The central argument of the UNESCO principles is that in school the demands placed on children to process language and information in a new way create special circumstances for learning, radically different, for most children, from the circumstances that prevailed for their "childish [preschool] purposes." In school, "new information and ideas are presented as fast as [they] can possibly absorb them." Simply, the "double burden" of academic language use and high concept load, plus only minimal control over the second language represents an unjustified and discriminatory imposition upon large numbers of children who are restricted to exclusive L2 schooling.

In a recent position statement on second language literacy instruction, the International Reading Association makes reference to the UNESCO principles:

> Proficiency in the dominant language [in this book "national language" – see Glossary for "dominant"] is the goal of language and literacy instruction, and bilingualism or multilingualism is desirable. Families have the right to decide whether initial literacy instruction is delivered in the dominant language or the

home language. Where such a choice is not feasible, the right of the child to choose to be bilingual, bicultural, or monolingual, monocultural, and monoliterate must be honored and respected. The accumulated wisdom of research in the field of bilingualism suggests that while initial literacy learning in a second language can be successful, it is riskier than starting with the child's home language – especially for those children affected by poverty, low levels of parental education, or poor schooling. (Snow *et al.*, 1998)

The United Nations has adopted the principle that indigenous linguistic minorities have the right to education in their home language. The International Reading Association supports this position and also supports the rights of families to determine the language of initial literacy instruction for their children. Families have the right, when feasible, to have their children taught to read in their home language. They also have the right to have their children's initial literacy instruction delivered in the official language of instruction of their country of residence. (International Reading Association, 2001)

Glossary

Alphabetic: A system of writing is alphabetic if it is based on the principle that letters, or graphic symbols in general, correspond closely to phonological patterns of the language. The written symbols of the alphabet (not to be confused with the *Roman* alphabet, which is only one kind of alphabetic system) represent the sound system of the language, specifically the phonemes. Examples of non-alphabetic writing systems are Chinese, and the Cherokee and Cree syllabic scripts. Most of the writing systems that have been adopted by indigenous languages are alphabetic.

Autochthonous: Native, indigenous, or aboriginal to a given region.

Basic Interpersonal Communicative Skills (BICS): Contrast with the term **Cognitive Academic Language Proficiency (CALP)**. Interpersonal, conversational-type, communicative skills develop completely and universally in all normal children. BICS refers to a set of related language abilities in which, typically: comprehending and expressing meaning can rely to a significant degree on situational context clues and extensive shared background knowledge between persons, who, in addition, are able to collaborate in an interactive way to clarify meaning, (e.g. pointing to a concrete referent). BICS develops spontaneously and naturally as a part of everyday primary socialization of children, and depends on, basically: (1) attaining a certain minimal threshold of grammar and vocabulary knowledge in the language in question, and (2) learning the social rules and conventions of culturally appropriate interpersonal interaction. See related terms: **context-embedded, discourse, register,** and **pragmatic system.**

Borrowing: Refer to **codeswitching**

Boundaries: In reference to diglossia, the limits or confines that separate one language from another in a given speech community according to how both bilingual and monolingual speakers perceive the social functions of each language. For example, the indigenous language may be perceived as corresponding to certain domains (e.g. ceremonial occasions) and not others (e.g. a formal meeting with the school principal).

Codeswitching: In speaking or writing, when a bilingual shifts from one language system to another. This can occur: (1) in conversation, for example, when speakers switch languages between turns; (2) when one speaker switches in the middle of an utterance, between sentences; or (3) when one speaker switches within a sentence. *Borrowing* usually refers to "loan words" that are taken from one language and are integrated into another (e.g. in English: taco, résumé, hogan). However, in many situations of extensive and ongoing language contact, a significant number of "loan words" can be of very recent introduction into the host language, with bilinguals continuously "borrowing" in a spontaneous way; in fact, researchers have found it difficult to make a sharp distinction between codeswitching and borrowing. Often borrowing refers to switches involving single **lexical** items, contrasting this to codeswitching, involving switches between grammatical sequences (i.e., between the two linguistic systems); this distinction, however, is also difficult to maintain in all situations. Codeswitching and borrowing occur in all situations of language contact. Linguists study this phenomenon from the point of view of the social uses of language because it reflects how the languages in contact interact in the bilingual speech community, and also from the point of view of the combined grammatical patterns that are produced because this reveals aspects of the bilingual speaker's knowledge of the two languages.

Coherence: The characteristic of a discourse or **text** in which its elements are organized in a logical or structured manner; the different parts are connected in a meaningful way, for example chronologically in time in the case of narrative. In argumentative discourse: are points and counterpoints pertinent? Refer to the critical feature of **discourse**. Meanings in a text or discourse are linked, as in a dialogue for example, where shared knowledge indicates the relationship between the elements in question. In contrast to *cohesion*, a specific grammatical or lexical link is not necessary. For example:

> Coyote: Now I've finally caught you. Come over here so I can eat you up.
> Opossum: One moment, let me to go down into my burrow to say goodbye to the earth.

Especially in the context of the story in which Coyote's attempts to capture Opossum have been frustrated several times already, Opossum's response is taken as coherent, even though there is no explicit reference to Coyote's request, or any other direct link to his words (such as: "no I will not", or "you are not going to eat me"). Coherence refers to a discourse that can be either in the form of a dialogue (as in a conversation), a monologue (as in a speech or lecture), or a text. *Cohesion* and *cohesive ties* refer to the relationship between different elements in a text at the **lexical** (related to words and word meanings) or **syntactical** level. A specific tie or connection can be identified between the two elements. For example:

> Coyote: It was you who deceived me, wasn't it?
> Opossum: No, it was not I; the one who did it was the opossum that takes care of the sheep.

"You" and "I" are linked, as are "deceived" and "did." Cohesive ties indicate how words and propositions are related, or linked; for example, who or what a pronoun refers to within the text. Cohesion and coherence refer to different ways that discourses and texts are constructed (i.e., in a way so that they form a unified whole). However cohesion and coherence work together in an interdependent way. For example, the cohesive link that ties "deceived" and "did" in the dialogue between Coyote and Opossum is not joined together automatically for the listener – "did" could conceivably refer to some other action. If the listener is mentally constructing a *coherent* dialogue in this scene, "did" is then linked to "deceived."

Competence: In general referring to the mental grammar, or knowledge of the structure of a language that a speaker or learner has acquired. This includes the ability to create and understand novel sentences governed by rules that the learner has constructed. For example, a bilingual's competence in a second language can be incomplete or partial. Linguists make an important distinction between competence (knowledge) and performance, the latter referring to the actual use of the language in expression, comprehension, communication, etc. For example, actual language performance can be affected by a number of incidental or accidental factors (lack of attention or distractions, fatigue, a temporary physical impediment of some sort) which do not affect the underlying knowledge that the speaker possesses; i.e. these factors do not change competence. The term *discourse competence*, in turn, refers to knowledge related to language and discourse patterns beyond the sentence level, and theoretically would correspond to a different cognitive domain from that of the knowledge of phonology and syntax, for example.

Concurrent translation: The now-outmoded practice of providing the same information in a second language learner's L1 immediately following its presentation in the L2 for the purpose of ensuring comprehension. Generally, two negative consequences result: (1) if the student expects a translation to his or her primary language, teachers unintentionally promote the tendency on the part of the learner to pay less attention to the L2 input. Without the "benefit" of translation, L2 learners will be more likely to apply the L2 comprehension strategies that they have at their disposal, resulting in *more comprehensive input*, and more language learning. (2) Teachers themselves will be less likely to make the necessary modifications in their delivery when presenting the lesson in the student's L2 (see Chapter 4 – Language Learner Sensitive Discourse), which results in *less comprehensible input*.

Context-embedded: Refers to comprehension, for example, that depends to a significant degree on the physical situation in which the message occurs. A less obvious variety of context-dependent communication is when prior knowledge, background information, or shared assumptions are so complete that comprehension of the message or text requires little processing of new information in the message or text itself. Comprehension depends less on the actual words that make up the **discourse**, than on access to contextual information.

Cognitive Academic Language Proficiency (CALP): Refers to a set of related language abilities that are typically learned in school and are closely tied to literacy. Unlike everyday, face-to-face, conversational, uses of language, CALP-type language abilities require higher degrees of attention to the text or discourse itself. This is because: (1) concrete, situation-embedded, context clues may not be readily available (e.g. in an academic lecture or an essay); (2) the information content consists of more abstract concepts, concepts that are new or unfamiliar, and/or that involve mentally keeping track of a greater number of these concepts while processing the information at hand. CALP is typically associated with schooling and literacy, but these kinds of language ability can also develop to a high degree of proficiency in oral tradition contexts. For a contrasting term, refer to **Basic Interpersonal Communicative Skills (BICS).** For more discussion see Notes 13, 16 and 20, and in particular, Chapter 8. Cummins (2000:70) defines CALP as "expertise in understanding and using literacy-related aspects of language."

Dialect: In reference to a language, a dialect is a variety of the *same* language, spoken by a community of persons (an ethnic group, social class, speakers living in a geographical region of the territory or country where the language is spoken). Dialects are typically associated with particular pronunciation patterns, and differences in grammar and vocabulary. *Dialectical variation* (referring to these differences) is common to all languages. This diversity within a language can be

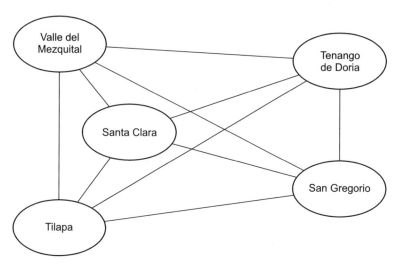

Figure 5 Network of the Dialects of Otomí

represented graphically (Figure 5) whereby some dialects can be said to be more "closely related" than others. Manrique Casteñeda (1988:28) provides the above example from the Otomí (Hñähñú) language.

The numerically largest dialect (or dialect spoken by the socially and economically most powerful group), or the one which is perceived as being most prestigious or "cultured," may, with time, come to be considered the *standard* dialect. Thus, "Standard English," "Standard Spanish," etc. are also dialects among all the others used for communication by native speakers of English, Spanish, and so forth. It follows then that "standard dialects" are not inherently more expressive or complete than "non-standard dialects." In regard to indigenous languages, a common incorrect use of the term dialect distinguishes between "language" corresponding to the national language and "dialect" as corresponding to the indigenous languages; the connotation in this incorrect use of the terms is that "dialects" are not as refined, are less structured grammatically, and are not suitable for writing. ILs are languages in the same way that NLs are: they both have a complete grammatical system, and adequate linguistic means for generating new lexical items for new concepts and artifacts. "Varieties" that beginning or intermediate learners of a language speak (that by definition reflect incomplete or partial competence) are not dialects, in and of themselves. Contrast with **register**.

Diglossia: Where the term bilingualism is used to describe how two languages coexist or interact within an individual, diglossia refers to the relationship between two languages in contact in society. For example the concept is applied to situations where it is likely that one language is associated with certain social functions and the other with different uses, circumstances and/or purposes (see Notes 9 and 10 for further discussion, and **boundaries** for a related term).

Discourse: Speech or writing about a topic, subject, or theme that is treated at some length; usually speech or writing beyond the sentence level. Discourse can be interactive, as in a conversation (dialogue), or produced by a single speaker or writer (in a "monologic" fashion). The critical feature of discourse is that the sequence of sentences or utterances forms an integrated whole; they are related to one another in some coherent way, and they constitute a recognizable instance of language that is, as a unit, meaningful (at least potentially so). When referring to *discourse competence*, the distinction can be made between different kinds of knowledge that the speaker has acquired or learned that in turn underlie abilities in different kinds of discourse (different ways of using language). In the case of Cummins' (2000) differentiation between BICS and CALP, the first describes a type of discourse ability that is required for normal, culturally appropriate, conversational uses of language; rules (specific to one's speech community) related to social interaction in face-to-face communication play an important role. CALP, which shares a number of underlying competencies with conversational ability, could be described as an ability, or complex of abilities, that relies on a different set of knowledge structures, in this case related to literacy, artistic genres, formal speech, and academic uses of language. See glossary entries for **register, pragmatic system,** and **competence.**

Dominant language: Synonymous in this book with primary language. For a bilingual, it is the language in which the person possesses native-speaker competence, and where the other language is "weaker" in some significant way. The reader should take note, that for many Indian students (as is common also for many other bilingual individuals), the dominant or primary language may be the second language (in chronological terms) that was learned. In the language that was acquired first, because of language loss, competence may be partial or incomplete. Thus, by definition the balanced bilingual does not have a dominant language. For clarity, in this book, the use of the term dominant language in the social sense (related to higher status, prestige, power) is avoided.

Dramatic irony: In literature, in particular in narrative and theater, where a contradiction or incongruity arises between the developing situation, or scene, and the words pronounced by a character (or between the situation and his or her actions).

Error: In general, errors refer to language patterns that are produced (usually in reference to a specific aspect of linguistic knowledge such as **syntax**) such that a native speaker of the language would judge them as non-native, immature, or incorrect; errors reflect partial knowledge of the language system a child is acquiring as an L1, or a language a student is learning as an L2. Not to be confused with *mistakes,* which all speakers make in performance as a result of factors not related to their actual knowledge of the language structure in question (e.g. lack of attention, "slips of the tongue"). A useful distinction in regard to second language learners' errors is that between *local* and *global* errors. The first refers to a non-native pattern that does not affect meaning or comprehension of the message. Global errors, on the other hand, involve major components of sentence structure or violate grammatical rules that make it difficult or impossible to assign meaning to the sentence as a whole. For example, in the sentence: "But since the river which it crosses my land flooded ... we had built a wall, my house is saved." the movement of "but since" to the front of the sentence would be a global error; the insertion of "it," a local error.

Ethnolinguistic vitality: Refers to the cultural and social factors that contribute to the maintenance and continued development of the language of a given speech community. For example, a strong and cohesive ethnic identity on the part of a minority language community will make it easier to resist language shift, as will support for the IL from educational and other community institutions, favorable demographic trends in relation to the majority, etc. See Muñoz Cruz (1987) and Hornberger (1987).

Expository text: A prose **genre**, usually associated with the general category of non-fiction, for the purpose of communicating ideas, transmitting information, explaining concepts, relating events, analyzing phenomena, ideas, propositions, and so forth. Expository often refers to the kind of written discourse, or genre, that is characteristic of textbooks in the academic subjects of social studies, science, and mathematics. The essay is a typical example, in contrast to narrative. Expository can also refer to oral genres associated with the above-mentioned purposes.

Extralinguistic information: Context support that helps a listener or reader, especially a second language learner, construct meaning from an utterance or text. The context support in this case is non-linguistic in nature (e.g. a visual illustration, a chart or graphic representation, or even shared background knowledge, that provides additional information complementing, repeating, or in some other way supporting the message received).

Foreshadowing: In literature, and in general, to prefigure, or indicate what is to come. Important in the comprehension of narratives, for example, in regard to the ability to look forward and look backward in a text, and mentally construct a coherent story.

Formulaic: Refers to an expression where the individual words, together, make up a single item, similar to conversational routines and idioms where the expression functions as a single unit of meaning (for example, a set form of words used in a ceremony or ritual).

Genre: A category of composition or a formal discourse of an identifiable type, oral or written, characterized by a particular style, form or structure. Examples include: narrative, poetic, journalistic, legal, academic or **expository**, and ceremonial. In this book, the term is used in a restricted sense to refer to *non-conversational* discourses.

Grammatical: Refers to sentences, or major parts of a sentence that form a unit (such as a phrase or a clause). A sentence is grammatical if it conforms to the rules of a native speaker's linguistic competence. Such a grammatical **competence** may follow the rules of a non-standard dialect or non-prestige variety of a language. The reader will note that this definition is different from the notion of conforming to a *prescriptive* grammar, which specifies what may be considered proper or correct usage (as described in published grammar manuals). The latter is always closer to, or coincides with, the standard variety of a language that is taught in school and is found in language arts textbooks.

Immersion: Content-based language instruction in its many variants and applications, put into practice on a large scale in Canada, and to a lesser extent in the United States and other countries. Immersion, strictly defined, ensures that second language students receive comprehensible input in the target language at all times, thus providing the optimal conditions for second language learning. Not to be confused with *submersion*, which is content teaching delivered (typically in a situation where native speakers of the L2 comprise a majority of the class) in such a way that the language of instruction is *not* comprehensible to the L2 learners. Immersion teaching can be applied to learning the national language (NL) as an L2, to a foreign language, to or an indigenous language in a community where the NL is the primary language of many children.

Indigenization: Coming from the field of Christian missionary work, indigenization refers to the idea that, to be successful, missionary work in the foreign fields needs to be put in the hands of the local community as soon as possible. Interpolated into the field of education, educational programs in a minority language community might be more successful and more permanent if staffed by teachers from that community. Therefore, the training of teachers from the same ethnic group as the students is a priority of the education program.

Input: Language data to which a language learner, in particular, is exposed. Input can be visual or auditory. Implicit in the definition is that input is potentially processible, that the learner can actually use the data in some way (for example: utilize the information received to build up knowledge of the language system). Krashen (1991) considers *comprehensible input* as a necessary condition of language acquisition. When input is processed and turned into knowledge some authors then refer to this stage of language processing as "intake" (Sharwood-Smith, 1994).

Integration: The inclusion of an ethnic group, nationality, or language minority into the opportunity structure of society as a whole, in the sense of removing barriers to social and economic advancement and eliminating discriminatory practices directed toward individuals belonging to the disfavored group. Today, in North and South America, such obstacles to advancement are rarely codified into law (e.g. legally sanctioned segregation and discriminatory social regulations that apply to or make reference to "race" or ethnic group), but rather are the consequence of historical inequities, and present social and economic policies, that may have, nevertheless, the same effect. In this book, integration is to be taken as contrasting to the concept of forced assimilation that would imply one kind or another of coercive incorporation, for example, of a cultural or linguistic minority. In the case of non-voluntary assimilation, cultural practices and language might be excluded from community institutions and generally devalued in favor of the majority culture and language. *Integration* in reference to pedagogical practices is to be taken in the usual and customary sense.

Language shift: Language erosion or loss, *socially*. Shift refers to the displacement of one language by another on the level of a community or region. The expanding language is almost always the language of wider communication. Not to be confused with other kinds of language change, such as the evolution of the structures and forms of a language over time.

Learner language: A second language learner will typically fall short of native-speaker competence in his or her **target language**, even after many years of study. As learning proceeds, the learner comes closer and closer to native-speaker levels. These intermediate stages can be described as forms of a learner language. Common features of a learner language include: patterns that are transferred from the first language, and generalizations that learners make based on their perceptions of how the second language system works. When speaking, for example, transfer and generalization can result in errors or in correct target language forms. In the literature on L2 learning, learner language is synonymous with "interlanguage."

Lexical: Refers to the lexicon, the mental dictionary that consists of the total set of words that a first language or second language learner knows. Researchers have studied, for example, if bilinguals store lexical items in different lexicons corresponding to each language, or if the vocabulary of the two languages is stored in a more integrated way.

Lingua franca: Any language that is used extensively among speakers of other languages (although some individuals may be native speakers of the lingua franca and be monolingual) for interethnic, cross-cultural, or interregional communication. Examples include: Latin in Medieval Europe, Náhuatl in Mesoamerica, and Quechua in South America during the 15th and 16th centuries, and Swahili in Eastern Africa today.

Literary: Here and throughout this book "literary" is used to refer to *written literature*. The reader will note, however, that separating oral **genres** out from the category of literature appears somewhat arbitrary. For example, the renowned oral tradition scholar Albert Lord (1991:21) observes that "although the two worlds, the oral and the written, of thought and its expression, exhibit some striking and important differences, they are not separate worlds...Oral literature did not need writing to become literature, and it continued long after writing was invented." Ong (1982), on the other hand, prefers to maintain the distinction between literature and traditional oral poetry and narrative. In our definition of the terms *literary* and *literature*, we emphasize their association with writing, as we wish to underscore the "important differences" between oral and written forms. At the same time, it is important to reiterate Lord's observation that the oral genres of the formal, aesthetic, ceremonial, and narrative type not only represent a precursor to written literature, but that there also exists a fundamental continuity between these non-conversational oral forms and literature.

Metalinguistic awareness: The consciousness or awareness of language itself: its forms, structures, patterns, etc. More specifically, viewing language as an object of reflection or study in which the learner or speaker deliberately manipulates the forms of the language. Children appear to spontaneously manifest the beginnings of this aspect of language development when they experiment with rhymes, and invent jokes involving word play. Young bilingual children make reference to bilingualism itself, or to some interesting aspect of it, translation equivalents, and other contrasting features that distinguish one language from another. However, metalinguistic awareness typically continues to develop in formal learning settings (school, religious education, higher levels of the development of story telling, etc.).

Metaphoric: Refers to figurative language that implies some kind of relationship. Metaphors belong to the broad category of *figures of speech,* where words denote objects or ideas to suggest a likeness or analogy. Such figurative language is common in all genres as well as in ordinary conversation.

Native, native: When capitalized *Native* is synonymous with indigenous or autochthonous, as in Native American, and not to be confused with its reference to linguistic competence (*native*), characteristic of the knowledge of a person's primary language.

Parallelism: A literary technique where two elements of a text or discourse are juxtaposed in some way to create an effect. A kind of repetition, for example where the author reiterates a linguistic structure for aesthetic purposes or to emphasize a meaning relationship.

Phonology, phonological: The study of phonology has as its focus the description of distinctive sound units called *phonemes*. Phonemes refer to the classes of these significantly different speech sounds in a language that can normally be perceived by a native speaker. They are the smallest units of sound that allow a native speaker of a language to distinguish two words. In English there are about 40. Other languages have different classes of roughly the same number. Phonemes are not to be confused with phones or allophones, which refer to variations at a lower level of representation. For example, the first vowel in the word "coffee" is pronounced differently by speakers of English who speak different dialects. To native speakers and learners alike, such variations are noticeable, but especially on the part of the former are perceived as "equivalent." These variants could be considered allophones of the same phoneme. Other kinds of allophonic variation are barely noticeable as in some of the variations of /t/ in English: *tin, stint, kit*; the different sounds of /t/ in *button, pitted and truck* are more easily distinguished one from the other, but nevertheless they too belong to the same "family" – the phoneme /t/. Study Chapter 4 in Akmajian *et al.* (1995).

Pragmatic system: The aspect of a speaker's knowledge of language use that allows him or her to interpret messages in a socially appropriate way, how meaning is obtained by linking the words of an utterance with real world or cultural knowledge. For example, to fully understand a message in actual communication, the listener must interpret the words that are spoken in relation to the specific situation in which the *speech act* occurs. Students, when they are in class, must be attentive to this aspect of language use and how the patterns may differ culturally. The teacher's utterances, spoken to a student in class: "why are you standing?" and "where is your book?" should be taken as questions only sometimes, usually not. The correct interpretation will depend on the context of the utterance, on who is speaking to whom, and the intentions of the speaker.

Prestige: In reference to the social relations among languages in contact, prestige refers to speakers' perceptions about the relative value or standing of a language – strictly an estimation in the eyes (and ears) of the members of a given speech community regarding superiority, elegance, expressiveness, and general worthiness and utility. For example the high prestige language or variety may be perceived as the most appropriate vehicle for educational and economic advancement.

Prosody: How speech varies according to the following characteristics of sound: loudness, rhythm, rate of speech, and intonation. Like other aspects of linguistic knowledge, for example, intonation patterns are rule-governed. A certain pattern may serve to mark grammatical function as in the variation in intonation that can be given to: "No" (a question, a statement, or a command). Prosody is an important aspect of **pragmatic** knowledge, the rules for interpreting prosodic patterns varying from one culture to another. See the discussion on intercultural communication in Chapter 5, and in Note 26.

Redundancy: The degree to which a text or an utterance provides more information than is absolutely necessary for it to be comprehensible. All languages allow for a certain amount of natural, built-in, redundancy, which can vary depending on the circumstances. Containing more information than is "necessary" helps the reader or listener by providing a kind of back up, or repetition, that decreases the chance of error. For example, in listening to the sentence "Those coyotes are always getting into trouble," if the listener does not "hear" the plural marker "s" in "coyotes," there is still enough redundancy in the message to ensure that he or she understands that more than one coyote is getting into trouble. Generally, in language addressed to L2 learners, increasing the amount of redundancy in the message (without, of course, violating grammatical rules) makes input more comprehensible.

Register: A situationally appropriate speech act or text, a **discourse** that corresponds to a given social situation or a given language function. Registers vary according to topic, setting, the relationship that exists between the speakers, and the purpose, objective or function of the interaction (Lessow-Hurley, 2000: 34). Not to be confused with *dialect*, which is a variety of a language that a person speaks from childhood and describes how he or she speaks all the time across different contexts (unless the speaker is "bi-dialectical" and can switch from one to the other). Thus, in principle, no dialect is incompatible with the different registers that a person learns for different purposes, functions, and social situations. It follows, for example, that children who speak a non-standard dialect do not have to replace this dialect with the standard dialect to learn and use academic registers. Speakers of a given dialect learn to be proficient in a number of registers. For example CALP would be considered a kind of register (or complex of related registers), compatible in principle with all dialects of a language.

Reported speech: A style in narrative, for example, where the narrator relates to the reader or listener the words of one of the characters, sometimes called "indirect speech" or "indirect style," implying perhaps that the speaker's words are not reported as they were actually pronounced. For example: *The coyote said that he was going to find the opossum and eat him up.* This is sometimes contrasted to "direct speech" where the narrator implies that the quote indeed represents the exact words spoken (The opossum replied: "it was not I"). However, see Tannen (1989) on how, in practice, it is difficult to maintain a strict separation between these categories.

Representational speech: Using language to represent ideas symbolically, implying a certain degree of abstraction. In regard to the early development of literacy-related language, primary caregivers may respond to children's utterances by interpreting and expanding upon them, in effect treating the younger learner as a communicative partner capable of the symbolic use of language involving concepts beyond the simple expression of basic immediate needs and intentions in the here and now (Faltis, 2001: 15-18).

Scaffolding: Refers to a kind of assistance or support that learners receive from an adult, or peer who has attained a higher level of proficiency, making it possible for the learners to solve problems that normally would be beyond their capabilities if they attempted them independently.

Schema: A mental representation of complex patterns of events, scenes, different kinds of knowledge, and so forth. Knowledge that is stored, or represented, in the mind and which is connected to networks of related categories of knowledge.

Situational factors: Contextual factors. In regard to language learning, the setting in which learners interact with other learners and native speakers, formal classroom setting or informal setting, frequency of interaction, topics, etc.

Syntax, syntactical: Syntax refers to the internal *structure* of sentences, the manner in which words are arranged so that the resulting sequence results in a grammatical sentence or phrase. While syntax concerns itself with the rules that govern the formation of sentences (e.g. word order), grammar is a broader category, referring to other aspects of language structure and meaning as well.

Target language: In reference to language teaching situations, a second language that a person is learning. The term target language is generally not used to refer to the acquisition of a child's primary (first) language.

Text: A meaningful instance of language, typically beyond the single word level. In this book, the term "text" is used to refer to written language or written discourse (refer to **expository** text). For other authors, text is defined more broadly, synonymous with discourse, oral or written.

Universal Grammar (UG): The innate, genetically endowed, knowledge that children have access to about how language ("in general") is structured and patterned. This unconscious knowledge enables children to acquire any particular language during the first six years in a manner that is universally successful, regardless of social or cultural circumstance. Under normal conditions of exposure to a spoken or signed language, children construct the grammar of their first language (first *languages*, in the case of a bilingual child) from primary linguistic data (i.e. attending to examples of well-formed words, phrases, and sentences); explicit instruction and corrective feedback are unnecessary. UG also refers to the "basic design underlying the grammar of all human languages" (Pinker, 1994: 483). For related concepts, see Notes 3 and 24.

Vernacular: In this book the term refers to a mother tongue of a given language community that is spoken on a daily basis within a defined region, locality, or group of localities, especially for interpersonal communication. Vernacular languages usually refer to local or regional languages, in contrast to a language of wider communication spoken at the national level that is also associated with formal uses and institutional contexts. The latter may also enjoy official status; a vernacular usually does not.

Appendix A

Coyote and the Shadow people

Coyote and his wife were dwelling there. His wife became ill. She died. Then Coyote became very, very lonely. He did nothing but weep for his wife.

There the death spirit came to him and said, "Coyote, do you pine for your wife?" – "Yes, friend, I long for her ..." replied Coyote. "I could take you to the place where your wife has gone, but, I tell you, you must do everything just as I say; not once are you to disregard my commands and do something else." – "Yes," replied Coyote, "yes, friend, and what else could I do? I will do everything you say." Then the ghost told him, "Yes. Now let us go." Coyote added, "Yes, let it be so that we are going."

They went, There he said to Coyote again, "You must do whatever I say. Do not disobey" – "Yes, yes, friend. I have been pining so deeply, and why should I not heed you?" Coyote could not see the spirit clearly. He appeared to be only a shadow. They started and went along over a plain. "Oh there are many horses; it looks like a round-up," exclaimed the ghost. "Yes," replied Coyote, though he really saw none, "Yes, there are many horses."

They had arrived now near the place of the dead. The ghost knew that Coyote could see nothing but he said, "Oh look, such quantities of service berries! [fruit from a Service Tree, belonging to the same family as Mountain Ash and Rowan Tree] Let us pick some to eat. Now when you see me reach up, you too will reach up and when I bend down, you too will pull your hands down." – "Yes," Coyote said to him, "so be it, thus I will do." The ghost reached up and bent the branch down and Coyote did the same. Although he could see no berries he imitated the ghost in putting his hand to and from his mouth in the manner of eating. Thus they picked and ate berries. Coyote watched him carefully and imitated every action. When the ghost would put his hand into his mouth Coyote would do the same. "Such good service berries these are," commented the ghost. "Yes, friend, it is good that we have found them," agreed Coyote. "Now let us go." And they went on.

"We are about to arrive," the ghost told him. "There is a long, very, very long lodge. Your wife is in there somewhere. Just wait and let me ask someone." In a little while the ghost returned and said to Coyote, "Yes, they have told me where your wife is. We are coming to a door through which we will enter. You will do in every way exactly what you see me do. I will take hold of the door flap, raise it up, and bending low, will enter. Then you too will take hold of the door flap and do the same." They proceeded now in this manner to enter.

It happened that Coyote's wife was sitting right near the entrance. The ghost said to Coyote, "Sit here beside your wife." They both sat. The ghost added, "Your wife is now going to prepare food for us. "Coyote could see nothing, except that he was sitting there on an open prairie where nothing was in sight; yet he could feel the presence of the shadow. "Now she has prepared our food. Let us eat." The ghost reached down and then brought his hand to his mouth. Coyote could see nothing but the prairie dust. They ate. Coyote imitated all the movements of his companion. When they had finished and the woman had apparently put the food away, the ghost said to Coyote, "You stay here. I must go to see some people."

He went out but returned soon. "Here we have conditions different from those you have in the land of the living. When it gets dark here it has dawned in your land and when it dawns for us, it is growing dark for you." And now it began to grow dark and Coyote seemed to hear people whispering, talking in faint tones, all around him. Then darkness set in. Oh, Coyote saw many fires in a long-house. He saw that he was in a very very large lodge and there were many fires burning. He saw the various people. They seemed to have shadow-like forms but he was able to recognize different persons, he saw his wife sitting by his side.

He was overjoyed, and he joyfully greeted all his friends who had died long ago. How happy he was! He would march down the aisles between the fires, going here and there, and talk with the people. He did this throughout the night. Now he could see the doorway through which he and his friend had entered. At last it began to dawn and his friend came to him and said, "Coyote, our night is falling and in a little while you will not see us. But you must stay right here. Do not go anywhere at all. Stay right here and then in the evening you will see all these people again." "Yes, friend. Where could I possibly go? I will spend the day here."

The dawn came and Coyote found himself alone sitting there in the middle of the prairie, he spent the day there, just dying from the heat, parching from the heat, thirsting from the heat, Coyote stayed here several days. He would suffer through the day, but always at night he would make merry in the great lodge.

One day his ghost friend came to him and said. "Tomorrow you will go home. You will take your wife with you." – Yes, friend, but I like it here so much, I am having a good time and I should like to remain here." "Yes" the ghost replied: "nevertheless you will go tomorrow, and you must guard against your inclination to do foolish things. Do not yield to any queer notions, I will advise you now what you are to do. There are five mountains. You will travel for five days. Your wife will be with you but you must never, never, touch her. Only after you have crossed and descended from the fifth mountain you may do whatever you like," "Yes friend," replied Coyote.

When dawn came again, Coyote and his wife started. At first it seemed to him as if he were going alone, yet he was dimly aware of his wife's presence as she walked along behind. They crossed one mountain, and now Coyote could feel more definitely the presence of his wife; like a shadow she seemed. They went on and crossed the second mountain. They camped at night at the foot of each mountain. They had a little conical lodge which they would set up each time. Coyote's wife would sit on one side of the fire and he on the other. Her form appeared clearer and clearer.

The death spirit, who had sent them, now began to count the days and to figure the distance Coyote and his wife had covered. "I hope that he will do everything right and take his wife through to the world beyond," he kept saying to himself.

Here Coyote and his wife were spending their last night, their fourth camping, and on the morrow she would again assume fully the character of a living person. They were camping for the last time and Coyote could see her clearly as if she were a real person who sat opposite him. He could see her face and body very clearly, but only looked and dare not touch her.

But suddenly a joyous impulse seized him; the joy of having his wife again overwhelmed him. He jumped to his feet, and rushed over to embrace her. His wife cried out, "Stop! Stop! Coyote! Do not touch me. Stop!" Her warning had no effect. Coyote rushed over to his wife and just as he touched her body she vanished. She disappeared – returned to the shadow-land.

When the death-spirit learned of Coyote's folly he because deeply angry. "You invenerate doer of this kind of thing! I told you not to do anything foolish. You, Coyote, were about to establish the practice of returning from death. Only a short time away the human race is coming, but you have spoiled everything and established for them death as it is."

Here Coyote wept and wept. He decided, "Tomorrow I shall return to see them again." He started back the following morning and as he went along he began to recognize the places where he and his spirit friend had passed before. He found the place where the ghost had seen the herd of horses, and now he began to do the same things they had done on their way to the shadow-land. "Oh, look at the horses; it looks like a round-up." He went on until he came to the place where the ghost had found the service berries. "Oh, such choice service berries! Let us pick and eat some." He went through the motions of picking and eating berries.

He went on and finally came to the place where the lodge had stood. He said to himself, "Now when I take hold of the door flap and raise it up you must do the same." Coyote remembered all the little things his friend had done. He saw the spot where he had sat before. He went there, sat down, and said, "Now, your wife has brought us food. Let us eat." He went through the motions of eating again. Darkness fell, and now Coyote listened for the voices, and he looked all around. He looked here and there, but nothing appeared. Coyote sat there in the middle of the prairie. He sat there all night but the lodge didn't appear again nor did the ghost ever return to him.

Recorded from his mother and translated by Archie Phinney, first published in *Nez Perce Texts, Columbia University Contributions to Anthropology*, Vol. 25 (1935), also in *Reading the Fire* (1983) by Jarold Ramsey.

Appendix B

The Opossum and the Coyote

This is what happened one day.

The coyote and the opossum and God our Father.
The coyote wanted to eat God's children. He said to Him: Give me your children, I will eat them.

God said to Coyote: Yes you can eat them, but you must fast. If you fast you will be able to eat My children. God called Opossum and He said to him: Coyote will fast, you will do lots of mischief to him.
So coyote left and said, well I'll fast, I won't eat anything. Not a single thing, not a thing.

He came along walking, hungry with the fast, he met the opossum sitting on top of a maguey.
Opossum says: You, Coyote, come here, come, drink a little pulque, drink a little pulque.
He says: No, I won't drink, I will fast, that's what God told me.
I will fast so I will be able to eat His children.
Take it, drink, and I won't accuse you. God won't see you.
The coyote, since he was already thirsty says: OK, I'll drink.
He lowered his mouth to the maguey. The opossum pushed him inside.
He got good and stuck. His head got stuck.
The opossum ran away, ran away. There the coyote was writhing.
He says: Now where do I find him? I'm going to really eat him up.
I'm really going to eat the opossum up. Really I'm going to eat him.

He goes and goes, he falters, walks, looking for him.
He finds the opossum. He's holding up a bolder, he's holding it up.
Now I'm going to eat you, says the coyote, Now I'm going to eat you.
Why did you deceive me?
I was drinking the pulque and all of a sudden you push me in.
My head got stuck. The opossum says: Not I, I'm not the one who got your head stuck, said the opossum, I wasn't the one, I'm not the one who got your head stuck.
It was the Pulque Opossum.
No. It was you.
Not me, look, you see, here I'm the Bolder Opossum, because I'm holding up the boulder so that it doesn't fall.
And the coyote looked up and saw that the clouds were moving.
See how the boulder is already falling, he says.
Are you going to help me, said the opossum, Are you going to help me?

239

You're going to help me? If not, it's going to fall on top of us.
The coyote also leaned up against it, like he was holding it up, holding it up. He started to push hard, and he closed his eyes, but hard, he pushed.
The opossum said: Hard, push, and the coyote, really, he even closed his eyes, pushing hard.
Then the opossum runs away, the coyote was now getting really tired.
He's doing it like this, then he says: let's see; no one is coming.
The opossum gets away again, runs away.
He says: Iiiiih! and now, and now it's going to fall. Zaz
He starts to let it go, let it go. He realizes that it's not true that it will fall.
It's because the clouds are moving, and it looks as if the bolder is falling.
Now he says: wherever I find him I'm going to eat him up, eat him up, and no longer will he be able to do these things to me.

He runs fast. He's already tired from all the work. He's looking for him.
This coyote goes looking for him. Now he sees him.
The opossum is herding. He has many sheep.
Now he says: I'll eat him up.
Why, why did you deceive me?
I was holding up the rock that was about to fall, and it wasn't true.
He says: He's the Boulder Opossum.
Me, look. I am the Sheep Opossum. I take care of the sheep.
Why don't you eat one of my sheep?
He says: Hmmmm!, but I am fasting and I told God that I will fast.
Come on, eat one of my sheep, over there, grab one.
I'm leaving now. I'll give them to you, as a present, all of my sheep, all of them.
And the coyote, since he was hungry, said right away: I'm going to eat well.
The opossum runs away.
He starts to follow them; run after them. All of a sudden he makes them angry and they jump on him, on top of the coyote.
They were nothing but dogs. The opossum deceived him, he really deceived the coyote. They bit the coyote all over.
So now wherever I find him, that opossum, I'm going to eat him up.
Why is he deceiving me so much? For that I will eat him up.

He went looking for him, but he got tired, he couldn't anymore.
Walking, enduring, then he saw that he was eating lots of prickly pears.
Eating a lot on top of a nopal, eating a lot. The opossum eating, eating.
Now he says: Why did you deceive me?
Supposedly they were sheep, and it wasn't true. They were nothing but dogs.
He says: Coyote, it was he that deceived you. He is the Sheep Opossum.
Me, look, I'm the Prickly Pear Opossum. I'm the Prickly Pear Opossum.
Now eat a prickly pear, see, delicious, sweet.
The coyote says: Well, if you give it to me, but don't accuse me, because God said that I will fast.
No, I won't accuse you. The opossum pealed the prickly pear.
Now he says: Close your eyes and open your mouth Coyote.
Now he closed his eyes real tight and opened his mouth.
Since he pealed the prickly pear, the opossum threw him the prickly pear fruit.
Hmmmm! Delicious! And he eats another one.

Do you want another? Yes!
Now the opossum cuts another prickly pear. But close your eyes; open your mouth. He threw it to him with the spines on.
The coyote screams: Ay ay ay! My mouth is full of spines, scratching himself all over.
The opossum already ran far away. He says now, indeed, wherever I find him, I will eat him up good that opossum.
Why is he doing such things to me?

Somewhere I'll find him.
Now, for sure, I will eat you.
Here the opossum is sitting. He's working on a grass mat [petate],working, he hurries to make the grass mat.
Now he says: I will eat you.
Why have you deceived me so much?
You were going to peal the prickly pear and it wasn't true.
You threw it to me, like that, with spines.
He says: Not I, look, I am the Grass Mat Opossum, I'm the Grass Mat Opossum.
That one who deceived you, that one is the Prickly Pear Opossum.
Look, I'm hurrying to make the grass mat, because, look, the rain and the hail are already approaching.
It's going to hail really hard. If you want now, I'll make you a grass mat so you can cover yourself, so you don't freeze to death.
I'm going to eat you because it is you who is deceiving me.
No, I already told you, that one is the Prickly Pear Opossum, I'm the Grass Mat Opossum.
Look, I'll make you the grass mat because the rain is approaching fast. Now I will make you the grass mat because the hail is already approaching fast. I'm telling you, OK, sit down here, he says to the coyote.
Sit down here. I will show you how, how you make a grass mat.
Now they finished it, big like this. Then he says: Go inside, and I'll tie you up so that you don't get wet, so you don't freeze.
The coyote goes in, he sits down all the way inside.
And the opossum, like this, like this, [ties him up] real well, and he even hangs him from a tree. But listen, over there, the hail is already approaching, but strong. The opossum showered him with rocks, hit him hard with rocks, hitting hard.
The coyote screamed and screamed.
He fell and broke the rope. So there he continued to writhe.
The opossum ran away, he escaped, he ran away, he left him stoned,
just like that, stoned.
Now, the coyote says: wherever I find him,
I'm going to eat him up, no longer will he deceive me.

He wanders around searching, and since he is fasting he's already tired.
Over there he goes searching. He finds him again taking care of turkeys, but lots of turkeys. Now, really I'm going to eat you. You are the one that has already done so many things to me. You've already deceived me many times, now I'm going to eat you.
Now I'm not going to let you go, now I eat you.

The opossum says: That one that deceived you was the Grass Mat Opossum.
Me, look, I am the Turkey Opossum. Here, I take care of them,
just turkeys, they're all turkeys, look. It appears that you are hungry.
Yes! God told me that I will fast; and if I can endure my fast,
I will be able to eat His children.
He says: Aha, well, eat a turkey, and don't eat me because it was
the Grass Mat Opossum who deceived you. Yes, it was he,
so, you're going to eat my turkeys.
Yes, I want to, I'm very hungry.
Here, I'll leave them to you, as a present. And I'm leaving, now I'm leaving.
Then the coyote becomes happy. Hmmmmm.
He says: now I'm going to eat well. The opossum already escaped, he ran away.
The coyote says: Hmmmmm, right now I'm going to eat them.
He starts to chase them, he's chasing them all over. He can't
capture them, and he continues chasing, and all of a sudden he gets tired.
They stopped and flew away. They weren't turkeys really, they weren't
turkeys that he left, rather they were vultures; he had left vultures.
For that he says: Now for sure wherever I find him I'll eat him up,
I'll eat him up, I'll eat him up, because, I'll eat him.

He came to a place where the opossum was sitting, like this;
so he says now I'm going to eat you. So the opossum says: If you want
to eat me, permit me at least that I say to the earth that I'm leaving,
because I am going to your stomach. Let me tell the earth that now I'm leaving.
Where the opossum was sitting, there was his burrow.
Here, where the opossum was sitting behind his back was his burrow.
He says to the coyote: Wait for me, wait for me. He went into his burrow.
The coyote waits and waits and waits. The opossum never appears;
So now for that reason he can't eat God's children.

Here this story ends.

Translation from the Náhuatl *In tlacual uan in coyotl*. Recorded in San Isidro
Buensuceso, Tlaxcala, Mexico. Narrator: Reyes Arce, in Navarrete Gómez and
Francis (1999)

Appendix C

Sample cloze passages

(Actual cloze stories that were completed by Mexican bilingual students who participated in a study of biliteracy development)

1. Training passage

Training passage in Spanish, in preparation for indigenous language cloze task.

El asno y el lobo
Un asno estaba en el campo comiendo hierba tranquilamente, cuando de pronto salió de entre los árboles un lobo hambriento, con muchas ganas de comérselo. Pero el asno, que no era nada tonto, intento rápidamente un truco, y comenzó a cojear y a _____: ¡Ay mi pata! ¡Ay mi _____! Y le dio al lobo: Ya sé que me vas a _____. Está bien, y te felicito, porque veo que tienes buen _____.

árbol	pata
gusto	grande
llorar	comer
tarde	para

Pero mira: tengo una espina _____ clavada en la pata. Si no quieres que se te atraviese en la garganta cuando me comas, te recomiendo que me la _____ ahorita. El lobo le respondió: Tienes mucha _____. A ver, levanta esa pata para quitarte la _____.

espina	niño
afuera	razón
cuatro	estoy
tremenda	quites

2. Náhuatl cloze passage (fragment)

Yolkatsitsin
Nin tenkualak in palankakuatl, uan nauyakuatl kijtlakua in yolyeso _____ uan niman miki. Ninke kuamej kuak takuaj tlatla yenonik in yeuejka tlatlakaj Mexikamej okin tokayotijke "Tlekuamej." Senka _____. Axan in tetajmej "Lacadones" kitlatlajtia in kuatl amo xikkuajkua in _____ amo xikmikti. Ninke yolkamej momatij ijtek in _____ motlakuitlauia tleka kikuaj chauil, uan kuak in kuamej ye uejuei kikuaj kimichimej uan tosantin, kuak itech in mili kaj _____ in kuamej kikuaj. Miek tlatokakej kinkauaj matlajpiakan in masakuatl,

243

_____ ijtek nin senkal kampa amo kikua makalakikan in kimichimej kuatiuej in tlaol. Ninakatl in masakuatl _____ mieke kimatij kuaske.

yajti	chauil
machautikan	nitlakuya
chapantok	kijyomiktia
nokonej	popotl
uelik	mili
itstlakatini	temajtijke
kakajtinemi	tekitl

Appendix D

UNESCO (1953) Declaration

Excerpts from the UNESCO (1953) declaration on the use of vernacular languages in education[35]

Towards the end of 1951, specialists from all parts of the globe met at UNESCO House, Paris, to discuss in particular the use of vernacular languages. The meeting considered its main task to be the provision of some answer to two important questions: under what circumstances is the use of the vernacular possible in education; and what measures might be taken to facilitate and encourage its use? The meeting recorded its findings in a draft report, which is now published in the pages that follow.

It is through his mother tongue that every human being first learns to formulate and express his ideas about himself and about the world in which he lives.

Every child is born into a cultural environment; the language is both part of, and an expression of, that environment. Thus the acquiring of this language (his "mother tongue") is a part of the process by which a child absorbs the cultural environment; it can, then, be said that this language plays an important part in molding the child's early concepts.

In learning any foreign language a child may find difficulty in mastering the alien vocabulary and syntax sufficiently to express his ideas in it. Where the foreign language belongs to a wholly alien culture he is faced with the added and much greater difficulties; to interpret to himself the new ideas in terms of his own medium of thought - his mother tongue - and to express his own ideas and thought through the new modes of the alien tongue. Ideas which have been formulated in one language are so difficult to express through the modes of another, that a person habitually faced with this task can readily lose his facility to express himself. A child faced with this task at an age when his powers of self-expression even in is mother tongue are but incompletely developed, may possibly never achieve adequate self-expression. For these reasons it is important that every effort should be made to provide education in the mother tongue.

On educational grounds we recommend that the use of the mother tongue be extended to as late a stage in education as possible. In particular, pupils should begin their schooling through the medium of the mother tongue because they understand it best and because to begin their school life in the mother tongue will make the break between home an school as small as possible.

Instead of running about and playing and shouting, [in school, the young child] is usually expected to sit still and be quiet; to concentrate, to do what he is told instead of what he wants to do, to listen and learn and answer questions. New information and ideas are presented to him as fast as he can possibly absorb them.

If the language in which all these bewildering new communications are made is also different from the mother tongue, the burden on the child is correspondingly increased. To expect him to deal with new information or ideas presented to him in an unfamiliar language is to impose on him a double burden, and he will make slower progress." (pp. 45–48)

In reply to the often cited objections to bilingual education the authors point out:

That there is nothing in the structure of any language which precludes it from becoming a vehicle of modern civilization.

That the child "has learnt [his or her mother tongue] enough for his own childish purposes,... the school is not merely teaching the child his mother tongue, it is using his mother tongue as the most effective means of teaching him other things.

And that "an equal or better command of the second language can be imparted if the school begins with the mother tongue as the medium of instruction, subsequently introducing the second language as a subject of instruction." (p. 49)

Appendix E

Sample Plates from the *Entrevista Bilingüe (Bilingual Interview)*

Scenes for Testing Vocabulary Knowledge

Market
Front yard/Exterior of house
Interior of house
Corn field

Narrative Strips for Description of Story Scenes

The celebration
The fight

Taken from Francis (1992a),
illustrations by María Antonieta Castilla

Market

Front yard/Exterior of house

Interior of house

Corn field

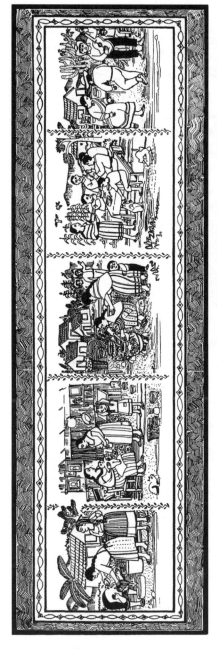

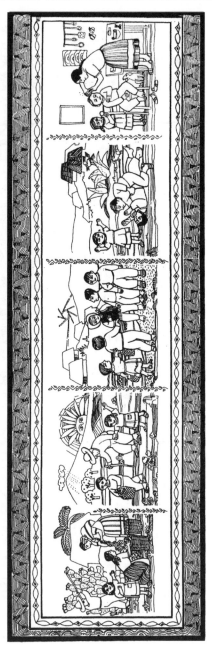

The celebration   The fight

References

Adams, M.J. (1990) *Beginning to Read: Thinking and Learning about Print*. Urbana-Champaign: Center for the Study of Reading, University of Illinois.

Aguirre Beltrán, G. (1973) *Teoría y Práctica de la Educación Indígena*. Mexico DF: Secretaría de Educación Pública.

Aguirre Beltrán, G. (1983) *Lenguas Vernáculas: Su Uso y Desuso en la Enseñanza, la Experiencia de México*. Mexico DF: Ediciones de la Casa Chata.

Aguilar Camín, H. (1998) México social. *Proceso*, No. 1141.

Ahenakew, F. and Wolfart, H.C. (eds) (1998) *The Counseling Speeches of Jim Kâ-Nîpitêhtêw*. Winnipeg: The University of Manitoba Press.

Akmajian, A., Demmers, R., Farmer, A. and Harnish, R. (1995) *Linguistics: An Introduction to Language and Communication*. Cambridge: MIT Press.

Albó, X. and D'Emilio, L. (1990) Lenguas autóctonas y educación en Bolivia. *Perspectivas* 20, 359–368.

Alianza de Profesores Indígenas Bilingües (1992) Autodeterminación indígena, colonialismo interno (Declaration presented at the fifth session of the Indigenous Populations Work Group, United Nations, Geneva, Switzerland, 1987). In J. Juncosa (ed.) *Educación Indígena: Transmisión de Valores, Bilingüismo e Interculturalismo*. Quito: Abya-yala.

Amadio, M. and Zúñiga, M. (1990) Bolivia. In F. Chiodi (ed.) *La Educación Indígena en América Latina, Tomo I*. Quito: Abya-yala.

Amery, R. (2000) *Warrabarna Kaurna: Reclaiming an Australian language*. Lisse: Swets & Zeitlinger.

Arguedas, J.M. (1938) *Canto Kechwa con un Ensayo sobre la Capacidad de Creación del Pueblo Indio y Meztizo*. Lima: Bustamante y Ballivián.

Arizona Department of Education (1983) *American Indian Language Proficiency Assessment: Considerations and Resources*. Phoenix, Arizona.

Arviso, M. and Holm, W. (1990) Native American language immersion programs: Can there be bilingual education when the language is going (or gone) as a child language? *Journal of Navajo Education* 8, 39–47.

Asher, J. (2000) *Learning Another Language Through Actions* (6th edn). Los Gatos, CA: Sky Oaks Productions (first published in 1977).

Atzatzi, P. (1991) La Danza de los Vaqueros Vasarios. Escuela de Antropología, Universidad Autónoma de Puebla (unpublished monograph).

Baetens Beardsmore, H. (1986) *Bilingualism: Basic Principles*. Clevedon: Multilingual Matters.

Baker, C. (2001) *Foundations of Bilingual Education and Bilingualism*. Clevedon: Multilingual Matters.

Bauman, R. (1977) *Verbal Art as Performance*. Rowley, MA: Newbury House Publishers.

253

Bennett, J. and Berry, J. (1990) Cree literacy in the syllabic script. In D. Olson and N. Torrence (eds) *Literacy and Orality*. New York: Cambridge University Press.

Bernard, H.R. (1992) Preserving language diversity. *Human Organization* 51, 150–159.

Bialystok, E. (1991) Metalinguistic dimensions of bilingual language proficiency. In E. Bialystok (ed.) *Language Processing in Bilingual Children*. New York: Cambridge University Press.

Bialystok, B. (2001) Metalinguistic aspects of bilingual processing. *Annual Review of Applied Linguistics* 21, 169–181.

Bialystok, E. and Cummins, J. (1991) Language, cognition and education of bilingual children. In E. Bialystok (ed.) *Language Processing in Bilingual Children*. New York: Cambridge University Press.

Bialystok, E. and Hakuta, K. (1994) *In Other Words: The Science and Psychology of Second Language Acquisition*. New York: Basic Books.

Birdsong, D. (1989) *Metalinguistic Performance and Interlinguistic Competence*. New York: Springer-Verlag.

Birdsong, D. (ed.) (1999) *Second Language Acquisition and the Critical Period Hypothesis*. Mahwah, NJ: Lawrence Erlbaum.

Bloom, P. (2000) *How Children Learn the Meanings of Words*. Cambridge: MIT Press.

Board of Indian Commissioners (1880) *Report of the Board of Indian Commissioners*. Washington, DC: US Government Printing Office (Eleventh Annual Report for 1879).

Bowra, C.M. (1963) *Primitive Song*. New York: The New American Library.

Bratt Paulston, C., Chen, P. and Connery, M. (1993) Language regenesis: A conceptual overview of language revival, revitalization and reversal. *Journal of Multilingual and Multicultural Development* 14, 275–286.

Bruner, J. (1986) *Actual Minds, Possible Worlds*. Cambridge: Harvard University Press.

Burnaby, B. (1996) Aboriginal language maintenance, development, and enhancement. In G. Cantoni (ed.) *Stabilizing Indigenous Languages*. Flagstaff: Northern Arizona University.

Burnaby, B. and Anthony, R. (1985) Orthography choice for Cree language in education. In B. Burnaby (ed.) *Promoting Native Language Systems in Canada*. Toronto: Ontario Institute for Studies on Education.

Burns, P., Roe, B. and Ross, E. (1999) *Teaching Reading in Today's Elementary Schools*. New York: Houghton Mifflin.

Cantoni, G. (1997) Keeping minority languages alive: The school's responsibility. In J. Reyhner (ed.) *Teaching Indigenous Languages*. Flagstaff: Northern Arizona University.

Cantoni, G. (1999) Using TPR-Storytelling to develop fluency and literacy in Native American languages. In J. Reyhner, G. Cantoni, and R. St Clair (eds) *Revitalizing Indigenous Languages*. Flagstaff: Northern Arizona University.

Carrell, P. (1989) Metalinguistic awareness and second language reading. *Modern Language Review* 73, 121–134.

Carrell, P., Devine, J., and Eskey, D. (1988) *Interactive Approaches to Second Language Reading*. New York: Cambridge University Press.

Castillo, I. (1945) La alfabetización en lenguas indígenas: El Proyecto Tarasco. *América Indígena* 5 (2), 139–151.

Castro, C.A. (1956) La lingüística en el Centro Coordinador Tzeltal-Tzotzil. *América Indígena* 16, 139–158.

Cerrón-Palomino, R. (1993) Normalización en lenguas andinas. In W. Kuper (ed.) *Pedagogía Intercultural Bilingüe: Fundamentos de la Educación Bilingüe*. Quito: Abya-Yala.

Cerrón-Palomino, R. and López, L.E. (1990) La escritura en lenguas indígenas y la experiencia de Oaxaca. *América Indígena* 50, 265–290.

Chatry-Komarek, M. (1987) *Libros de Lectura para Niños de Lengua Vernácula a Partir de una Experiencia Interdisciplinaria en el Altiplano Peruano*. Eschborn, Germany: GTZ.

Chávez-Oller, M.A., Chihara, T., Weaver, K.A. and Oller, J.W. (1994) When are cloze items sensitive to constraints across sentences? In J.W. Oller and J. Jonz (eds) *Cloze and Coherence*. Toronto: Bucknell University Press.

Chiodi, F. (1990) Ecuador. In F. Chiodi (ed.) *La Educación Indígena en América Indígena, Tomo I* (pp. 329–543). Quito: Abya-yala.

Chiodi, F. (1993) Los problemas de la educación bilingüe intercultural en el area de lenguaje. In W. Kuper (ed.) *Pedagogía Intercultural Bilingüe: Fundamentos de la Educación Bilingüe*. Quito: Abya-Yala.

Chomsky, N. (1999) On the nature, use, and acquisition of language. In W. Ritchie and T.K. Bhatia (eds) *Handbook of Child Language Acquisition*. New York: Academic Press.

Cifuentes, B. (1992) Language policy in Mexico. *International Journal of the Sociology of Language* 96, 9–17.

Cisneros Paz, E. (1989) Tlatelolco y la educación indígena. *Pedagogía* 20, 81–90.

Citarella, L. (1990) México, Perú. In F. Chiodi *La Educación Indígena en América Latina, Tomo I* (pp. 9–156), *Tomo II* (pp. 7–226). Quito: Abya-yala.

Cloud, N., Genesee, F. and Hamayan, E. (2000) *Dual Language Education: A Handbook for Enriched Education*. Boston: Heinle and Heinle.

Cohen, A. (1994) *Assessing Language Ability in the Classroom*. Boston: Heinle and Heinle.

Collier, J. (1941) Nuevos conceptos sobre la unidad indígena. *América Indígena* 1, 11–15.

Collier, J. (1945) Indianismo vs. racismo? *América Indígena* 5, 241–255.

Collier, V. and Thomas, W. (1998) Assessment and evaluation. In C. Ovando and V. Collier (eds) *Bilingual and ESL Classrooms: Teaching in Multicultural Contexts*. New York: McGraw Hill.

Comás, J. (1956) La lengua vernácula y el bilingüismo en la educación. *América Indígena* 16, 93–109.

Condori Mamani, G. (1977) *Autobiografía* (edited by R. Valderrama Fernández and C. Escalantes Gutiérrez). Cuzco: Centro de Estudios Rurales Bartolomé de las Casas.

Coronado, G. (1988) Alfabetización en lengua vernácula: Consideraciones sociolingüísticas. *Papeles de la Casa Chata* 3, 57–62.

Coronado, G. (1989) De las prácticas comunicativas a las políticas lingüísticas. In G. Coronado (ed.) *De la Realidad al Deseo: Hacia un Pluralismo Viable*. Mexico DF: Cuadernos de la Casa Chata.

Coronado, G. (1992) Educación bilingüe en México: Propósitos y realidades. *International Journal of the Sociology of Language* 96, 53–70.

Corvalán, G. (1988) Bilingualism in Paraguay. In C. Bratt Paulston (ed.) *International Handbook of Bilingualism and Bilingual Education*. New York: Greenwood Press.

Crago, M., Allen, S. and Hough-Eyamie, W. (1997) Exploring innateness through cultural and linguistic variation. In M. Gopnik (ed.) *The Inheritance and Innateness of Grammar.* Oxford: Oxford University Press.

Crawford, J. (1995) Endangered Native American languages: What is to be done, and why? *Bilingual Research Journal* 19, 17–38.

Crawford, J. (1996) Seven hypotheses on language loss: Causes and cures. In G. Cantoni (ed.) *Stabilizing Indigenous Languages.* Flagstaff: Northern Arizona University.

Crawford, J. (1997) California's Proposition 227: A post mortem. *Bilingual Research Journal* 21, 1–30.

Cumming, A. (1990) Metalinguistic and ideational thinking in second language composing. *Written Communication* 7, 482–511.

Cummins, J. (1989) Language and literacy acquisition in bilingual contexts. *Journal of Multilingual and Multicultural Development* 10, 17–29.

Cummins, J. (1991) Language development and academic learning. In L. Malavé amd G. Duquette (eds) *Language, Culture and Cognition.* Clevedon: Multilingual Matters.

Cummins, J. (1996) *Negotiating Identities: Education for Empowerment in a Diverse Society.* Sacramento: California Association for Bilingual Education.

Cummins, J. (2000) *Language, Power and Pedagogy: Bilingual Children in the Crossfire.* Clevedon: Multilingual Matters.

Cummins, J. and Swain, M. (1983) Analysis-by-rhetoric: Reading the text or the reader's own projections? A reply to Edelsky *et al. Applied Linguistics* 4, 23–41.

Cummins, J. and Swain, M. (1987) *Bilingualism in Education.* New York: Longman.

Danesi, M. (1991) Revisiting the research findings on heritage language learning: Three interpretative frames. *The Canadian Modern Language Review* 47, 650–659.

Davies, A. (1990) *Principles of Language Testing.* Cambridge: Basil Blackwell.

DeFrancis, J. (1989) *Visible Speech: The Diverse Oneness of Writing Systems.* Honolulu: University of Hawaii Press.

DeKeyser. R. (2000) The robustness of critical period effects in second language acquisition. *Studies in Second Language Acquisition* 22, 499–533.

de la Cruz, V. (1992) La flor de la palabra (Guie' sti' didxaza). In C. Montemayor (ed.) *Los Escritores Indígenas Actuales II.* Mexico DF: Consejo Nacional para la Cultura y las Artes.

de la Cruz, V. and de la Cruz, G. (1990) Didxaguca' sti' lexu ne gueu' [The story of the rabbit and the coyote]. In C. Inchaustegui and V. Juárez (eds) *Animales Fantásticos y más Leyendas.* Mexico DF: CONAFE.

Denham, K., George, K., Rensink, E. and Sarr, J. (2000) Incorporating literary style prior to literacy in the elementary tribal school. In N. Ostler and B. Rudes (eds) *Endangered Languages and Literacy: Proceedings of the Fourth FEL Conference.* Charlotte: University of North Carolina.

Devine, J. (1988) The relationship between general language competence and second language reading proficiency: Implications for teaching. In P. Carrell, J. Devine and D. Eskey (eds) *Interactive Approaches to Second Language Reading.* New York: Cambridge University Press.

DGEI (Dirección General de Educación Indígena) (1986) *Manual para la Enseñanza de Lecto-escritura en Lengua Náhuatl.* Mexico DF: Secretaría de Educación Pública.

DGEI (Dirección General de Educación Indígena) (1988) *Noamoch tlen se Xiutl Tlamachtilistli, Libro Náhuatl, Primer Grado.* Mexico DF: Secretaría de Educación Pública.

DGEI (Dirección General de Educación Indígena) (1990a) *Prontuario de Estadística Educativa Indígena.* Mexico DF: Secretaría de Educación Indígena.

DGEI (Dirección General de Educación Indígena) (1990b) *Fundamentos para la Modernización de la Educación Indígena.* Mexico DF: Secretaría de Educación Pública.

Díaz, R.M. (1985) Bilingual cognitive development: Addressing three gaps in current research. *Child Development* 56, 376–388.

Díaz-Couder, E. (1990) Comunidades y dialectos: Acerca de la función social de la diversidad dialectal en las zonas indígenas del sur de México. *Papeles de la Casa Chata* 5, 29–39.

Díaz-Rico, L. and Weed, K. (1995) *The Crosscultural, Language and Academic Development Handbook.* Boston: Allyn and Bacon.

Dick, G.S., Estell, D.W. and McCarty, T. (1994) Saad naakih bee'enootííljí na'alakaa: Restructuring the teaching of language and literacy in a Navajo community school. *Journal of American Indian Education* 33, 31–45.

Dick, G.S. and McCarty, T. (1994) Navajo language maintenance and development: Possibilities for community-controlled schools. *Journal of Navajo Education* 11, 15–20.

Dick, G.S. and McCarty, T. (1997) Reclaiming Navajo: Language renewal in an American Indian community school. In N. Hornberger (ed.) *Indigenous Literacies in the Americas: Language Planning from the Bottom Up.* Berlin: Mouton de Gruyter.

Edelsky, C. (1996) *With Literacy and Justice for All: Rethinking the Social in Language and Education.* London: Taylor & Francis.

Edelsky, C., Hudelson, S., Flores, B., Barkin, F., Altwerger, B. and Jilbert, C. (1983) Semilingualism and language deficit. *Applied Linguistics* 4, 1–22.

Education Committee of the Navajo Nation Council (2000) *Diné Cultural Content Standards for Students.* Window Rock, AZ: Office of Diné Culture, Language and Community Service.

Edwards, H. and Kirkpatrick, A. (1999) Metalinguistic awareness in children: A developmental progression. *Journal of Psycholinguistic Research* 28, 313–329.

Ellis, R. (1993) The structural syllabus and second language acquisition. *TESOL Quarterly* 27, 91–113.

Ellis, R. (1997) *SLA Research and Language Teaching.* Oxford: Oxford University Press.

Ellis, R. (1998) *Second Language Acquisition.* Oxford: Oxford University Press.

Ethnologue: Languages of the World (1999). Dallas: Summer Institute of Linguistics. At http://www/ethnologue.com/web.asp.

Faltis, C.J. (2001) *Joinfostering: Adapting Teaching for the Multilingual Classroom.* Columbus: Merrill.

Feldman, C.F. (1991) Oral metalanguage. In D. Olson and N. Torrance (eds) *Literacy and Orality.* New York: Cambridge University Press.

Ferguson, C.A. (1959) Diglossia. *Word* 15, 325–340.

Fishman, J. (1967) Bilingualism with and without diglossia; Diglossia with and without bilingualism. *Journal of Social Issues* 23, 29–38.

Fishman, J. (1991) *Reversing Language Shift.* Clevedon: Multilingual Matters.

Fishman, J. (1996) What do you lose when you lose your language? In G. Cantoni (ed.) *Stabilizing Indigenous Languages.* Flagstaff: Northern Arizona University.

Fishman, J. (2001) *Can Threatened Languages Be Saved? Reversing Language Shift Revisited.* Clevedon: Multilingual Matters.

Flores Farfán, J.A. (1996) *Adivinanzas Nahuas.* Mexico DF: Centro de Investigaciones y Estudios Superiores en Antropología Social.

Fradd Homlar, S. and McGee Larrinaga, P. (1994) *Instructional Assessment: An Integrative Approach to Evaluating Student Performance.* New York: Addison-Wesley.

Francis, N. (1991) Educación bilingüe: La tradición oral en la adquisición de la lectoescritura. *Revista Latinoamericana de Estudios Educativos* 21, 49–84.

Francis, N. (1992a) Evaluación del bilingüismo: Una propuesta metodológica. *América Indígena* 52, 51–74.

Francis, N. (1992b) Procesos de lectoescritura en segunda lengua: Resultados preliminares de un estudio en las escuelas bilingües del Valle del Mezquital. *Lectura y Vida* 13, 31–39.

Francis, N. (1997) *Malintzin: Bilingüismo y Alfabetización en la Sierra de Tlaxcala.* Quito: Ediciones Abya-yala.

Francis, N. (1998a) Bilingual children's reflections on writing and diglossia. *International Journal of Bilingual Education and Bilingualism* 1, 1–29.

Francis, N. (1998b) Mezquital, Malintzi y Misión de Chichimecas: La conciencia del lenguaje en el desarrollo de la alfabetización bilingüe. *Lectura y Vida* 19, 21–30.

Francis, N. (1999a) Bilingualism, writing and metalinguistic awareness: Oral-literate interactions between first and second languages. *Applied Psycholinguistics* 20, 533–561.

Francis, N. (1999b) Applications of cloze procedure to reading assessment in special circumstances of literacy assessment. *Reading Horizons* 40, 23–46.

Francis, N. (2000a) The shared conceptual system and language processing in bilingual children: Findings from literacy assessment in Spanish and Náhuatl. *Applied Linguistics* 21, 170–205.

Francis, N. (2000b) Rincones de lectura comes to San Isidro: New contexts for biliteracy and language maintenance. *Language, Culture and Curriculum* 13, 31–50.

Francis, N. (2000c) An examination of written expression in bilingual students' "non-academic" language: Assessment of sense of story structure and interlinguistic transfer. *International Journal of Applied Linguistics* 10, 27–60.

Francis, N. and Hamel, R.E. (1992) La redacción en dos lenguas: Escritura y narrativa en tres escuelas bilingües del Valle del Mezquital. *Revista Latinoamericana de Estudios Educativos* 22, 11–36.

Francis, N. and Navarrete Gómez, P.R. (1999) *Narrativa de la Tradición Oral Náhuatl.* Tlaxcala: Colegio de Historia de Tlaxcala.

Francis, N. and Navarrete Gómez, P.R. (2000) La narrativa como sitio de intercambio entre el náhuatl y el español: Un análisis de la alternancia lingüística. *Estudios de Cultura Náhuatl* 31, 359–391.

Francis, N. and Nieto Andrade, R. (1996) Stories for language revitalization in Náhuatl and Chichimeca. In G. Cantoni (ed.) *Stabilizing Indigenous Languages.* Flagstaff: Northern Arizona University.

Francis, N. and Nieto Andrade, R. (2000) Mexico: The challenge of literacy and multilingualism. *Childhood Education* 76, 374–380.

Francis, N. and Ryan, P. (1998) English as an international language of prestige: Conflicting perspectives and shifting ethnolinguistic loyalties. *Anthropology and Education Quarterly* 29, 25–43.

Fromkin, V.A. (ed.) (2000) *Linguistics: An Introduction to Linguistic Theory.* Oxford: Blackwell.

Garibay, A.M. (1963) *Panorama Literario de los Pueblos Nahuas.* Mexico DF: Editorial Porrúa.

Garner, R. (1994). Metacognition and self-monitoring strategies. In S.J. Samuels and A.E. Farstrup (eds) *What Research Has to Say about Reading Instruction.* Newark, DE: International Reading Association.

Gass, S. (1997) *Input, Interaction, and the Second Language Learner.* Mahwah, NJ: Lawrence Erlbaum.

Gass, S. (2000) Fundamentals of second language acquisition. In J. Rosenthal (ed.) *Handbook of Undergraduate Second Language Education.* Mahwah, NJ: Lawrence Erlbaum Associates.

Gee, J.P. (1989) Literacy, discourse and linguistics. *Journal of Education* 171, 75–96.

Gee, J.P. (2001) Educational linguistics. In M. Aronoff and J. Rees-Miller (eds) *The Handbook of Linguistics.* Oxford: Blackwell.

Genesee, F. (1987) *Learning Through Two Languages: Studies of Immersion and Bilingual Education.* New York: Newbury House Publishers.

Genesee, F. (1991) L'immersion et l'apprenant défavorisé. *Etudes de Linguistique Appliquée* 82, 77–93.

Genesee, F. and Upshur, J. (1996) *Classroom-based Evaluation in Second Language Education.* New York: Cambridge University Press.

Geva, E. and Wang, M. (2001) The development of basic reading skills in children: A cross-language perspective. *Annual Review of Applied Linguistics* 21, 182–204.

Gombert, J.E. (1992) *Metalinguistic Development.* Chicago: University of Chicago Press.

Gonzalbo, P. (1988) La lectura de evangelización en la Nueva España. In *Historia de la Lectura en México* (Seminario de Historia de la Educación en México de El Colegio de México). Mexico DF: El Colegio de México.

Goodman, K. (1992) Whole language research: Foundations and development. In S.J. Samuels and A.E. Farstrup (eds) *What Research Has to Say about Reading Instruction.* Newark, DE: International Reading Association.

Goodman, Y. (1995) Miscue analysis for classroom teachers: Some history and some procedures. *Primary Voices K-6* (3), 2–11.

Gregg, K. (1996) The logical and developmental problems of second language acquisition. In W. Ritchie and T. Bhatia (eds) *Handbook of Second Language Acquisition.* New York: Academic Press.

Grimes, B. (1999) *Ethnologue: Languages of the World.* Dallas: Summer Institute of Linguistics. At http://www.ethnologue.com/web.asp.

Gruzinski, S. (1991) *La Colonización de lo Imaginario: Sociedades Indígenas y Occidentalización en el México Español, Siglos XVI–XVIII.* Mexico DF: Fondo de Cultura Económica.

Hall, M.A. (1978) *The Language Experience Approach for Teaching Reading: A Research Perspective.* Newark, DE: International Reading Association.

Halliday, M. (1989) *Spoken and Written Language.* Oxford: Oxford University Press.

Hamel, R.E. (1993) Linguistic human rights for indigenous peoples in Latin America. In T. Skutnabb-Kangas and R. Phillipson (eds) *Linguistic Human Rights.* New York: Cambridge University Press.

Hamel, R.E. (1995) The inroads of literacy in the Hñahñú communities in Central Mexico. *International Journal of the Sociology of Language* (Special Issue: Vernacular Literacy in Nonmainstream Communities) 119, 13–42.

Hamel, R.E. (1997) Language conflict and language shift: A sociolinguistic framework for linguistic human rights. *International Journal of the Sociology of Language* 127, 105–134.

Hamel, R.E. and Sierra, M.T. (1983) Diglosia y conflicto intercultural: La lucha por un concepto o la danza de los significantes. *Boletín de Antropología Americana* 8, 89–108.

Hammerly, H. (1987) The immersion approach: Litmus test of second language acquisition through classroom communication. *The Modern Language Journal* 71, 395–401.

Harley, B., Allen, P., Cummins, J. and Swain, M. (1990) *The Development of Second Language Proficiency.* New York: Cambridge University Press.

Harrison, R. (1989) *Signs, Songs, and Memory in the Andes: Translating Quechua Language and Culture.* Austin: University of Texas Press.

Hasler, A. (1987) El problema de la escritura del náhuatl. *Colección Pedagógica Universitaria* 15, 87–98.

Hatch, E. (1983) *Psycholinguistics: A Second Language Approach.* Rowley, MA: Newbury House.

Hausler, M. and Masayesva Jeanne, L. (1987) Young Hopi writers and readers. *Journal of the National Association for Bilingual Education* 11, 83–92.

Heath, S. (1972) *Telling Tongues: Language Policy in Mexico, Colony to Nation.* New York: Teachers College Press.

Heaton, J.B. (1991) *Classroom Testing.* New York: Longman.

Hedge, T. (2001) *Teaching and Learning in the Language Classroom.* Oxford: Oxford University Press.

Hernández-Chávez, E. (1984) The inadequacy of English immersion education as an educational approach for language minority students in the United States. In *Studies on Immersion Education.* Sacramento: California State Department of Education.

Hidalgo, M. (1994) Bilingual education, nationalism and ethnicity in Mexico: From theory to practice. *Language Problems and Language Planning* 18, 185–207.

Hill, J. and Hill, K. (1986) *Speaking Mexicano: Dynamics of Syncretic Language in Central Mexico.* Tucson: University of Arizona Press.

Hinman, S.D. (1869) *Journal of the Rev. S.D. Hinman Missionary to the Santee Sioux Indians.* Philadelphia: McCalla & Stavely.

Hinton, L. (1994) *Flutes of Fire: Essays on California Indian Languages.* Berkeley, CA: Heyday Books.

Hinton, L. and Ahlers, J. (1999) The issue of "authenticity" in California language restoration. *Anthropology and Education Quarterly* 30, 56–67.

Holm, A. and Holm, W. (1995) Navajo language education: Retrospect and prospects. *The Bilingual Research Journal* 19, 141–167.

Holm, W. (1993) On the use of the Navajo language in Navajo Head Start centers: Preliminary considerations. *Journal of Navajo Education* 10, 63–45.

Holm, W., Silentman, I. and Wallace, L. (1996) Navajo language teaching in immersion classrooms. *Journal of Navajo Education* 8, 30–41.

Hopi Cultural Preservation Office, The Hopi Tribe (1997) *Hopi Language Fluency Survey* (Draft). Kykotsmovi, Arizona.

Hornberger, N. (1987) *Bilingual Education and Language Maintenance: A Southern Peruvian Quechua Case.* Dordrecht: Foris.

Hornberger, N. (1989) Can Peru's rural schools be agents for Quechua language maintenance? *Journal of Multilingual and Multicultural Development* 10, 145–159.

Hornberger, N. (1990) Teacher Quechua use in bilingual and non-bilingual classrooms of Puno, Peru. In R. Jacobson and C. Faltis (eds) *Language Distribution Issues in Bilingual Schooling.* Clevedon: Multilingual Matters.

Hornberger, N. (ed.) (1996) *Indigenous Language Literacies in the Americas: Language Planning from the Bottom Up.* Berlin: Mouton de Gruyter.

Hornberger, N. (1997) Literacy, language maintenance, and linguistic human rights: Three telling cases. *International Journal of the Sociology of Language* 127, 87–104.

Hornberger, N. (1998) Language policy, language education, language rights: Indigenous, immigrant, and international perspectives. *Language in Society* 27, 439–458.

Horowitz, R. (1990) Discourse organization in oral and written language: Critical contrasts for literacy and schooling. In J. de Jong and D. Stevenson (eds) *Individualizing the Assessment of Language Abilities.* Clevedon: Multilingual Matters.

Iapi Oaye (1874) Editorial. *Iapi Oaye* 3 (1), 4.

INEGI (Instituto Nacional de Estadística Geografía e Información) (1990a) *XI Censo General de Población y Vivienda (Tlaxacala).* Mexico DF: INEGI.

INEGI (Instituto Nacional de Estadística Geografía e Información) (1990b) *La Población Hablante de Lengua Indígena en México.* Mexico DF: INEGI.

International Reading Association (2001) *Second Language Literacy Instruction.* Newark, DE: IRA.

Iverson, P. (1994) Speaking their language: Robert W. Young and the Navajos. In M.C. Szasz (ed.) *Between Indian and White Worlds: The Cultural Broker.* Norman, OK: University of Oklahoma Press.

Jackendoff, R. (1994) *Patterns in the Mind: Language and Human Nature.* New York: Harper Collins.

Jacobson, L. (1998) Turning the tide. *Education Week,* October 7.

Jacobson, R. and Faltis, C. (1990) *Language Distribution Issues in Bilingual Schooling.* Clevedon: Multilingual Matters.

Johansson, P. (1993) *La Palabra de los Aztecas.* Mexico DF: Trillas.

Johnson, R. and Swain, M. (1997) *Immersion Education: International Perspectives.* New York: Cambridge University Press.

Jordan, C. (1995) Creating cultures of schooling: Historical and conceptual background of the KEEP/Rough Rock collaboration. *The Bilingual Research Journal* 19, 83–100.

Joseph, J. (1997) Hopi language perpetuation efforts. *Hopi Tutuveni* 7 (5) 7–13.

Jung, I. (1992) *Conflicto Cultural y Educación: El Proyecto de Educación Bilingüe: Puno/ Perú.* Quito: Abya-yala.

Kamaná, K. and Wilson, W. (1996) Hawaiian language programs. In G. Cantoni (ed.) *Stabilizing Indigenous Languages.* Flagstaff: Northern Arizona University.

Ka'awa, M. and Hawkins, E. (1997) Incorporating technology into a Hawaiian language curriculum. In J. Reyhner (ed.) *Teaching Indigenous Languages.* Flagstaff: Northern Arizona University.

King, J. (1999) Lessons from Maori schooling experience: 13 years of immersion schools. In N. Ostler (ed.) *Proceedings of the Third Foundation for Endangered Languages (FEL) Conference.* Bath, UK: FEL.

King, J. (2001) Te Kohanga Reo: Maori language revitalization. In L. Hinton and K. Hale (eds) *The Green Book of Language Revitalization in Practice.* New York: Academic Press.

King, K. (2001) *Language Revitalization Processes and Prospects: Quechua in the Ecuadorian Andes.* Clevedon: Multilingual Matters.

Kipp, D. (2000) *Encouragement, Guidance, Insights, and Lessons Learned for Native Language Activists Developing their own Tribal Language Programs.* St Paul, MN: Grotto Foundation.

Krashen, S. (1991) Bilingual education: A focus on current research. *Focus: Occasional Papers in Bilingual Education.* Washington DC: National Clearing house for Bilingual Education.

Krashen, S. (1996) A gradual exit, variable threshold model for limited English proficient children. *NABE News* 19, 1–17.

Krashen, S. (1999) *Condemned Without a Trial: Bogus Arguments Against Bilingual Education.* Portsmouth, NH: Heinemann.

Krashen, S. and Biber, D. (1988) *On Course: Bilingual Education's Success in California.* Sacramento: California Association for Bilingual Education.

Krauss, M. (1996) Status of Native American language endangerment. In G. Cantoni (ed.) *Stabilizing Indigenous Languages.* Flagstaff: Northern Arizona University.

Kubiszyn, T. and Borich, G. (2000) *Educational Testing and Measurement: Classroom Application and Practice.* New York: John Wiley.

Lambert, W. (1990) Persistent issues in bilingualism. In B. Harley, P. Allen, J. Cummins and M. Swain (eds) *The Development of Second Language Proficiency.* New York: Cambridge University Press.

Lankford, G. (1987) *Native American Legends: Tales from the Natchez, Caddo, Biloxi, Chicksaw and other Nations.* Little Rock: August House.

Lapkin, S., Swain, M. and Shapson, S. (1990) French immersion research agenda for the 90s. *The Canadian Modern Language Review* 46, 638–674.

Leander, B. (1972) *In Xochitl in Cuicatl: Flor y Canto.* Mexico DF: Instituto Nacional Indigenista.

Leap, W. L. (1993) *American Indian English.* Salt Lake City: University of Utah Press.

Leavitt, R. (1991) Language and cultural content in Native education. *Canadian Modern Language Review* 47, 266–279.

LeBlanc, R. (1992) Les programmes d'immersion et l'habliteé à communiquer. *Etudes de Linguistique Appliquée* 88, 67–82.

Leeds, B. (1994) *Writing in a Second Language: Insights from First and Second Language Teaching and Research.* White Plains, NY: Longman.

León-Portilla, M. (1976) *Culturas en Peligro.* Mexico DF: Alianza Editorial Mexicana.

León-Portilla, M. (1992a) *Literaturas Indígenas de México.* Mexico DF: Fondo de Cultura Económica.

León-Portilla, M. (1992b) *Fifteen Poets of the Aztec World.* Norman, OK: University of Oklahoma Press.

León-Portilla, M. (1996) *El Destino de la Palabra: De la Oralidad y los Códices Mesoamericanos a la Escritura Alfabética.* Mexico DF: Fondo de Cultura Económica.

Lessow-Hurley, J. (2000) *The Foundations of Dual Language Instruction*. White Plains, NY: Longman.

Linn, R. and Gronlund, N. (1995) *Measurement and Assessment in Teaching* (7th edn). Englewood Cliffs, NJ: Prentice Hall.

Littlebear, R. (1992) TPR works! *NABE News* 15(6), 13.

Lockard, L. (1995) New paper words: Historical images of Navajo language literacy. *American Indian Quarterly* 19, 17–31.

Lockhart, J. (1990) Postconquest Nahua society and concepts viewed through Náhuatl writings. *Estudios de Cultura Náhuatl* 20, 91–115.

Lomakama, S. (1997) Language assessment sets off alarms. Interview in *Navajo-Hopi Observer*, December 3.

López, L.E. (1989) Problemática sociolingüística y educativa de la población Aymara-hablante en el Perú. *International Journal of the Sociology of Language* 77, 55–67.

López, L.E. (1995) Reformas del estado y política lingüística en Bolivia. *America Indígena* 55, 9–22.

Lord, A. (1991) *Epic Singers and Oral Tradition*. Ithaca, NY: Cornell University Press.

Loschky, L. and Bley-Vroman, R. (1993) Grammar and task-based methodology. In G. Crookes and S.M. Gass (eds) *Tasks and Language Learning: Integrating Theory and Practice*. Clevedon: Multilingual Matters.

Llanque Chana, D.(1992) Dimensión política de un alfabeto aymara y quechua. In J. Juncosa (ed.) *Educación Indígena: Transmisión de Valores, Bilingüismo e Interculturalismo Hoy*. Quito: Abya-yala.

MacLean, M. and d'Anglejan, A. (1986) Rational cloze and retrospection: Insights into first and second language reading comprehension. *The Canadian Modern Language Review* 42, 814–826.

MacSwan, J. (1999) *A Minimalist Approach to Intrasentential Code Switching*. New York: Garland Publishing.

MacSwan, J. (2000) The threshold hypothesis, semilingualism, and other contributions to a deficit theory view of linguistic minorities. *Hispanic Journal of Behavioral Sciences* 22, 3–45.

Maffi, L. (2001) Language, knowledge, and indigenous heritage rights. In L. Maffi (ed.) *On Biological Diversity: Linking Language, Knowledge, and the Environment*. Washington, DC: Smithsonian Institution Press.

Mandel-Morrow, L. (1988) Retelling stories as a diagnostic tool. In S.M. Glazer, L. Searfoss and L. Gentile (eds) *Reexamining Reading Diagnosis: New Trends and Procedures*. Newark, DE: International Reading Association.

Mandler, J.M. (1984) *Stories, Scripts and Scenes: Aspects of Schema Theory*. Hillsdale, NJ: Lawrence Erlbaum Associates.

Manrique Castañeda, L. (1988) *Atlas Cultural de México: Lingüística*. Mexico DF: Instituto Nacional de Antropología e Historia.

Martin-Jones, M. and Romaine, S. (1986) Semilingualism: A half-baked theory of communicative competence. *Applied Linguistics* 7, 26–37.

McCarthy, M. (1991) *Discourse Analysis for Language Teachers*. New York: Cambridge University Press.

McCarty, T. (1993) Federal language policy and American Indian education. *The Bilingual Research Journal* 17, 13–34.

McCarty, T. (1999) Schooling, resistance, and American Indian languages. *International Journal of the Sociology of Language* 132, 27–42.

McCarty, T., Wallace, S., Hadley Lynch, R. and Benally, A. (1991) Classroom inquiry and Navajo learning styles; A call for reassessment. *Anthropology and Education Quarterly* 22, 43–59.

McCarty, T. and Watahomogie, L. (1999) Indigenous education and grassroots language planning in the USA. *Practicing Anthropology* 20, 5–11.

McGroarty, M., Beck, A. and Butler, F. (1995) Policy issues in assessing indigenous languages: A Navajo case. *Applied Linguistics* 16, 323–343.

McLaughlin, B., Gesi Blanchard, A. and Osanai, Y. (1995) *Assessing Language Development in Bilingual Preschool Children*. Washington DC: National Clearing house for Bilingual Education.

McLaughlin, D. (1990) The sociolinguistics of Navajo literacy. *Journal of Navajo Education* 7, 28–36.

McLaughlin, D. (1992) *When Literacy Empowers: Navajo Language in Print*. Albuquerque: University of New Mexico Press.

Meneses Méndez, D. (1992) Bajche' mi' ña'tyañ i mel ye'tyel juñi xts' ibob (La visión del escritor indígena sobre sus escritos). In C. Montemayor (ed.) *Los Escritores Indígenas Actuales*. Mexico DF: Consejo Nacional para la Cultura y las Artes.

Messineo, C. (2000) Toba teachings: Analysis of oral genres for pedagogical purposes. *Latin American Indian Literatures Journal* 16, 18–46.

Met, M. (1994) Teaching content through a second language. In F. Genesee (ed.) *Educating Second Language Children: The Whole Child, the Whole Curriculum, the Whole Community*. New York: Cambridge University Press.

Milroy, L. and Muysken, P. (1995) *One Speaker, Two Languages: Cross-disciplinary Perspectives on Codeswitching*. New York: Cambridge University Press.

Modiano, N. (1972) *Indian Education in the Chiapas Highlands*. New York: Holt, Rinehart and Winston.

Modiano, N. (1988) Public school education in México. In C. Bratt Paulson (ed.) *International Handbook of Bilingualism and Bilingual Education*. New York: Greenwood Press.

Montemayor, C. (1992) *Los Escritores Indígenas Actuales*. Mexico DF: Consejo Nacional para la Cultura y las Artes.

Moya, R. (1990) Un decenio de educación bilingüe y participación indígena: Ecuador. *Perspectivas* 20, 369–382.

Montoya, V. (1983) Bolivia: La educación bilingüe en proyectos integrados. In N. Rodríguez, E. Masferrer and R. Vargas Vega (eds) *Educación, Etnias y Descolonización en América Latina*. Mexico DF: Instituto Indigenista Interamericano.

Muñoz Cruz, H. (1987) Factores de vitalidad en la lenguas indígenas. *México Indígena* 3, 16–20.

Myers-Scotton, C. (1993) *Duelling Languages: Grammatical Structure in Codeswitching*. Oxford: Clarendon Press.

Nahmad Sittón, S. (1999) Derechos lingüísticos de los pueblos indígenas de México. *International Journal of the Sociology of Language* 132, 143–162.

Navarrete Gómez, P.R. and Francis, N. (1999) *In Tlapuiltin tlen Otechcahuato to Cocolhuan (Narativa de la Tradición Oral Náhuatl)*. Tlaxcala: Archivo Histórico del Estado de Tlaxcala.

Northern Ute Tribe (1985) Ute language policy. *Cultural Survival Quarterly* 9, 16–19.

Nurss, J.R. and Hough, R.A. (1992) Reading and the ESL student. In S. Jay Samuels and A.E. Farstrup (eds) *What Research Has to Say about Reading Instruction*. Newark, DE: International Reading Association.

Nuttall, C. (1996) *Teaching Reading Skills in a Foreign Language*. Oxford: Heinemann.

Office of Diné Culture, Language and Community Service (2000) *Empowering Values of the Diné Individual*. Window Rock, AZ: Office of Diné Culture, Language and Community Service

Olson, D. (1991) Literacy and metalinguistic activity. In D. Olson and N. Torrence (eds) *Literacy and Orality*. New York: Cambridge University Press.

Olson, D. (1994) *The World on Paper*. New York: Cambridge University Press.

Ong, W. (1982) *Orality and Literacy: The Technology of the Word*. London: Methuen.

Ong, W. (1992) Writing is a technology that restructures thought. In P. Downing, S. Lima and M. Noonan (eds) *The Linguistics of Literacy*. Philadelphia: John Benjamins.

Ovando, C. and Collier, V. (1998) *Bilingual and ESL Classrooms: Teaching in Multicultural Contexts*. New York: McGraw Hill.

Pawley, C. (1985) How bilingual are French immersion students? *The Canadian Modern Language Review* 41, 865–876.

Pardo, M. T. (1993) El desarrollo de la escritura de las lenguas indígenas de Oaxaca. *Revista Iztapalapa* 29, 109–134.

Pease-Alvarez, C. and Vázquez, O. (1994) Language socialization in ethnic minority communities. In F. Genesee (ed.) *Educating Second Language Children*. New York: Cambridge University Press.

Pellicer, D. (1993) Oralidad y escritura de la literatura indígena: Una aproximación histórica. In C. Montemayor (ed.) *Situación Actual y Perspectivas de la Literatura en Lenguas Indígenas*. Mexico DF: Consejo Nacional para la Cultura y las Artes.

Pellicer, D. and Rockwell, E. (1991) La apropiación del castellano en las escuelas bilingües de Puno Perú: Revisión crítica de una estrategia de evaluación. Departamento de Investigaciones Educativas. Mexico DF: Instituto Politéctico Nacional (mimeo).

Peregoy, S.F. and Boyle, O.F. (2001) *Reading, Writing and Learning in ESL*. New York: Longman.

Pérez, B. and Torres-Guzmán, M.E. (1992) *Learning in Two Worlds: An Integrated Spanish/English Biliteracy Approach*. New York: Longman.

Phinney, A. (1935) *Nez Perce Texts: Columbia University Contributions to Anthropology* (Vol. 25). New York: Columbia University.

Piaget, J. (1952) *The Origins of Intelligence in Children*. New York: Norton.

Pinker, S. (1994) *The Language Instinct: How the Mind Creates Language*. New York: Harper Collins.

Pinker, S. (1999) *Words and Rules: The Ingredients of Language*. New York: Basic Books.

Platero, P. (2001) Navajo Head Start language study. In L. Hinton and K. Hale (eds) *The Green Book of Language Revitalization in Practice*. New York: Academic Press.

Poplack, S. (1980) Sometimes I'll start a sentence in Spanish y termino en español: Toward a typology of codeswitching. *Linguistics* 18, 581–618.

Porter, R. (1990) *Forked Tongue: The Politics of Bilingual Education*. New York: Basic Books.

Prem, H. and Riess, B. (1983) Autochthonous American writing systems: The Aztec and Maya examples. In F. Coulmas and K. Ehlich (eds) *Writing in Focus, Trends in Linguistics: Studies and Monographs 24*. New York: Mouton Publishers.

Ramsey, J. (1983) *Reading the Fire: Essays in the Traditional Indian Literatures of the Far West*. Lincoln: University of Nebraska Press.

Ray, B. and Seely, C. (1997) *Fluency Through TPR Storytelling: Achieving Real Language Acquisition in School*. Berkeley, CA: Command Performance Language Institute.

Reiss, E. (1967) *Elements of Literary Analysis*. New York: World Publishing Company.

Reyhner, J. (1992) *Teaching American Indian Students*. Norman, OK: University of Oklahoma Press.

Reyhner, J. (1993) American Indian language policy and school success. *The Journal of Educational Issues of Language Minority Students* 12 (Special Issue III), 35–59.

Reyhner, J., Cantoni, G., St Clair, R. and Parsons Yazzie, E. (eds) (1999) *Revitalizing Indigenous Languages*. Flagstaff: Northern Arizona University.

Reyhner, J. and Eder, J. (1989) *A History of Indian education*. Billings: Eastern Montana College.

Reyhner, J. and Eder, J. (1992) A history of American Indian education. In J. Reyhner (ed.) *Teaching American Indian Students*. Norman, OK: University of Oklahoma Press.

Reyhner, J., Martin, J., Lockhard, L., and Sakiestewa Gilbert, W. (eds) (2000). *Learn in Beauty: Indigenous Education for a New Century*. Flagstaff: Northern Arizona University.

Reyhner, J. and Tennant, E. (1995) Maintaining and renewing Native languages. *Bilingual Research Journal* 19, 279–304.

Richard-Amato, P. (1996) *Making it Happen: Interaction in the Second Language Classroom*. White Plains, NY: Longman.

Riggs, S.R. (1880) *Mary and I: Forty years with the Sioux*. Chicago: W.G. Holmes. (Reprinted in 1969 by Ross & Haines: Minneapolis, MN.)

Rockwell, E.M.R., Muñoz, H., Pellicer, D. and Quiroz, R. (1989) *Educación Bilingüe y Realidad Escolar: Un Estudio en Escuelas Primarias Andinas*. Mexico DF: Departamento de Investigaciones Educativas-CIEA-IPN.

Romaine, S. (1994) *Language in Society: An Introduction to Sociolinguistics*. New York: Oxford University Press.

Romero, M. and Parrino A. (1994) Planned alternation of languages (PAL): Language use and distribution in bilingual classrooms. *The Journal of Educational Issues of Language Minority Students* 13, 137–161.

Rosaldo, M. (1984) Words that are moving: The social meanings of Ilongot verbal art. In D. Brenneis and F. Myers (eds) *Dangerous Words: Language and Politics in the Pacific*. Prospect Heights, IL: Waveland Press.

Rosen, H. (1992) The power of story. *Teachers Networking* 11, 1–6.

Rosenblatt, L. (1994) The transactional theory of reading and writing. In R. Ruddell, M.R. Ruddell and H. Singer (eds) *Theoretical Models and Processes of Reading*. Newark, DE: International Reading Association.

Roth Seneff, A., Rodríguez, M.T. and Alarcón, L. (1986) *Lingüística Aplicada y Sociolingüística del Náhuatl en la Sierra de Zongolica*. Mexico DF: Cuadernos de la Casa Chata.

Rudes, B. (2000) When you choose, must you lose? Standard orthography versus dialect diversity. In N. Ostler and B. Rudes (eds) *Endangered Languages and Literacy: Proceedings of the Fourth FEL Conference*. Charlotte, NC: University of North Carolina.

Ruiz, R. (1988) Bilingualism and bilingual education in the United States. In C. Paulson (ed.) *International Handbook of Bilingualism and Bilingual Education.* New York: Greenwood Press.

Ruiz, R. (1995) Language planning considerations in indigenous communities. *Bilingual Research Journal* 19, 71–81.

Saguier, R. (1983) Las lenguas de Indoamérica. *El Correo de la UNESCO* 36, 12–14.

Schachter, J. (1988) Second language acquisition and its relationship to Universal Grammar. *Applied Linguistics* 9, 219–235.

Schachter, J. (1992) A new account of language transfer. In S.M. Gass and L. Selinker (eds) *Language Transfer in Language Learning.* Philadelphia: John Benjamins.

Scollon, R. and Scollon, S. (1981) *Narrative, Literacy and Face in Interethnic Communication.* Norwood, NJ: Ablex.

Scovel, T. (1998) *Psycholinguistics.* New York: Oxford University Press.

Shafer, S.M. (1988) Bilingual/bicultural education for Maori cultural preservation in New Zealand. *Journal of Multilingual and Multicultural Development* 9, 487–501.

Sharwood-Smith, M. (1994) *Second Language Learning: Theoretical Foundations.* New York: Longman.

Shearwood, P. (1987) Literacy among the Aboriginal peoples of the Northwest Territories. *Canadian Modern Language Review* 43, 630–642.

Shonerd, H. (1990) Domesticating the barbarous tongue: Language policy for the Navajo in historical perspective. *Language Problems and Language Planning* 14, 193–207.

Sierra, M. T. (1992) *Discurso, Cultura y Poder: El Ejercicio de la Autoridad en los Pueblos Hñähñús del Valle del Mezquital.* Mexico DF: Centro de Investigaciones y Estudios Superiores en Antropología Social.

Silver, S. and Miller, W. (1997) *American Indian Languages: Cultural and Social Contexts.* Tucson: University of Arizona Press.

Singleton, D. and Lengyel, Z. (1995) *The Age Factor in Second Language Acquisition.* Clevedon: Multilingual Matters.

Skutnabb-Kangas, T. (2000) *Linguistic Genocide in Education or Worldwide Diversity and Human Rights?* Clevedon: Multilingual Matters.

Slate, C. (1993) On reversing Navajo language shift. *Journal of Navajo Education* 10 (3), 30–35.

Slaughter, H. (1997) Indigenous language immersion in Hawai'i: A case study of Kula Kaiapuni Hawai'I, an effort to save the indigenous language of Hawai'i. In R.K. Johnson and M. Swain (eds) *Immersion Education: International Perspectives.* New York: Cambridge University Press.

Smith, F. (1988) *Understanding Reading: A Psycholinguistic Analysis of Reading and Learning to Read.* Hillsdale, NJ: Lawrence Erlbaum.

Snow, C.E., Burns, M.S. and Griffin, P. (1998) *Preventing Reading Difficulties in Young Children.* Washington DC: National Academy Press.

Snow, M.A. and Brinton D.M. (1997) *The Content-Based Classroom: Perspectives on Integrating Language and Content.* White Plains, NY: Longman.

Snow, M.A., Met, M. and Genesee, F. (1989) A conceptual framework for the integration of language and content in second/foreign language instruction. *TESOL Quarterly* 23, 210–217.

Spolsky, B. (1981) Bilingualism and biliteracy. *The Canadian Modern Language Review* 37, 473–485.

Spolsky, B. (1989) Maori bilingual education and language revitalization. *Journal of Multilingual and Multicultural Development* 10, 89–105.

Spolsky, B. and Irvine P. (1982) Sociolinguistic aspects of the acceptance of literacy in the vernacular. In F. Barkin, E. Brandt and J. Ornstein-Galicia (eds) *Bilingualism and Language Contact: Spanish, English and Native American Languages*. New York: Teachers College Press.

Stein, N. and Albro, E. (1997) Building complexity and coherence: Children's use of goal-structured knowledge in telling stories. In M. Bamberg (ed.) *Narrative Development: Six Approaches*. Mahwah, NJ: Lawrence Erlbaum.

Sulzby, E. (1994) Children's emergent reading of favorite storybooks: A developmental study. In R. Ruddell, M.R. Ruddell and H. Singer (eds) *Theoretical Models and Processes of Reading*. Newark, DE: International Reading Association.

Summer Institute of Linguistics (1984) *Cinco Cuentos en Chinanteco de Comaltepec*. Mexico DF: Summer Institute of Linguistics

Swain, M. and Johnson R. (1997) Immersion education: A category within bilingual education. In R. Johnson and M. Swain (ed.) *Immersion Education: International Perspectives*. New York: Cambridge University Press.

Swadesh, M. (1966) *El Lenguaje y la Vida Humana*. Mexico DF: Fondo de Cultura Económica.

Tannen, D. (1985) Relative focus on involvement in oral and written discourse. In D. Olson, N. Torrence and A. Hildyard (eds) *Literacy, Language, and Learning: The Nature and Consequences of Reading and Writing*. New York: Cambridge University Press.

Tannen, D. (1987) The orality of literature and the literacy of conversation. In J. Langer (ed.) *Language, Literacy and Culture: Issues of Society and Schooling*. Norwood, NJ: Ablex.

Tannen, D. (1989) *Talking Voices: Repetition, Dialogue, and Imagery in Conversational Discourse*. New York: Cambridge University Press.

Taylor, G. (1988) La tradición oral andina y la escritura. In L.E. López (ed.) *Pesquisas en Lingüística Andina*. Lima: Consejo Nacional de Ciencia y Tecnología.

Thornton, R. (1987) *American Indian Holocaust and Survival: A Population History Since 1942*. Norman, OK: University of Oklahoma Press.

Tierney, R., Carter, M. and Desai, L. (1991) *Portfolio Assessment in the Reading-Writing Classroom*. Norwood, MA: Christopher Gordon Publishers.

Torrence, N. and Olson, D. (1985) Oral and written competencies in the early school years. In D. Olson, N. Torrence and A. Hildyard (eds) *Literacy, Language, and Learning: The Nature and Consequences of Reading and Writing*. New York: Cambridge University Press.

Torrence, N. and Olson, D. (1987) Development of the metalanguage of literacy. *Interchange* 18, 136–146.

Troike, R. (1984) SCALP: Social and cultural aspects of language proficiency. In C. Rivera (ed.) *Language Proficiency and Academic Achievement*. Clevedon: Multilingual Matters.

UNESCO (1953) *The Use of Vernacular Languages in Education. Monographs on Fundamental Education VIII*. Paris: United Nations.

Valdés, G. (1997) Dual-language immersion programs: A cautionary note concerning the education of language-minority students. *Harvard Educational Review* 67, 391–427.

Valdés, M.L. and Menéndez, M.T. (1987) *Dinámica de la Población de Habla Indígena (1900–1980)*. Mexico DF: Instituto Nacional de Antropología e Historia.

Valdez-Pierce, L. and O'Malley, J.M. (1992) *Performance and Portfolio Assessment for Language Minority Students*. Washington, DC: National Clearinghouse for Bilingual Education.

Valencia, S.W., Jiebert, E.H. and Afflerbach, P. (1994) *Authentic Reading Assessment: Practices and Possibilities*. Newark, DE: International Reading Association.

van Dijk, T. (1990) *Estructuras y Funciones del Discurso*. Mexico DF: Siglo Veintiuno Editores.

Varese, S. (1990) Desafíos y perspectivas de la educación indígena en México. *Perspectivas* 20, 383–394.

Velie, A. (ed.) (1991) *American Indian Literature*. Norman, OK: University of Oklahoma Press.

Vygotsky, L. (1986). *Thought and Language*. Cambridge: MIT Press (first published in 1934).

Wagner, D.A., Spratt, J.E. and Ezzaki, A. (1989) Does learning to read in a second language always put the child at a disadvantage? Some counter evidence from Morocco. *Applied Psycholinguistics* 10, 31–38.

Warner, S. (2001) The movement to revitalize Hawaiian language and culture. In L. Hinton and K. Hale (eds) *The Green Book of Language Revitalization in Practice*. New York: Academic Press.

Wenden, A. (1998) Metacognitive knowledge and language learning. *Applied Linguistics* 19, 515–537.

Whitehead, M. (1997) *Language and Literacy in the Early Years*. London: Paul Chapman.

Whitmore, T. (1992) *Disease and Death in Early Colonial Mexico: Simulating Amerindian Depopulation*. San Francisco: Westview Press.

Widdowson, H.G. (1984) Reading and communication. In C. Alderson. *Reading in a Foreign Language*. London: Longman.

Wiley, T. (1996) *Literacy and Language Diversity in the United States*. Washington, DC: Center for Applied Linguistics.

Wilson, A. and Kamaná, K. (2000) Ku maka ihe laumeki: The tip of the spear in language revitalization. *Native Americas* 17, 32–37.

Williams, J.D. and Snipper, G.C. (1990) *Literacy and Bilingualism*. New York: Longman.

Window Rock School District (1981) *The Window Rock Oral Language Test: Navajo/ English Bilingual Proficiency*. Fort Defiance, AZ: Window Rock School District.

Wong, L. (1999) Authenticity and revitalization of Hawaiian. *Anthropology and Education Quarterly* 30, 94–115.

Woolfolk, A. (1996) *Educational Psychology*. Boston: Allyn and Bacon.

Yelland, G.W., Pollard, J. and Mercuri, A. (1993) The metalinguistic benefits of limited contact with a second language. *Applied Psycholingusitics* 14, 423–444.

Zepeda, O. (1995) The continuum of literacy in American Indian communities. *The Bilingual Research Journal* 19, 5–15.

Zúñiga, M. (1990) Políticas y experiencias educativas con poblaciones indígenas en el Perú. *Perspectivas* 20, 405–416.

Index